A Hands-On Tutorial and Guide

THOMAS F. GOLDMAN, J.D.

Thomas Edison State College
Professor Emeritus
Bucks County Community College

WORKING SMARTER SERIES

Prentice Hall

Boston   Columbus   Indianapolis   New York   San Francisco   Upper Saddle River
Amsterdam   Cape Town   Dubai   London   Madrid   Milan   Munich   Paris   Montreal   Toronto
Delhi   Mezico City   Sao Paolo   Sydney   Hong Kong   Seoul   Singapore   Taipei   Tokyo

Editor in Chief: Vernon Anthony
Senior Acquisitions Editor: Gary Bauer
Editorial Assistant: Megan Heintz
Director of Marketing: David Gesell
Marketing Manager: LeighAnn Sims
Senior Marketing Assistant: Les Roberts
Project Manager: Christina Taylor
Senior Operations Supervisor: Pat Tonneman

Senior Art Director: Diane Ernsberger
Cover Designer: Candace Rowley
Composition: Naomi Sysak
Printer/Binder: Edwards Brothers
Cover Printer: Coral Graphics
Text Font: Meridien
Copyeditor: Bret Workman

Microsoft® and Windows® are registered trademarks of the Microsoft Corporation in the U.S.A. and other countries. Screen shots and icons reprinted with permission from the Microsoft Corporation. This book is not sponsored or endorsed by or affiliated with the Microsoft Corporation.

Library of Congress Cataloging-in-Publication Data

Goldman, Thomas F.
  SmartDraw : a hands-on tutorial and guide / Thomas F. Goldman. -- 1st ed.
     p. cm. -- (Working smarter series)
  ISBN-13: 978-0-13-506434-4 (pbk. : alk. paper)
  ISBN-10: 0-13-506434-1 (pbk. : alk. paper)
  1. Computer graphics. 2. Presentation graphics software. 3. SmartDraw. I. Title.
T385.G63983 2010
006.6'86--dc22

                    2009000301

10 9 8 7 6 5 4 3 2

Prentice Hall
is an imprint of

PEARSON

www.pearsonhighered.com

ISBN-10:   0-13-506434-1
ISBN-13: 978-0-13-506434-4

Dedication

I dedicate this book to the hardest working and best teacher I have ever known, who has set a standard for teaching excellence that has earned him the respect of students and colleagues, and especially of an appreciative brother for whom he is the model of a truly great teacher.

Contents

SECTION 4 ■ Symbols (You Mean There Is More?)   64

Acknowledgments

This book would not have been possible without the vision and support of Paul Stannard, Founder, CEO, and creator of SmartDraw, who made his entire company available to me to write and produce this book.

Todd Savitt of SmartDraw provided encouragement and support by helping to develop the concept of the book and helping students gain access to a most remarkable program.

John Bradley, Dean and Professor Emeritus of the technology resource center at Bucks County Community College, is a technology-in-education visionary who has consistently given me guidance at every stage and spent countless hours reviewing the manuscript and working every tutorial.

Martin Goldman, Professor of Hospitality Management, who taught me what was needed and had his classes try out the tutorials.

My editor, Gary Bauer, for supporting another one of my ideas from conception to reality.

Introduction
(How Do I Use This Guide?)

- Using This Basics Tutorial and Guide
- Layout and Design of This Tutorial and Guide
- Using Your Mouse
- What If I Make a Mistake?
  - ▲ *Tutorial—Undo and Redo Last Action*
- Can I Do Every Tutorial in This Guide and Tutorial with My Version of SmartDraw?
- Tips and Notes
- History of Graphics
- Productivity
- Your Expectations

USING THIS GUIDE

This book was designed to be both a reference guide and a series of hands-on step-by-step tutorials on specific features of SmartDraw. As a reference guide it provides quick answers to questions, and as a hands-on step-by-step tutorial it helps you learn everything about SmartDraw (well, almost everything). Each section provides answers to the most frequently asked questions users have about the program as well as example procedures to guide you in learning and using the features and tools in the program. Be sure to save the individual documents created with SmartDraw in each tutorial for use in other tutorials and for reference.

LAYOUT AND DESIGN OF THIS GUIDE

Each tutorial answers a question by providing a brief explanation of the underlying concept and a step-by-step example of how to do it. The procedures are presented with the **GOAL, ACTION**, and **RESULT** in a step-by-step chart.

G O A L		

This section of the chart presents the goal of each step in the tutorial.

	A C T I O N	

This section specifies the action required to achieve the goal.

The action may be a mouse click, a keystroke, or a combination of both. In the step-by-step tutorials an **ACTION** such as **CLICK** will be in **BOLD**, and the text describing the item to be selected or text to be typed will be in *italics*. For example,

> **CLICK**
> *CLICK and RELEASE LEFT MOUSE BUTTON*
> *on border of object*

CLICK refers to a mouse click (generally the **LEFT MOUSE BUTTON** unless **RIGHT CLICK** appears). Clicking the **RIGHT MOUSE BUTTON** generally opens a menu of options or help text related to the specific action being taken (referred to as **Context Sensitive**). The following chart shows the most frequently used commands. Most actions, except for typing text, can be completed using the left mouse button and occasionally a keyboard key, such as the Control (Ctrl) or the Shift (Shift) key.

USING YOUR MOUSE

NOTES

The mouse pointer must be on the specific icon, symbol, or object mentioned before you click the mouse.

As each object is selected, selection handles will appear and stay on.

GOAL	ACTION	RESULT
SELECT SINGLE OBJECT	**CLICK** *CLICK and RELEASE LEFT MOUSE BUTTON on border of object*	
SELECT MULTIPLE OBJECTS	**PRESS and HOLD Ctrl KEY** **and** **CLICK** *on each of the objects to be selected*	
DRAG AND DROP	**CLICK and HOLD** *Place cursor on object, then click and hold left mouse button, and then* **MOVE** *Drag mouse to desired location* **RELEASE** *left mouse button*	
OPEN CONTEXT-SENSITIVE HELP MENU	**RIGHT CLICK MOUSE** *while on object*	
PROPORTION-ATE RESIZE	**HOLD Shift KEY and CLICK** *with mouse cursor on a selection handle* **DRAG** *selection handle until object is resized as desired* **RELEASE** *left mouse button*	

			R E S U L T

As you progress through the tutorial, the on-screen RESULT of the ACTION or a sample screen is presented for each step. This section of the chart shows you the actual displays you should see on your computer screen. If there are alternatives or options, a representative screen will be shown.

The following example shows how the steps will appear.

Starting SmartDraw

GOAL	ACTION	RESULT
START PROGRAM FROM DESKTOP	**CLICK** *the SmartDraw icon on your desktop or from the Windows Start menu*	SmartDraw 2009
START PROGRAM FROM PROGRAM LIST	**CLICK** **SELECT** ▶ **All Programs** **DOUBLE LEFT CLICK** ◆ SmartDraw 2009	▢ SmartDraw 2009 ◆ SmartDraw 2009 Uninstall SmartDraw 2009

WHAT IF I MAKE A MISTAKE?

SmartDraw is very forgiving software. You can **UNDO** (up to 100 steps) or **REDO** the last UNDO if you make a mistake undoing. Look for the **UNDO** and **REDO** arrows at the top of the page above the **Home** tab next to the **Smart Button**.

UNDO and REDO Last Action

GOAL	ACTION	RESULT
UNDO A MISTAKE	**CLICK** *Back arrow*	◆ ↶ ↷ Home

You can also use the standard Microsoft shortcut keyboard combination (pressing the Control and Z keys together (**Ctrl+Z**)) to undo the last keystroke action.

CAN I DO EVERY TUTORIAL IN THIS TEXT WITH MY VERSION OF SMARTDRAW?

All of the basic tutorials in this guide use the templates, symbols, and features found in the SmartDraw Standard version. SmartDraw, like many programs, is available in different versions: **Standard, Legal**, and **Healthcare**. The Standard version has no tabs for version selection. The Legal and Healthcare versions have tabs for selecting the version under the Smart Button.

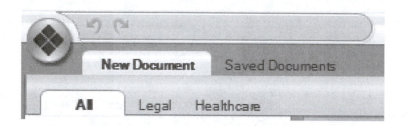

Users of the Legal or Healthcare versions should use the **All** tab to access the SmartTemplates and Examples used in the basic tutorial exercises. The legal and healthcare applications in the specialty application sections will require templates not found in the Standard version. The basic functionality, however, is the same in all versions; the only difference is in the additional specialized templates and examples in the Legal or Healthcare versions. Tutorials for specialty applications are presented in separate sections (Sections 8 through 13).

TIPS AND NOTES

Tips and **Notes** are inserted in the tutorials. These contain shortcuts, additional methods of completing the task, or other information you may find helpful. Each section also has a margin note showing other sections where the same topic or tools are also discussed.

HISTORY OF GRAPHICS

Graphics have been used to communicate and tell stories since the first humans drew pictures in caves to explain the animals in a hunt. The Egyptians raised graphics to a new level by drawing hieroglyphics on walls; but more importantly, they put them on a new material called paper. Today we create graphics in electronic form that can be sent over the Internet, shown on screens using projectors, or printed out on paper. What has also changed is the skill needed to produce graphics. Early creators of graphics needed to be skilled in crafts with the manual dexterity to draw and fill in areas between lines. SmartDraw has eliminated almost every skill required of the user except the ability to use a mouse, to click and drag, to drag and drop, and to type in text on a keyboard. It also helps to be able to figure out which symbols to use and where to place them (which requires some creativity, but not much). But so many public-domain samples and examples are available today that you can just copy most things, which is something that the first cave painters obviously could not do.

PRODUCTIVITY

A very wise man (actually, my Uncle Ralph) said "Tom, work smarter, not harder." Selecting the right tools to do the job is part of working smarter. The advantage of a program like SmartDraw is that it does most of the work for you, so you don't have to exert as much effort. Now *that* is working smarter.

Many of the graphics or forms you may need are already supplied as examples or templates in SmartDraw. In most cases a drawing can be used "as is," or easily modified to meet your needs. And you do not have to be a graphic artist or computer programmer, or possess great manual dexterity. The program anticipates what you want to do and the tools you need and provides context-sensitive tools and help on either side of the work space. Most users will need just the few tools provided on the left side, the SmartPanel. You will not have to search through the menus to find what you require to complete most projects. Context-sensitive help is provided on the right side of the working area (called the SmartHelp panel).

YOUR EXPECTATIONS

What can you expect from SmartDraw and from this guide? You DO NOT have to be an artist to create drawings and graphics. SmartDraw does most of the work for you, enabling you to create customized drawings that help you present ideas and communicate concepts. SmartDraw allows you to create needed graphics quickly and professionally with almost no training. There are no complicated keystroke combinations or hidden tricks; for most applications, the tools needed to create a graphic are presented in one place on the left side of the work space. Answers to questions are provided in context-sensitive help menus on the right side. Moreover, many projects can be completed without ever using the many other options and menu choices available at the top of the working screen.

As with anything new, there is a learning curve; but with SmartDraw it is a very short learning curve, so you will be able to create a graphic document the first time you use the program. With a little practice you will be able to use some of the powerful tools and features to create custom templates, symbols, and graphics.

A Hands-On Tutorial and Guide

Before We Really Start

So, What's It All About?

- How Can I Learn to Use SmartDraw?
- What Hardware Do I Need to Get Started?
- Why Do I Need an Internet Connection?
- What Can I Do with SmartDraw?
- Is There Anything I Should Do Before Installing SmartDraw?
- How Do I Install SmartDraw?
  - ▲ *Tutorial—Downloading and Installing SmartDraw from Website*
  - ▲ *Tutorial—Installing SmartDraw from a CD*
  - ▲ *Tutorial—Completing SmartDraw Installation*
  - ▲ *Tutorial—Starting SmartDraw*
- Where Can I Get More Answers?

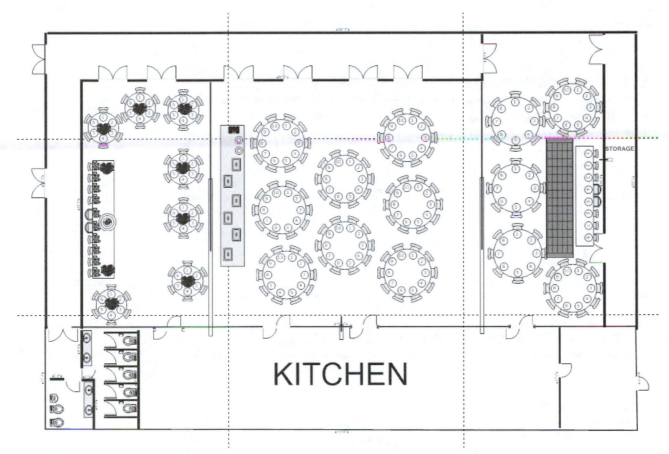

KITCHEN

Source: Created using SmartDraw Floor Plan SmartTemplates

HOW CAN I LEARN TO USE SMARTDRAW?

There are many methods of learning a new software program: reading the user's manual, using the online help, or randomly trying program features and menu choices. Few users, however, except the most dedicated ones, will consult the manual, help screens, or detailed training course material. This guide offers suggested hands-on training solutions to enable you to instantly use the program and its principal features with just a little guidance.

The SmartDraw program is easy to learn because it is intuitive. The features just seem to work as they are supposed to; the interface is forgiving, with the back arrow taking you back to the previous change you made in case you have second thoughts; and many samples and templates are provided that can be fully adapted or modified, so you may never need to create anything from scratch.

WHAT HARDWARE DO I NEED TO GET STARTED?

You must install SmartDraw on a computer that has enough hard drive space to store the program and data files and enough memory to run the program. You also should have an Internet connection to download additional content and updates and to gain access to the SmartDraw library of information.

Computer:	IBM-compatible PC with Windows® Vista, XP, or 2000
Operating memory:	256 MB RAM
Hard disk drive memory:	3 GB free hard disk space
Not really optional:	Internet connection

(Sorry, SmartDraw will not work on an Apple computer.)

WHY DO I NEED AN INTERNET CONNECTION?

First: Unless you have a CD of the program, you will need to connect to the SmartDraw website to download either the version of SmartDraw you purchased or the demo version.

Second: If you install SmartDraw by download only a portion of the full program is initially installed to save you Internet connection time. SmartDraw has so many samples, examples, and templates that only some of them are installed when you install the program. If you use a feature that was not installed in the initial download session, however, SmartDraw will download it automatically as long as you have an active Internet connection.

Third: The SmartDraw software is regularly updated. The updates are downloaded over the Internet.

Fourth: Additional documentation and tutorials may be downloaded from the SmartDraw website **http://www.smartdraw.com**.

Fifth: You may want to upgrade to a specialty version to complete a task. For example, a lawyer preparing for a case may need the Legal version; or a teacher giving a lecture on anatomy may want images from the Healthcare version.

WHAT CAN I DO WITH SMARTDRAW?

The SmartDraw graphics creation program provides hundreds of sample drawings. You can print or use many of these images without change; or edit or modify them using the thousands of symbols from SmartDraw's symbol and clip art library; or import web pages, Google maps, and personal pictures and images. SmartDraw's Legal and Healthcare versions offer more specialized examples as well as additional symbols, charts, and forms.

You can also use SmartDraw to create drawings and graphics for use in other presentation programs like Microsoft PowerPoint, export them to other programs like MS Word and Corel WordPerfect, or save them in popular image formats like PDF, JPEG, and GIF. The following documents and drawings are examples of the kinds of documents you can create.

**SmartDraw
Legal Version**

**Crime Scene
Reconstruction**

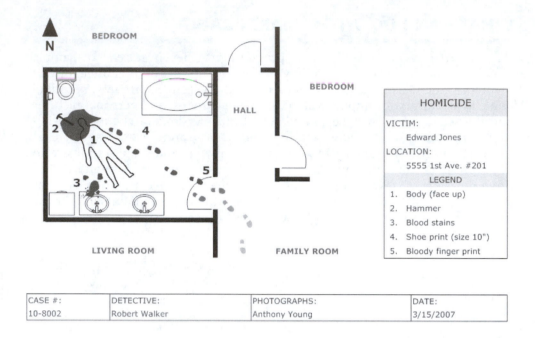

CASE #:	DETECTIVE:	PHOTOGRAPHS:	DATE:
10-8002	Robert Walker	Anthony Young	3/15/2007

**Accident Scene
Reconstruction**

ACCIDENT DESCRIPTION

Vehicle 1 made a right turn onto Camino del Sol and hit Vehicle 2 in the left rear panel. The driver of Vehicle 1 stated that the bush blocked his view of the street. Vehicle 2 was parked in a fire lane with no hazard lights indicating that it was stopped.
Damage is estimated at $1200. Both vehicles were driven from the accident scene and neither driver sustained injury.

INCIDENT NUMBER:	356516212-A
DATE:	3/15/2008
TIME:	16:18
SCALE	1:96

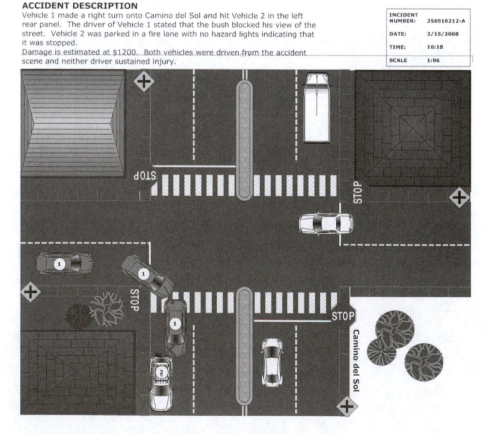

Timelines

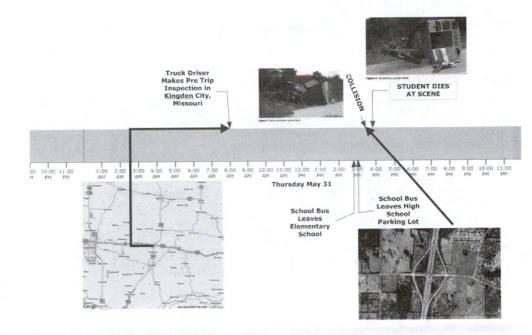

Truck Driver Makes Pre Trip Inspection in Kingden City, Missouri

COLLISION

STUDENT DIES AT SCENE

Figure 3. Tractor semitrailer, postbacident

Figure 4. School Bus, postbacident

10:00 PM 11:00 PM   1:00 AM 2:00 AM 3:00 AM 4:00 AM 5:00 AM 6:00 AM 7:00 AM 8:00 AM 9:00 AM 10:00 AM 11:00 AM 12:00 PM 1:00 PM 2:00 PM 3:00 PM 4:00 PM 5:00 PM 6:00 PM 7:00 PM 8:00 PM 9:00 PM 10:00 PM 11:00 PM

Thursday May 31

School Bus Leaves Elementary School

School Bus Leaves High School Parking Lot

SmartDraw Healthcare Version

Patient Education

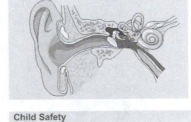

Thomas Family Practice Monthly Newsletter

October Issue

Ear Infections

Ear infections occur in the middle ear behind the eardrum. They often develop as a side effect of a cold or flu. Children have a hard time draining substances from their ears and these trapped substances can promote the growth of bacteria. Children who have an ear infection will seem irritable and they may also have trouble sleeping. The infected fluid puts pressure on the eardrums causing considerable pain and discomfort.

To treat ear infections, pediatricians will prescribe antibiotics to kill the bacteria and pain medication to help relieve any pain or fever. Even with an ear infection, children can play outside and even swim (as long as the eardrums are not torn). If you travel by plane, have the child swallow fluids or chew gum during take-off and landing.

Child Safety

Child safety tips:

- Lock away all household cleaners and medications.
- Place a pet's food and water out of the reach of children.
- Always secure your child in a car seat when in car
- Never leave a hot stove or BBQ unattended.
- Bolt bookshelves to the wall.
- Keep Ipecac Syrup handy for poisoning emergencies.
- Limit direct and lengthy sun exposure
- use high SPF sunblock.
- Have fire drills and discuss fire safety with your children.
- Buy only age-appropriate toys.
- Use safety gates near stairs.
- Cover all unused electrical outlets.

Old Town Center-New Town   555-555-1111

**SmartDraw
Standard
Version**

Charts

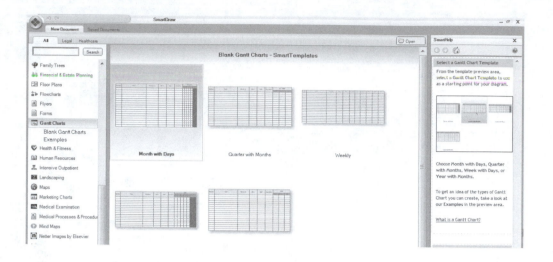

Real Estate

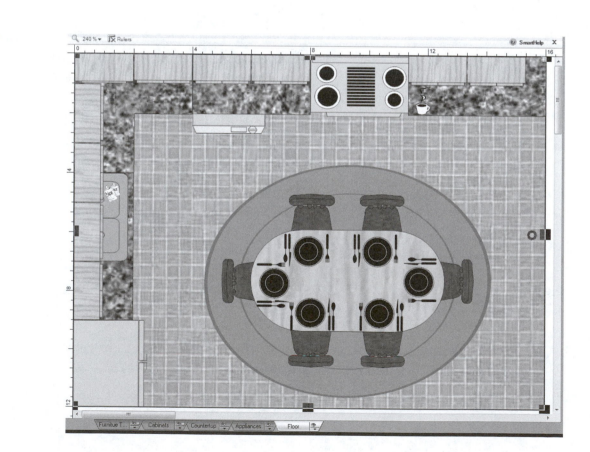

Teachers

Custom Forms

FIELD TRIP PERMISSION SLIP

Where: _____

When: _____

Transportation: _____

Cost: _____

Make checks payable to: _____

Additional comments: _____

_____

_____

Please return permission slip by _____

I give my child, _____, permission to attend the field trip to _____

on _____ from _____ to _____ .

I enclose _____ to cover the cost of the trip.

In case of an emergency, please contact _____ at _____

_____   _____

Parent's Signature   Date

**Lessons
and Displays**

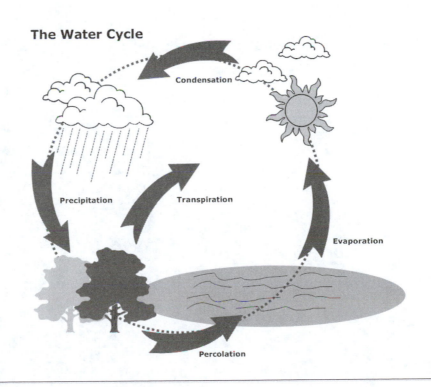

The Water Cycle

Condensation

Precipitation

Transpiration

Evaporation

Percolation

**Custom
Seating
Charts**

Seating Chart

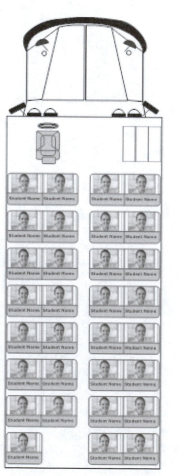

Restaurants

Menu Creation

YOUR LOGO

Tips for Designing a Menu

Your Menu Sets the Mood
Remember that your menu is part of your cuisine performance that offers a customer not only quality food, but also quality time.

Effective Titles
Highlight types of foods by including menu headings such as "Fresh from Garden" or "Our Specialties" rather than using generic terms such as Starters or Entrees.

Use Bold Lettering /Boxes
Impacting your special offers by using bold lettering or Boxing help direct customer towards your specials.
Consider boxing one out of every 7 to 10 items.

Signature Items
Put one or two signature items that your restaurant is famous for.

Menu Description
Keep food descriptions short, and Use wherever possible 'word pictures' rather than lengthy descriptions.

Using Symbols and Icons
Symbols and Icons can make your menu unique and draw attention to menu items that you would prefer to sell.

Too Much Choice, or Too Few Choice
Too much choice in a menu creates customer's confusion, and too few choice on a menu create customer's boredom.

Colored Paper
Consider the environment of your restaurant when choosing a paper for your menu. Some colors makes difficult to read in the dark setting.

Clean Menu
Keep your menu clean.

Inserting Your Photo:
To replace the photo on menu select the photo-container by clicking the photo. Then, on the Insert menu, click Picture, select your picture, and choose Replace.

Layout

CASHIER

CARTER FAMILY RESTAURANT

PEORIA, IL

DRINK/ SILVER   DRINK/ SILVER
TO KITCHEN   TO KITCHEN

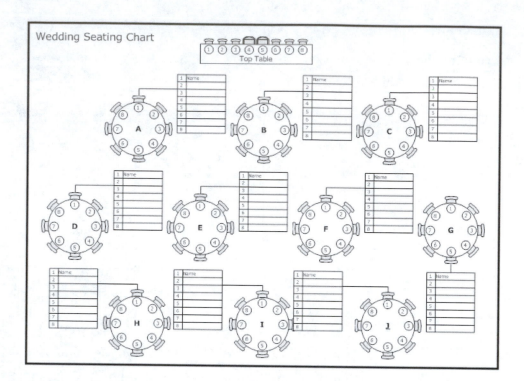

IS THERE ANYTHING I SHOULD DO BEFORE INSTALLING SMARTDRAW?

Before installing any software, close all other programs that may be running on your computer. You should also temporarily turn off your virus protection program during installation. The firewall on your system may need to be shut down or other steps taken to allow the program files to install.

HOW DO I INSTALL SMARTDRAW?

All versions of SmartDraw, including the trial or demo version, may be installed from a CD or downloaded from the SmartDraw website, http://www.smartdraw.com. If you have a registration or serial number you will need that number to activate your copy of the software.

N O T E S

Some Internet browsers may give you a choice to Save or to Run.

Some versions of Windows will ask if you want to run the program.

Installation should start automatically. If it does not, perform the "Start Installation Manually" step.

In the Destination Folder field, "C" is the default drive for the Program Files, the default directory.

Downloading and Installing SmartDraw from Website

GOAL	ACTION	RESULT
DOWNLOAD SOFTWARE FROM SMARTDRAW WEBSITE	**START** *your web browser* **ENTER** *SmartDraw URL, http://www.smartdraw.com* **CLICK** Click here to download SmartDraw.	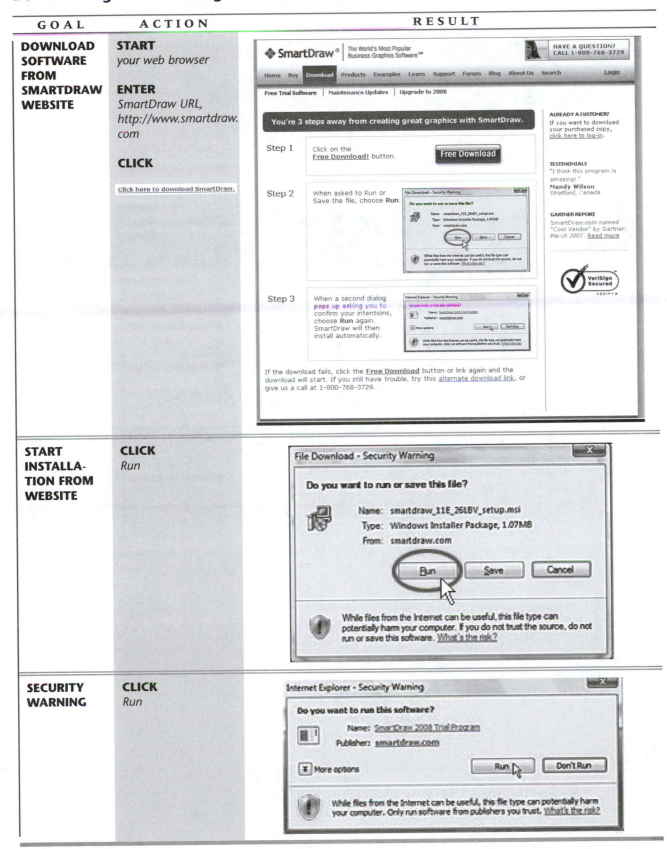
START INSTALLA-TION FROM WEBSITE	**CLICK** *Run*	
SECURITY WARNING	**CLICK** *Run*	

Installing SmartDraw from a CD

GOAL	ACTION	RESULT
INSTALL FROM CD	**INSERT** *CD into computer CD drive* **CLOSE** *drive door*	
START INSTALLA-TION MANUALY	**CLICK** *CD drive designation containing the SmartDraw installation file* **CLICK** *Setup*	

Completing SmartDraw Installation

GOAL	ACTION	RESULT
COMPLETE PROGRAM INSTALLA-TION	**CLICK** *Next and follow the instructions to install SmartDraw*	SmartDraw 2009 Welcome to the SmartDraw 2009 Setup program. This program will install SmartDraw 2009 on your computer. It is strongly recommended that you exit all Windows programs, including virus detection software, such as Norton Anti-Virus and McAfee, before running this Setup Program. Click Cancel to quit Setup and close any programs you have running. Click Next to continue with the Setup program. WARNING: This program is protected by copyright law and international treaties. Unauthorized reproduction or distribution of this program, or any portion of it, may result in severe civil and criminal penalties, and will be prosecuted to the maximum extent possible under law. SmartDraw Next > Cancel
SELECT DESTINATION FOR PROGRAM ON COMPUTER	**CLICK** *Next to select default location*	SmartDraw 2009 **Destination Location** Setup will install SmartDraw 2009 in the following folder. To install into a different folder, click Browse, and select another folder. You can choose not to install SmartDraw 2009 by clicking Cancel to exit Setup. **Destination Folder** C:\Program Files\SmartDraw 2009 Browse... SmartDraw < Back Next > Cancel

Starting SmartDraw

GOAL	ACTION	RESULT
START PROGRAM FROM DESKTOP	**CLICK** *the SmartDraw icon on your desktop or from the Windows Start menu*	SmartDraw 2009
START PROGRAM FROM PROGRAM LIST IF NO ICON APPEARS ON DESKTOP	**CLICK** **SELECT** ▶ **All Programs** **SELECT and DOUBLE CLICK** ◆ SmartDraw 2009	SmartDraw 2009 ◆ SmartDraw 2009 Uninstall SmartDraw 2009

WHERE CAN I GET MORE ANSWERS?

The SmartDraw® User's Guide may be downloaded from the SmartDraw website in PDF file format. A link is provided in the SmartDraw Help menu. To read a PDF file you will need to have the free Adobe Reader or some other reader installed on your computer.

N O T E

Additional tutorials and documentation are available at http://www.smartdraw.com.

SmartDraw®

User's Guide

Version 2009

SmartDraw.com

SmartDraw 2009 User's Guide User's Guide   • 1

The Basics: Using SmartDraw
(I Want to Get Going . . .)

- What Does the Work Space Look Like?
  - ▲ *Tutorial—SmartDraw Document Browser (Opening Screen) Features*
- Working Screen
  - ▲ *Tutorial—Application (Working) Screen Features*
- What Is the SmartDraw Button?
- What Is the Ribbon?
  - ▲ *Home Tab*
  - ▲ *Design Tab*
  - ▲ *Insert Tab*
  - ▲ *Page Tab*
  - ▲ *Table Tab*
  - ▲ *Chart Tab*
  - ▲ *Picture Tab*
  - ▲ *PowerPoint® Tab*
  - ▲ *Help Tab*

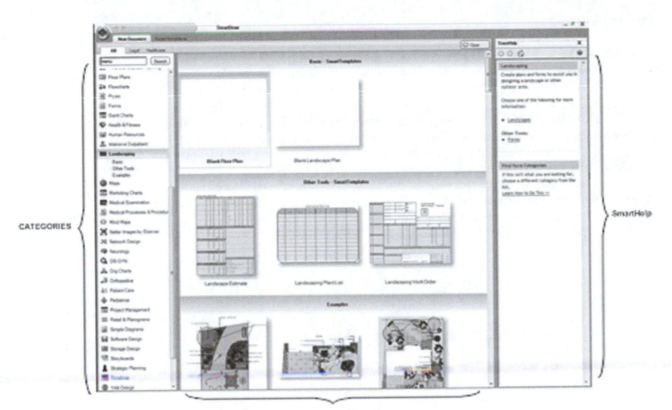

CATEGORIES

PREVIEW AREA

SmartHelp

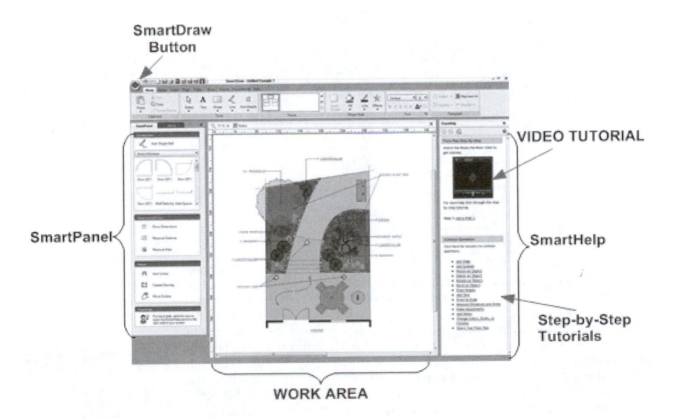

SmartDraw
Button

VIDEO TUTORIAL

SmartPanel

SmartHelp

Step-by-Step
Tutorials

WORK AREA

Source: Document Browser Category: Landscaping\Examples\Backyard

WHAT DOES THE WORK SPACE LOOK LIKE?

After the program is used for the first time, it has two screens: the opening screen, called the **Document Browser**, and the working screen, called the **Application Screen**, each of which has three panels. The first time you use SmartDraw, a screen appears with an option to create a new document. After that first use, the Document Browser will appear showing the last templates or examples you used.

As shown below, the Document Browser has tabs, **All, Legal**, or **Healthcare**, for selecting the version:. The templates for the selected version appear in the SmartTemplate list on the left. A search tool can be used to locate desired templates by key word.

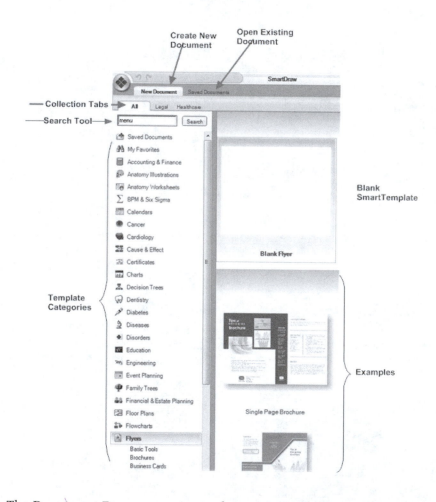

The Document Browser appears when you start or open SmartDraw. The Document Browser allows you to create a new document by selecting a type of template (SmartTemplate) or to open an existing document by selecting a Saved Document. After you select the desired template or document the Document Browser features will change to the Application Screen layout. Both screen layouts have three panels: left, middle, and right. The left panel in the Document Browser contains the list of SmartTemplates; the middle panel is the Preview Area, which shows examples of the selected category from the Templates List; and the right panel provides Help in selecting the templates.

TIP

Open SmartHelp (right panel) by clicking on the **?SmartHelp** button

SmartDraw Document Browser (Opening Screen) Features

GOAL	ACTION	RESULT
FEATURES OF THE DOCUMENT BROWSER (OPENING SCREEN)	**START** *SmartDraw* **CLICK** *All tab (left panel)* **CLICK** *Landscaping in SmartPanel* **CLICK** *Backyard SmartTemplate*	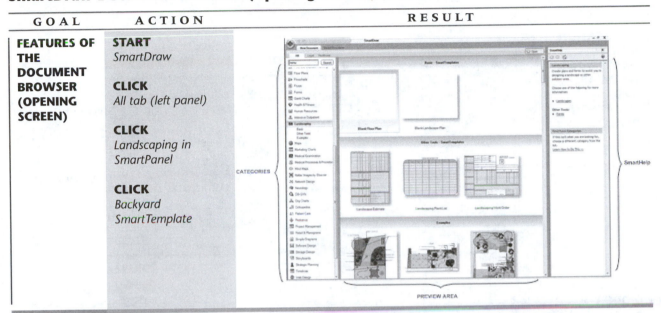

WORKING SCREEN

After you select a template or open an existing document from the Document Browser, the active SmartDraw program window changes to the **Application Screen**. The Application Screen provides **context-sensitive** help in the right panel (**SmartHelp panel**), and the most frequently used menu options for the template selected in the left panel (**SmartPanel**). Most documents can be completed using just the options shown in the SmartPanel, such as drawing a wall or adding text. This is one of the "working smarter" features that will save you time when looking for the needed menu options. The help provided in the SmartHelp panel is also context sensitive. Detailed help is provided for most of the specific features you will need to edit or complete the selected template. In many cases there is also a video tutor that shows you how to perform the operation; but this nullifies the advantage of the Smart system that makes tools and help available immediately at a mouse click, which is definitely not working smarter.

TIPS

Rulers may be turned on or off as needed.

The work area can be enlarged or reduced as desired.

NOTES

SmartPanel has the most frequently used items for the type of template.

SmartPanel is context-sensitive, based on the type of template selected.

Video tutorials are available in many categories such as the Floor Plans category.

The Home symbol will redisplay the list of topics in the SmartPanel.

Application (Working) Screen Features

GOAL	ACTION	RESULT
APPLICATION SCREEN, SMARTPANEL, WORK AREA, AND SMARTHELP PANEL	**CLICK** *?SmartHelp if the right panel is not open*	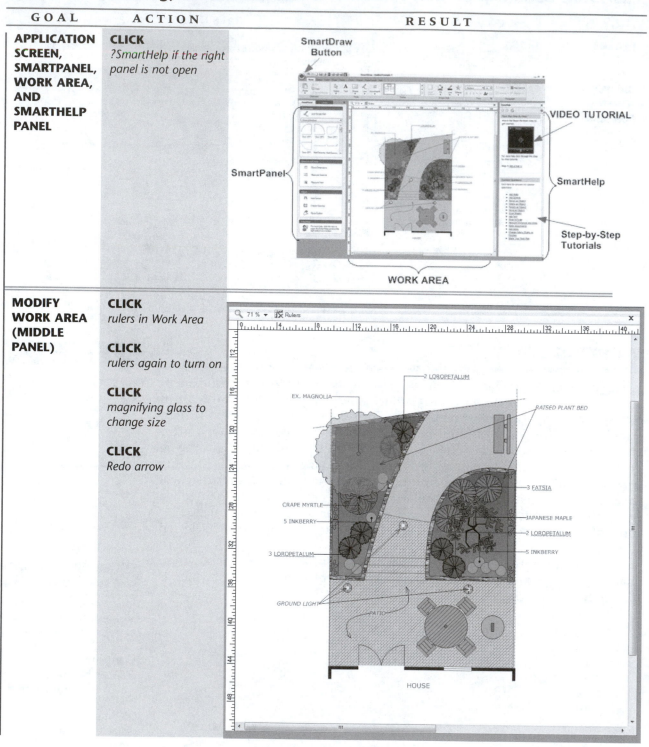
MODIFY WORK AREA (MIDDLE PANEL)	**CLICK** *rulers in Work Area* **CLICK** *rulers again to turn on* **CLICK** *magnifying glass to change size* **CLICK** *Redo arrow*	

Application (Working) Screen Features (*continued*)

GOAL	ACTION	RESULT
SMARTPANEL (LEFT PANEL)	**CLICK** *SmartPanel* **CLICK** *Library tab*	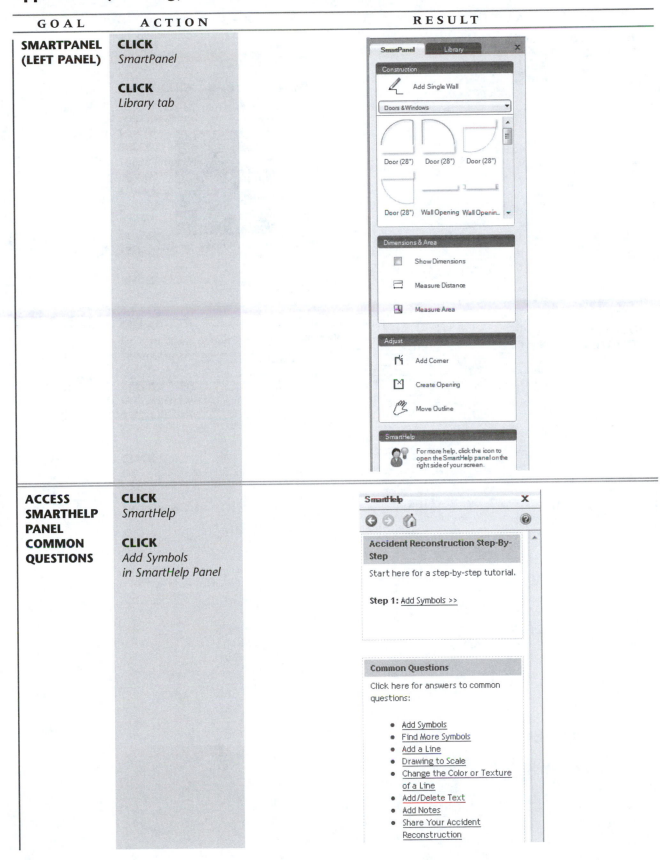
ACCESS SMARTHELP PANEL COMMON QUESTIONS	**CLICK** *SmartHelp* **CLICK** *Add Symbols in SmartHelp Panel*	

Application (Working) Screen Features (*continued*)

GOAL	ACTION	RESULT
VIEW VIDEO TUTORIAL	**CLICK** *Arrow button*	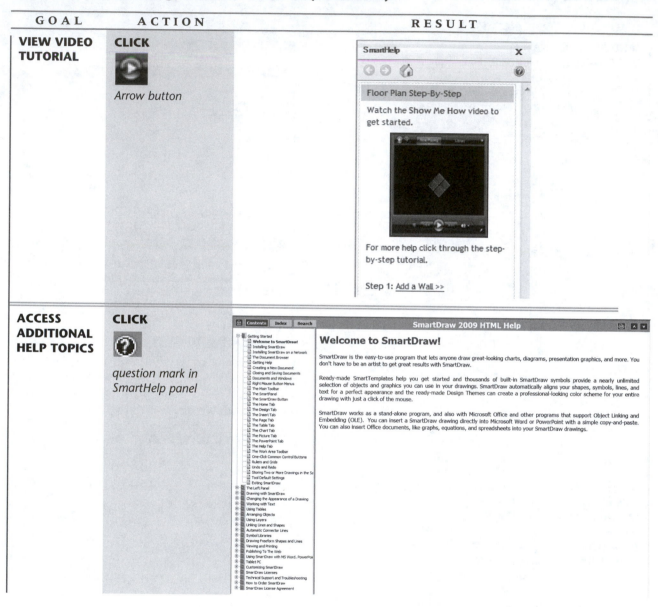
ACCESS ADDITIONAL HELP TOPICS	**CLICK** *question mark in SmartHelp panel*	

Application (Working) Screen Features (*continued*)

GOAL	ACTION	RESULT
DISPLAY CONTEXT-SENSITIVE HELP TOPICS	**CLICK** in SmartHelp panel **CLOSE** SmartDraw	

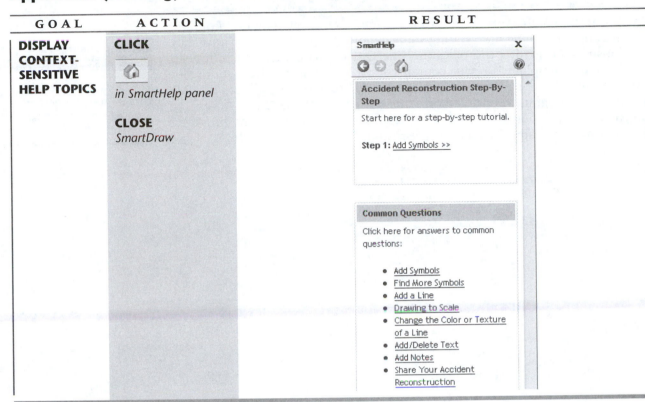

SmartDraw has many context-sensitive screens and features. These anticipate the action you want to perform, based on the template selected, and provide the most appropriate options without your manually searching for them.

All of the features and menu options in the main Ribbon menu grouping can be accessed and used if appropriate for the application. Those that are not appropriate or do not apply to the selected activity are grayed out (for example, the chart types that are usable only in Charts). You can select a completely unrelated type of blank template and complete a document using options from the Ribbon menus; but, again, you lose the advantage of the Smart system that provides tools and help immediately at a mouse click.

WHAT IS THE SMARTDRAW BUTTON?

The **SmartDraw Button** on the Application Screen opens a menu of options for opening and saving files, setting some default options for SmartDraw files, and closing and exiting the program. The Quick Access bar, which appears only when a template is open, contains shortcuts to selected functions like Open, Save, Print, or Export (which sends a file to another program like MS Word if that program is installed on your computer). Some Quick Access bar shortcuts (e.g., Export to LexisNexis® CaseMap) appear only if the programs they open are already installed on your computer.

Microsoft Office users will recognize the similarity of the SmartDraw button to the Smart Button introduced in Microsoft Office 2007. Most of the functions in the top group (**New, Open, Save, Save As, etc.**) conform to the standard usage found in many software applications.

The second group (**Print, Export,** and **Email**) contains additional options to print a document, to send it as an email, or to direct it to an outside SmartDraw partner for bulk or specialty printing.

The **Export** option menu in SmartDraw allows you to send files to other programs, such as MS Word, Excel, or PowerPoint, or to save files in other file formats, such as PDF, JPEG, or GIF. Clicking the Quick Access button or the menu listing will perform the same function.

Choose Format to Export Graphic as

» PDF

» Word

» PowerPoint

» Excel

» WordPerfect

» HTML

» JPEG

» PNG

» GIF

» TIFF

» BMP

» Metafile

» Enhanced Metafile

Options (in the third group) allows you to customize the basic features in SmartDraw to suit the way you want to use them.

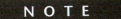

N O T E

You must have the appropriate programs installed to open files saved in the available formats, such as, the Adobe Reader for PDF files.

Select How Lines and Shapes Interact

☑ Allow Lines to Link

☑ Allow Shapes to Link to Lines

☑ Allow Shapes to Link

☑ Allow Lines to Join

☑ Hide Ribbon Area

Utilities includes a conversion utility to convert files from other programs, such as Microsoft Visio, to SmartDraw file format.

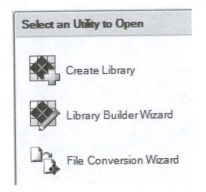

Select an Utility to Open

Create Library

Library Builder Wizard

File Conversion Wizard

WHAT IS THE RIBBON?

The Ribbon contains menus and options. Desired features and menu options in the main Ribbon menu grouping can be accessed and used for any document. Any options or menus that are not appropriate or do not apply to the selected activity (such as chart types that are useable only in Charts) appear grayed out. You could also select a completely unrelated blank template and complete a document using the options and menu choices from the Ribbon menus; but this would involve a bit more work.

The Ribbon has a number of **tabs**. These tabs contain **groups** of related menus, which contain drawing options and settings.

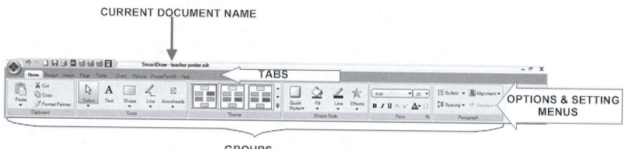

CURRENT DOCUMENT NAME

TABS

OPTIONS & SETTING MENUS

GROUPS

The groups of menus in each tab are shown below. Each of the menus and options is discussed later in the tutorials that explain their use and function.

HOME TAB

DESIGN TAB

INSERT TAB

PAGE TAB

TABLE TAB

CHART TAB

PICTURE TAB

POWERPOINT® TAB

HELP TAB

Templates and Examples
(Do I Have to Start from Scratch?)

- The Basics: What Do I Need to Know to Get Started?
- What If I Need Help Completing a Project?
  - ▲ *Tutorial—Steps for Creating a Gantt Chart Using a SmartTemplate*
- What Types of Help Are Available?
  - ▲ *Tutorial—SmartHelp Panel Features*
- Are There Limitations on Using Examples?
- How Do I Select and Edit an Example or Template?
  - ▲ *Tutorial—Selecting a SmartTemplate or Example*
- What Are the Absolute Basics to Start Working?
  - ▲ *Tutorial—Setting up the Work Space*
- Why Are There Menu Items in the SmartPanel?
  - ▲ *Tutorial—Using SmartPanel Options to Draw a Wall*
- How Do I Draw Lines and Arrows?
  - ▲ *Tutorial—Drawing Lines and Arrows*
- How Do I Work with Shapes?
  - ▲ *Tutorial—Working with Shapes*
- How Do I Resize Shapes?
  - ▲ *Tutorial—Resizing Shapes*
- How Do I Connect Shapes with Lines and Arrows?
  - ▲ *Tutorial—Using Connection Points*
- What Are Connection Points and Anchors?
  - ▲ *Tutorial—Connection Points Menu*
- How Do I Add Text?
  - ▲ *Tutorial—Adding Text*

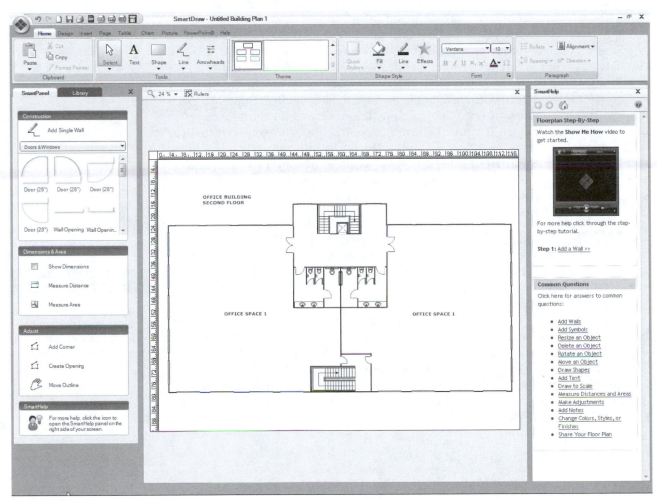

Source: Document Browser Category: Floor Plans\Office Building 1-First Floor

THE BASICS: WHAT DO I NEED TO KNOW TO GET STARTED?

Many projects can be completed using the basic functions of drawing lines and arrows, adding or editing text, and adding symbols from the symbols library to program templates or examples. These templates are called **SmartTemplates**. Many of the most commonly requested graphics and documents have already been created and made available in SmartDraw as SmartTemplates. You may modify the template examples without fear of erasing or losing the originals; SmartTemplates are a permanent part of the SmartDraw program and are not changed by editing or customization.

The most commonly used menu options, like drawing a wall, are linked to SmartTemplates and are displayed for easy access and use in the SmartPanel when a SmartTemplate is selected. An initial selection of symbols is also displayed in the SmartPanel in the symbol library based on the category of SmartTemplate selected. SmartTemplates have default settings that are associated with the category of template, such as the ability of lines and arrows to anchor automatically to shapes in charts. These defaults are context-sensitive items related to the application or tool being used. The tutorials and videos displayed in the SmartHelp panel are also context sensitive. For example, selecting the SmartTemplate for floor plans will display help for all of the steps in creating a floor plan, as well as any related video tutorial.

WHAT IF I NEED HELP COMPLETING A PROJECT?

If anything sounds confusing or you want a little help, the SmartPanel provides step-by-step help, and in many cases video instruction, for each category in the Document Browser based on the SmartTemplate selected. A sample of the help available from the SmartHelp panel for creating a Gantt chart is shown below. Even for seasoned business professionals, making a timeline of dependent events (a Gantt chart) can be a daunting task without a program like SmartDraw. The demonstration below shows how simple it can be to create a Gantt chart for a home renovation. The starting point is selecting the correct SmartTemplate from the Document Browser, in this case the Blank Gantt Charts-Month with Days.

The tasks include:

1. Select Paper and Paint
2. Purchase Materials
3. Strip Wall Paper
4. Repair Plaster
5. Let Plaster Dry
6. Paint First Coat
7. Let Paint Dry
8. Tape Areas
9. Paint Second Coat
10. Clean Up
11. Fourth of July Party

> **TIP**
>
> For personal projects unselect holidays when you will work at home.

The finished Gantt chart for a home renovation

Number	Task	Resource	Start	End	Duration	June																															July				
						1	2	3	4	5	6	7	8	9	10	11	12	13	14	15	16	17	18	19	20	21	22	23	24	25	26	27	28	29	30	1	2	3	4	5
1	SELECT PAPER and PAINT	DECORATORS	6/1/2009	6/5/2009	4																																				
2	PURCHASE MATERIALS	Home Supply	6/5/2009	6/7/2009	2																																				
3	STRIP WALLPAPER		6/5/2009	6/8/2009	3																																				
4	REPAIR PLASTER		6/8/2009	6/10/2009	2																																				
5	LET PLASTER DRY		6/10/2009	6/12/2009	2																																				
6	PAINT FIRST COAT		6/11/2009	6/14/2009	3																																				
7	LET PAINT DRY		6/14/2009	6/15/2009	1																																				
8	TAPE AREA		6/15/2009	6/16/2009	1																																				
9	PAINT SECOND COAT		6/16/2009	6/20/2009	4																																				
10	CLEAN UP		6/20/2009	6/26/2009	6																																				
11	FOURTH OF July PARTY		7/4/2009	7/5/2009	1																																				

Steps for Creating a Gantt Chart Using a SmartTemplate

GOAL	ACTION	RESULT
SELECT GANTT CHART SMARTTEMPLATE OPEN SMARTHELP PANEL	**START** *SmartDraw* **CLICK** *Gantt Charts in Document Browser* **CLICK** *Month with Days* **CLICK** *?SmartHelp*	
USE SMARTPANEL OPTIONS TO SET START DATE	**CLICK** *Start Date in SmartPanel* **ENTER** *June 1 2009* **CLICK** *OK*	

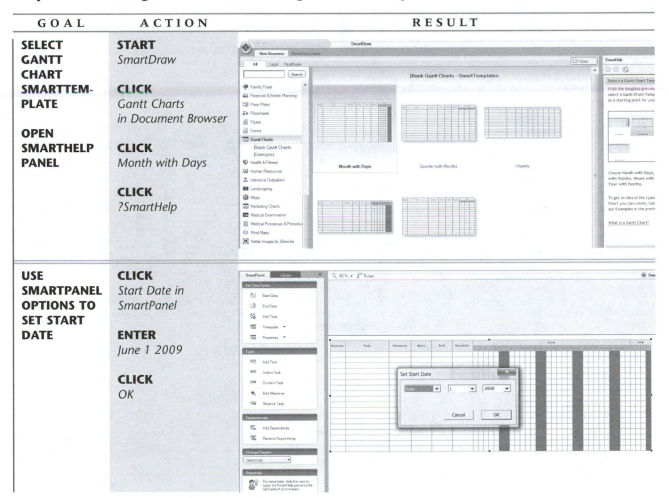

Steps for Creating a Gantt Chart Using a SmartTemplate (*continued*)

GOAL	ACTION	RESULT
USE SMARTPANEL OPTION TO SET END DATE	**CLICK** *End Date in SmartPanel* **ENTER** *July 4 2009* **CLICK** *OK*	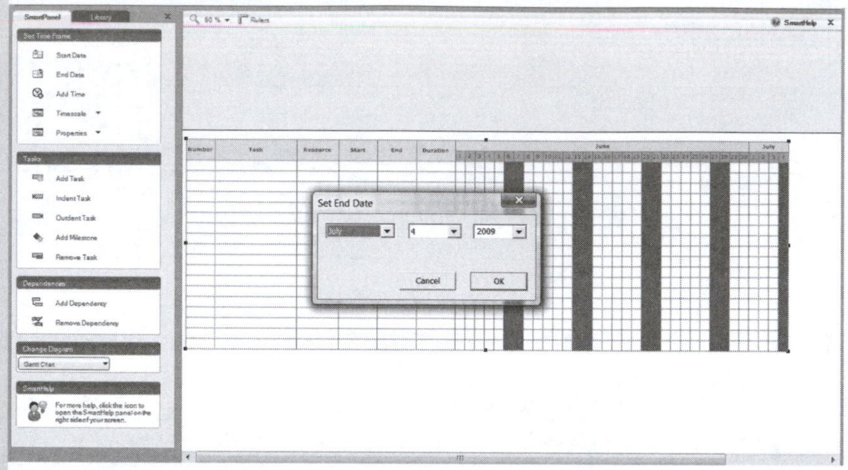
USE SMARTPANEL OPTIONS TO SET PROPERTIES	**CLICK** *Properties SmartPanel* **CLICK** *Sun and Sat to make them work days* **CLICK** *None in Standard Holidays* **CLICK** *OK*	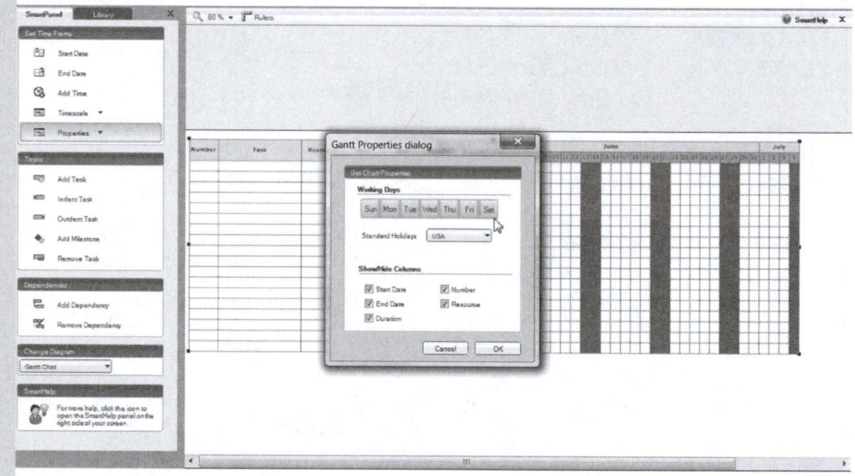
USE SMARTPANEL OPTIONS TO ADD TASK **Option:** Enter the rest of the tasks as shown above.	**CLICK** *Add Task* **TYPE** *Select Paper (the first task)* **TYPE** *Purchase Materials (the second task)*	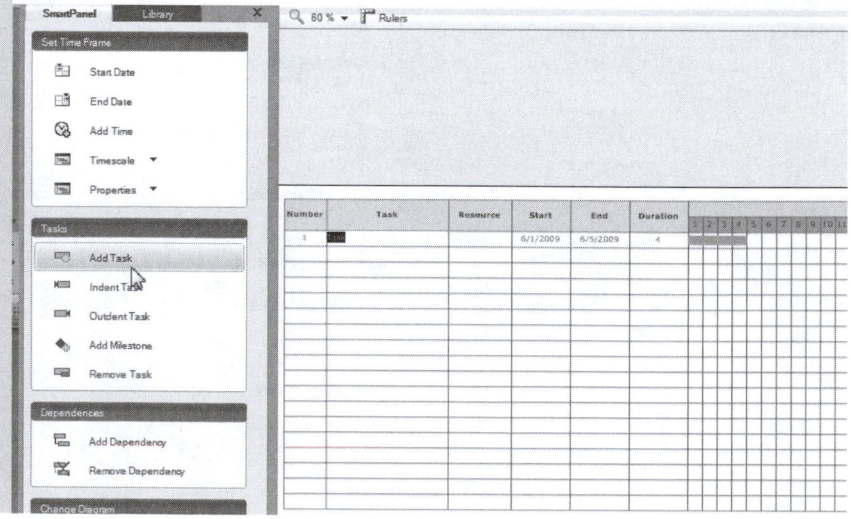

Steps for Creating a Gantt Chart Using a SmartTemplate (*continued*)

GOAL	ACTION	RESULT
USE MOUSE TO DRAG TIMELINE TO MOVE TO DIFFERENT DAY AND CHANGE LENGTH OF TIMELINE	**SELECT** *Task 2 timeline* **CLICK** *on selection handle at end of line for Task 2* **DRAG and DROP** *to move to day 6*	<table><tr><td>Number</td><td>Task</td><td>Resource</td><td>Start</td><td>End</td><td>Duration</td><td>1 2 3 4 5 6 7 8 9</td></tr><tr><td>1</td><td>SELECT PAPER and PAINT</td><td>DECORATORS</td><td>6/1/2009</td><td>6/5/2009</td><td>4</td><td></td></tr><tr><td>2</td><td>PURCHASE MATERIALS</td><td>Home Supply</td><td>6/1/2009</td><td>6/5/2009</td><td>4</td><td></td></tr></table>
CHANGE LENGTH OF TIMELINE	**SELECT** *Task 2 timeline* **CLICK** *left selection handle of Task 2* **DRAG and DROP** *to resize for 2 days (5–6)*	<table><tr><td>Number</td><td>Task</td><td>Resource</td><td>Start</td><td>End</td><td>Duration</td><td>1 2 3 4 5 6 7 8</td></tr><tr><td>1</td><td>SELECT PAPER and PAINT</td><td>DECORATORS</td><td>6/1/2009</td><td>6/5/2009</td><td>4</td><td></td></tr><tr><td>2</td><td>PURCHASE MATERIALS</td><td>Home Supply</td><td>6/5/2009</td><td>6/9/2009</td><td>4</td><td></td></tr></table>
CHANGE LENGTH OF LINE USING DURATION	**CLICK** *4 in Task 1 Duration column* **TYPE** *1*	

You may close this document now; it will not be used in any future tutorials.

WHAT TYPES OF HELP ARE AVAILABLE?

The SmartHelp panel provides answers to questions commonly asked about the type of template selected. The chart below shows the Gantt Charts Step-By-Step Show Me How video. There are video tutorials for most of the most frequently used SmartTemplates. The videos provide a short overview of the steps to create or modify a template as shown in the selected screen for the Gantt chart, similar to the tutorial you just completed. These videos are particularly helpful when using a new SmartTemplate or for refreshing your memory on how to create a document you use infrequently. Commonly asked questions are listed for the function in the SmartTemplate selected. The answers provided are those you might otherwise obtain from the User's Guide or from the Help desk. Having the answers instantly available with a mouse click is a real time saver. The chart below shows the contents of the Gantt charts help material. Selecting a different SmartTemplate, such as that for a floor plan, will not show these features. This is one reason for selecting the correct template type for your project.

SmartHelp Panel Features

SMARTHELP PANEL	VIDEO INSTRUCTIONS	STEP-BY-STEP HELP

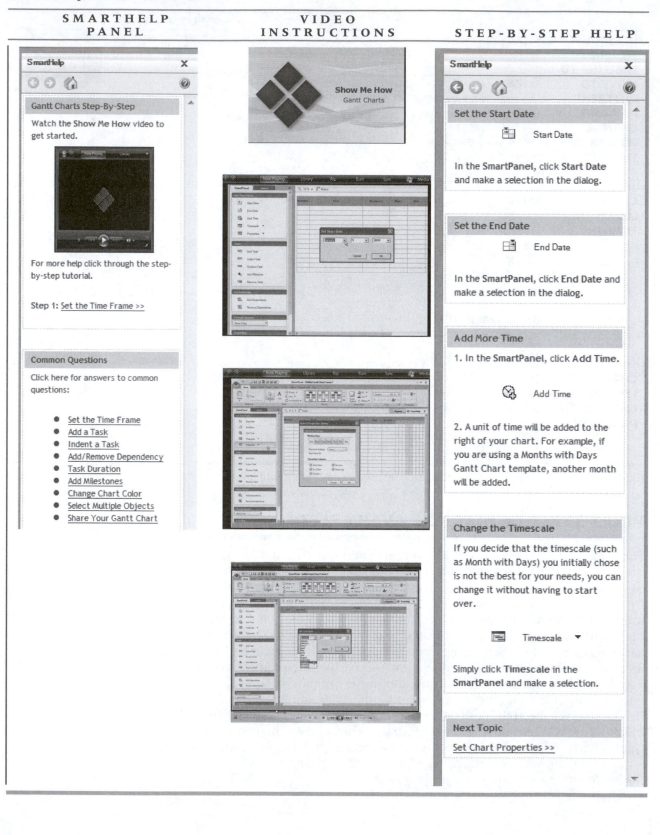

SmartHelp   X

Gantt Charts Step-By-Step

Watch the **Show Me How** video to get started.

For more help click through the step-by-step tutorial.

Step 1: Set the Time Frame >>

Common Questions

Click here for answers to common questions:

- Set the Time Frame
- Add a Task
- Indent a Task
- Add/Remove Dependency
- Task Duration
- Add Milestones
- Change Chart Color
- Select Multiple Objects
- Share Your Gantt Chart

Show Me How
Gantt Charts

SmartHelp   X

Set the Start Date

Start Date

In the SmartPanel, click **Start Date** and make a selection in the dialog.

Set the End Date

End Date

In the SmartPanel, click **End Date** and make a selection in the dialog.

Add More Time

1. In the SmartPanel, click **Add Time**.

Add Time

2. A unit of time will be added to the right of your chart. For example, if you are using a Months with Days Gantt Chart template, another month will be added.

Change the Timescale

If you decide that the timescale (such as Month with Days) you initially chose is not the best for your needs, you can change it without having to start over.

Timescale ▼

Simply click **Timescale** in the SmartPanel and make a selection.

Next Topic

Set Chart Properties >>

You can also use your Internet connection to obtain online help from the SmartDraw Encyclopedia of Business Graphics as shown below.

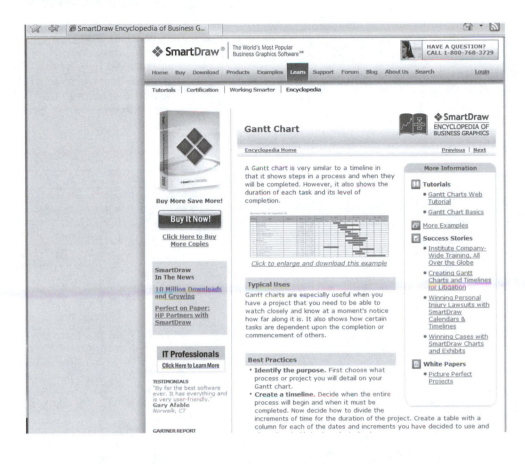

The key to all of this help is selecting the correct SmartTemplate for the project from the Document Browser.

ARE THERE LIMITATIONS ON USING EXAMPLES?

Examples are useful in deciding what type of document or graphic you need and can create. In many cases the example may be exactly what you want; or you may decide to use the example but experience a problem with some of the features and options. For example, some of the features and option selections may have been locked or set to a default. Most of these features and options can be unlocked or reset, for example, a document where the lines have been set to anchor to a shape at a specific point. If you select an example that does not allow you do what you want, you may just need to change the options to those you desire. Many of these options and settings will be shown as you work through the tutorials and can be used as a guide for future document creation.

HOW DO I SELECT AND EDIT AN EXAMPLE OR TEMPLATE?

Review the available template examples to find the one that is closest to the type of graphic or document you wish to create. Initially, while you learn the basics, it may be easier to edit or modify a template example. If none is close to what you need, select a blank template in the desired category to benefit from the context-sensitive SmartPanel menus and SmartHelp panel information.

N O T E

The SmartPanel and SmartHelp change to show commonly used menus and Help for the type of template selected (context sensitive).

Selecting a SmartTemplate or Example

GOAL	ACTION	RESULT
START SMARTDRAW FROM DESKTOP	**DOUBLE CLICK** SmartDraw 2009 *the SmartDraw icon on your desktop or from the Windows Start menu* **OR** *if there is no icon on the desktop then go to the next step*	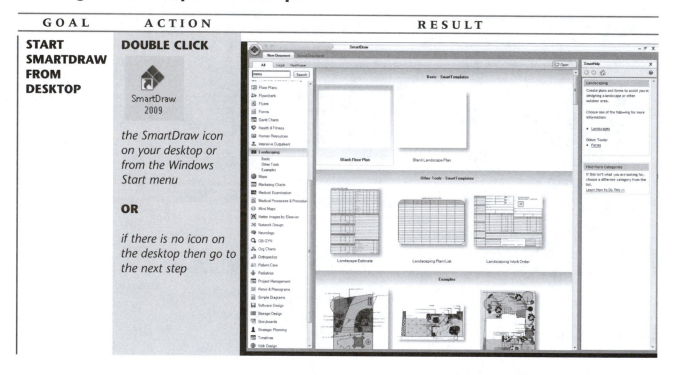

Selecting a SmartTemplate or Example (*continued*)

GOAL	ACTION	RESULT
START SMARTDRAW FROM PROGRAM LIST IF THERE IS NO SMARTDRAW ICON ON THE DESKTOP	**CLICK** **SELECT** ▶ **All Programs** **DOUBLE CLICK** ◆ SmartDraw 2009	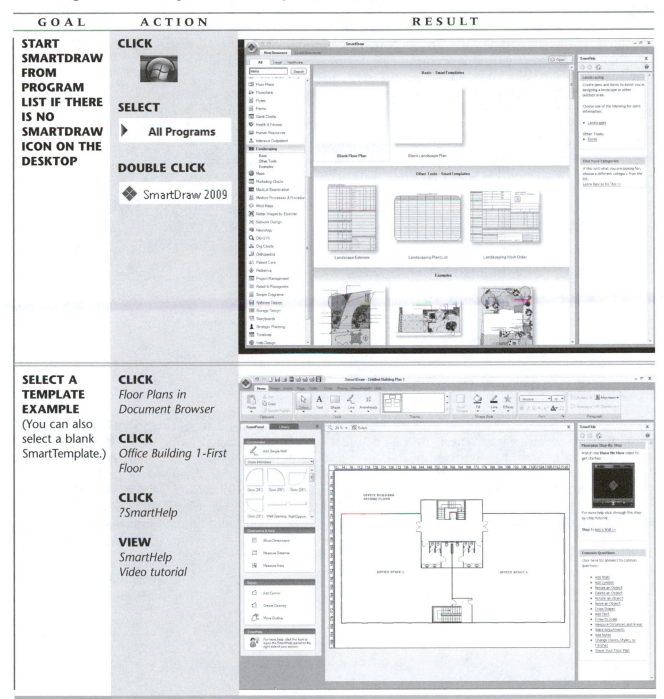
SELECT A TEMPLATE EXAMPLE (You can also select a blank SmartTemplate.)	**CLICK** *Floor Plans in Document Browser* **CLICK** *Office Building 1-First Floor* **CLICK** *?SmartHelp* **VIEW** *SmartHelp Video tutorial*	

WHAT ARE THE ABSOLUTE BASICS TO START WORKING?

A mouse is all you need to work on a document or graphic except for editing or adding text, when you will need your keyboard. If you have a tablet PC, you may also use your tablet "pen" instead of the mouse.

Templates and objects (symbols, lines, arrows, and text boxes) are selected using the **LEFT MOUSE BUTTON**. A single left click will select the desired template or object. A left mouse **CLICK and HOLD** will allow you to **DRAG and DROP** an object from one location to another (e.g., from the symbol library in the SmartPanel to the work space).

Symbols, lines, and text boxes can all be selected with a left mouse click on their border. Each object in the work area has a border around it that illuminates when the mouse cursor passes over it.

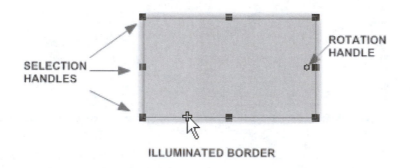

When the border appears it will also have markers at the corners and sometimes along the edges. These are called **selection handles**. The use of selection handles will be discussed below. A single left mouse click on the border will turn on the border; a single left mouse click outside the object will turn it off. Selecting an object makes it available for editing or modification.

A few basic work space settings can make work easier. A grid and rulers may be added to the work area to help visualize and place symbols and lines. The work area can be adjusted to show a larger or smaller view of the work area. Each of these work area options may be changed at any time without making any change to your document or graphic.

TIP

Context-sensitive option menus are opened by a **RIGHT MOUSE CLICK**.

NOTE

Grid lines can be useful in drawing lines and placing objects. They may be turned off or on at any time.

Setting Up the Work Space

GOAL	ACTION	RESULT
ADJUST DOCUMENT TO FIT WORK AREA	**CLICK** *Down arrow next to magnifying glass to open Zoom menu* **CLICK** *50%*	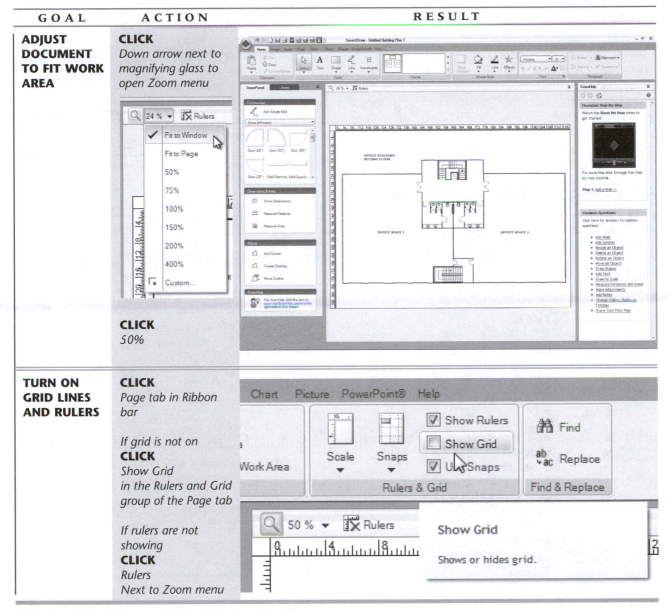
TURN ON GRID LINES AND RULERS	**CLICK** *Page tab in Ribbon bar* *If grid is not on* **CLICK** *Show Grid in the Rulers and Grid group of the Page tab* *If rulers are not showing* **CLICK** *Rulers Next to Zoom menu*	

This template will be used in the following tutorial.

WHY ARE THERE MENU ITEMS IN THE SMARTPANEL?

Most of the features you will need for a particular template, such as the Add a Wall option that appears when you select a Floor Plan template, are displayed in the SmartPanel on the left of your screen. This is a time saver that allows you to create your document without using the menu options accessed by selecting a tab and menu in the ribbon at the top of the screen. SmartDraw adds additional specialty features to the SmartPanel, such as the Add Corner and Create Opening used with Walls, that are not usually needed in other types of templates. The most frequently used symbols are also preloaded into the symbols area.

Using SmartPanel Options to Draw a Wall

GOAL	ACTION	RESULT
ADD A WALL Wall length is shown as you draw the wall.	*If not open* **CLICK** *Floor Plans in Document Browser* **CLICK** *Office Building 1-First Floor* **CLICK** *Add Single Wall in SmartPanel Menu* **PLACE MOUSE CURSOR** *at starting point* **CLICK and HOLD** *left mouse button and drag mouse to end point* **RELEASE** *left mouse button*	

HOW DO I DRAW LINES AND ARROWS?

Lines and arrows are drawn using the same techniques used for drawing the single wall example shown in the previous tutorial. You add lines and arrows by selecting the desired style from the Line menu or Arrow menu in the **Tools group** in the **Home tab**. After you select the line or arrow style, the mouse cursor, now appearing as a pencil, is placed at the starting point of the desired line or arrow. Then you click and hold the left mouse button while dragging the cursor to the end point of the line or arrow and then release it. Lines, arrows, or walls may be moved, resized, or rotated. All objects, including lines, walls, arrows, and symbols, must first be **SELECTED** by clicking on the object, which illuminates the selection handles or rotation marks. Remember to click (left mouse button) on another spot on the work area to **UNSELECT** the object when you are finished editing.

N O T E S

A wall is a type of line with special characteristics and properties.

Depending on the style selected, the arrowhead will appear at the beginning or at the end of the line.

Drawing Lines and Arrows

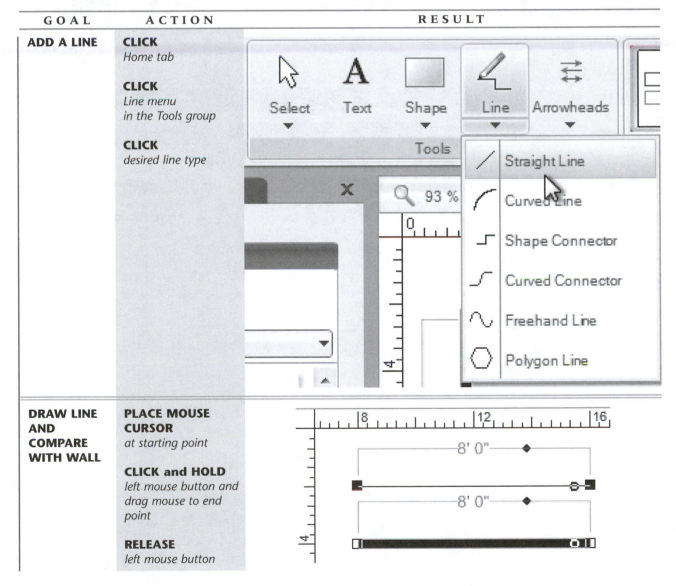

GOAL	ACTION	RESULT
ADD A LINE	**CLICK** *Home tab* **CLICK** *Line menu in the Tools group* **CLICK** *desired line type*	
DRAW LINE AND COMPARE WITH WALL	**PLACE MOUSE CURSOR** *at starting point* **CLICK and HOLD** *left mouse button and drag mouse to end point* **RELEASE** *left mouse button*	

Drawing Lines and Arrows (*continued*)

GOAL	ACTION	RESULT
ADD A CURVED LINE	**CLICK** *Line menu* **CLICK** *Curved Line* **DRAW** *a curve from one side to the other*	 **OFFICE SPACE 1**
SELECT ARROW TYPE	**CLICK** *Arrowheads menu* **CLICK** *Both (Arrow type)*	
DRAW ARROW	**PLACE MOUSE CURSOR** *at starting point* **CLICK and HOLD** *left mouse button and drag mouse to end point* **RELEASE** *left mouse button*	

Drawing Lines and Arrows (*continued*)

GOAL	ACTION	RESULT
CHANGE THICKNESS OR COLOR OF LINE OR ARROW	**SELECT** *line or arrow in drawing*	
	CLICK *Line in Shape Style group in Home tab*	
	CLICK *Thickness*	
	CLICK *desired version (in menu) or*	
	CLICK *desired color*	
	CLOSE FILE	

HOW DO I WORK WITH SHAPES?

Shapes are frequently used in flyers, organization charts, flow charts, and similar types of documents. Shapes may also be a part of symbols created with SmartDraw. Shapes are useful in many applications as building blocks that may be edited and resized to fit specific needs, such as creating a custom symbol or changing its shape using the Shape menu.

TIPS

The last shape selected appears in the menu until a new shape is chosen. Just click on the menu button to reuse the same shape.

Unselect items by pressing the Esc key or double clicking the mouse on a blank area of the work space.

NOTES

When a shape is selected, the cursor appears as an old-fashion rubber stamp.

A selected shape stays illuminated as other shapes are selected.

Working with Shapes

GOAL	ACTION	RESULT
OPEN A BLANK TEMPLATE	**CLICK** *Flyers category in Document Browser* **CLICK** *Blank Flyer*	**Blank Flyer**
SELECT AND ADD SINGLE SHAPE	**CLICK** *Home tab* **CLICK** *Shape menu* **CLICK** *Oval*	Shape Line Arrowheads Rectangle Rounded Rectangle Oval Square Circle Rounded Square
USE STAMPING TOOL TO ADD SHAPE TO DOCUMENT	**CLICK** *cursor in work area*	

Working with Shapes (*continued*)

GOAL	ACTION	RESULT
SELECT NEW SHAPE TO ADD TO DOCUMENT	**CLICK** *Shape menu* **CLICK** *Square*	
ADD NEW SHAPE TO DOCUMENT	**CLICK** *cursor in work area*	
ADD SAME SHAPE MULTIPLE TIMES	**HOLD** *Shift key down* **CLICK** *desired shape in SmartPanel* **MOVE** *cursor to work area* **STAMP (CLICK)** *shape multiple times in work area* **UNSELECT**	

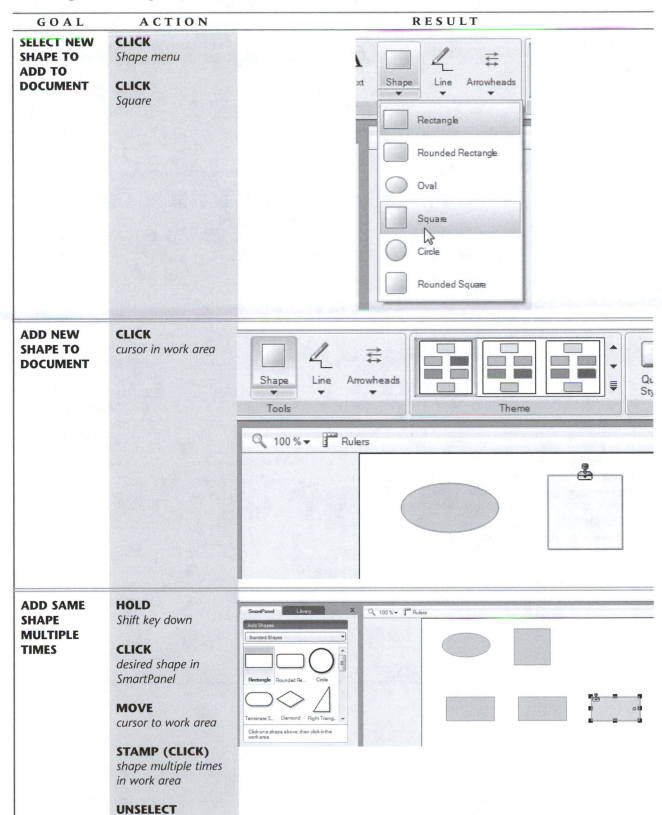

Working with Shapes (*continued*)

G O A L	A C T I O N	R E S U L T
FILL A SINGLE SHAPE WITH COLOR	**SELECT** *desired shape in document* **CLICK** *Fill menu* **CLICK** *desired color*	
SELECT MULTIPLE SHAPES AT THE SAME TIME AND FILL ALL SELECTED SHAPES WITH COLOR	**HOLD** *Shift key down* **SELECT** *desired shapes* **CLICK** *Fill* **CLICK** *Hatch and* **CLICK** *desired pattern*	

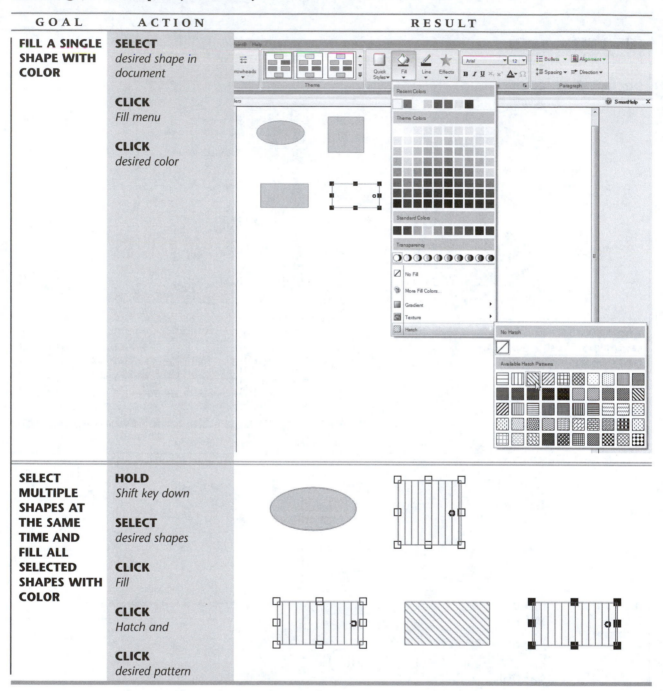

HOW DO I RESIZE SHAPES?

There are two methods to resize shapes and most objects like symbols, lines, and text boxes. You may click and hold the mouse on the object's selection handles and drag it to the new size or change the object's dimensions by typing the new dimensions. Length and width relationships may be maintained by using the **Proportionally** option in the **Grow Options Menu** area of the **Shape Properties box**.

A right mouse click will open context-sensitive menus and options.

Dimensions change as you drag selection handles.

Nonproportional length or width changes may be made by clicking and dragging the middle selection handles on an object. This horizontal or vertical selection will allow you to change individual sides without changing the dimensions of the other sides. The Undo arrow (Crtl+Z) may be used to return an object to the original size.

You may also resize most shapes and objects by changing the dimensions shown with the object. This is usually the easiest method when a specific size is desired. Clicking the cursor on the existing dimensions shown will change their appearance and allow you to type in new dimensions, similar to typing text in a text box. Some objects and shapes, such as the triangle shape, cannot be resized using this method.

Resizing Shapes

GOAL	ACTION	RESULT
SELECT RESIZING PROPERTIES AND SELECT SHOW DIMENSIONS AND TOTAL AREA	**SELECT** *rectangle in work area* **RIGHT CLICK** *mouse button* **CLICK** *Proportionally in Grow options in Shape Properties box* **CLICK** *Show Area* **CLICK** *OK*	Shape Properties Grow: ⦿ Proportionally ○ Horizontally only ○ Vertically only ○ No restrictions ☐ Allow sides to be independently adjusted (Applies only to certain shapes) Select the way the shape can be re-sized. Proportional growth maintains a symbol's original shape and prevents distortion. OK / Cancel / Help Show Dimensions: ○ Always ⦿ Only when selected ○ Never Show Area: ☑ Always show the area of the shape Linking: ☐ Allow shape to link to borders ☐ Allow shape to link to cells in table Check these boxes to allow the shape to attach to the border of another shape or to attach inside a cell in a table. ☐ Do not check spelling Checking this box turns off spelling correction for any text contained inside the shape. ☐ Print as Transparent Checking this box marks the shape as transparent so that it will print properly. ☐ Allow Image Drop Checking this box allows images to be dropped into the shape.

Resizing Shapes (*continued*)

GOAL	ACTION	RESULT
RESIZE WITH CURSOR	**SELECT** *rectangle shape* **CLICK and HOLD** *selection handle* *and* **DRAG** *to desired size*	
RESIZE BY TYPING DESIRED DIMENSION	**SELECT** *rectangle shape* **CLICK** *on the dimension to be changed (2.10)* **TYPE** *new dimension (1.91)* **PRESS** *Enter key* **CLOSE FILE**	

HOW DO I CONNECT SHAPES WITH LINES AND ARROWS?

Lines and shapes may be anchored or not anchored. Anchored lines and arrows move as the shapes to which they are anchored move. Lines that are not anchored will remain in the place where they were drawn, just as other objects on the work space remain in place when other objects are moved. Depending on the diagram and the relationships, you may want to connect the lines so you can move the shape and retain the connection.

Shapes may be set up to allow connections to be made in specific places on the outside edge of the shape or in customized locations within the shape. Each shape has a default connection setting that provides select points along the shape's edges.

Using Connection Points

GOAL	ACTION	RESULT
OPEN A BLANK TEMPLATE **TURN OFF OPTION FOR LINES TO LINK**	**CLICK** *Blank Flyer in Flyers category of Document Browser* **CLICK** *Oval in SmartPanel* **CLICK** *on work area* **CLICK** *Rectangle in SmartPanel* **CLICK** *on work area* **CLICK** *SmartDraw button* **CLICK** *Options* **UNCLICK** *Allow Lines to Link*	

Menu items:
- New
- Open
- Save
- Save As ▸
- Print ▸
- Export ▸
- Email ▸
- **ABC** Spellcheck ▸
- Options ▸
- Utilities ▸
- Close
- **X** Exit SmartDraw

Select How Lines and Shapes Interact

- ☐ Allow Lines to Link
- ☐ Allow Shapes to Link to Lines
- ☐ Allow Shapes to Link
- ☐ Allow Lines to Join
- ☐ Hide Ribbon Area

Using Connection Points (*continued*)

GOAL	ACTION	RESULT
CONNECT SHAPES WITH STRAIGHT LINE	**CLICK** *Home tab* **CLICK** *Line menu* **CLICK** *Straight Line* **PLACE MOUSE CURSOR** *at starting point on left shape* **CLICK and HOLD** *left mouse button and drag mouse to shape on right* **RELEASE** *left mouse button* **UNSELECT** *Line*	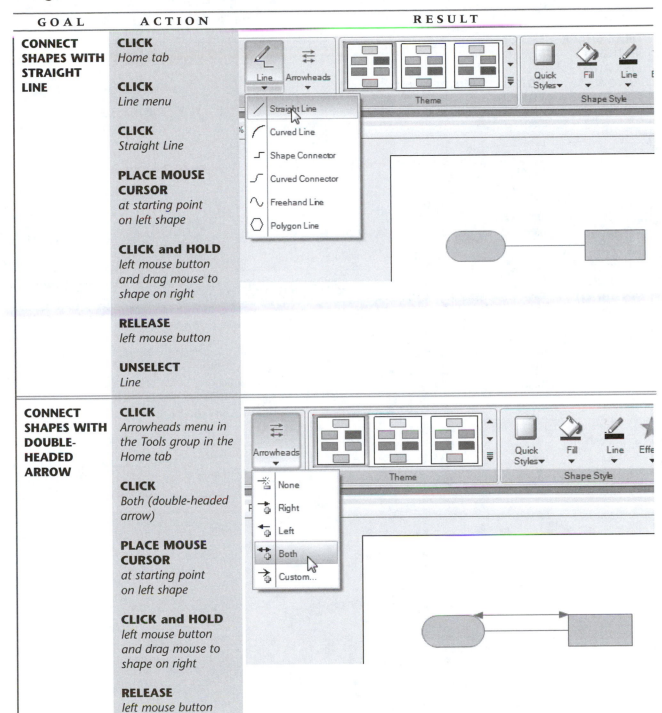
CONNECT SHAPES WITH DOUBLE-HEADED ARROW	**CLICK** *Arrowheads menu in the Tools group in the Home tab* **CLICK** *Both (double-headed arrow)* **PLACE MOUSE CURSOR** *at starting point on left shape* **CLICK and HOLD** *left mouse button and drag mouse to shape on right* **RELEASE** *left mouse button*	

Using Connection Points (*continued*)

G O A L	A C T I O N	R E S U L T
DRAG SHAPE WITHOUT LINE AND ARROW	**SELECT** *shape on right* **HOLD LEFT MOUSE BUTTON** *and drag selected shape down the work area* **CLICK** *Undo arrow (Ctrl +Z)* **UNSELECT** *all objects*	
TURN ON OPTION TO LINK LINES	**CLICK** *SmartDraw button* **CLICK** *Options* **CLICK** *Allow Lines to Link*	

Home · Design · Insert · Page · Table · Chart · Picture · PowerPoint® · H

New

Open

Save

Save As ▸

Print ▸

Export ▸

Email ▸

ABC Spellcheck ▸

Options ▸

Utilities ▸

Close

✕ Exit SmartDraw

Select How Lines and Shapes Interact

☑ Allow Lines to Link

☐ Allow Shapes to Link to Lines

☐ Allow Shapes to Link

☐ Allow Lines to Join

☐ Hide Ribbon Area

Using Connection Points (*continued*)

GOAL	ACTION	RESULT
DRAW DOUBLE-HEADED ARROW AND A SHAPE CONNECTOR LINE	**CLICK** *Arrowheads menu* **CLICK** *Both* **CLICK** *Line menu* **CLICK** *Curved line* **PLACE** *cursor on top middle of one shape and drag cursor to top middle of the other shape* **CLICK** *Line menu* **CLICK** *Shape Connector* **PLACE** *cursor on one of the connection points on bottom of one shape and draw to connection point on bottom of other shape*	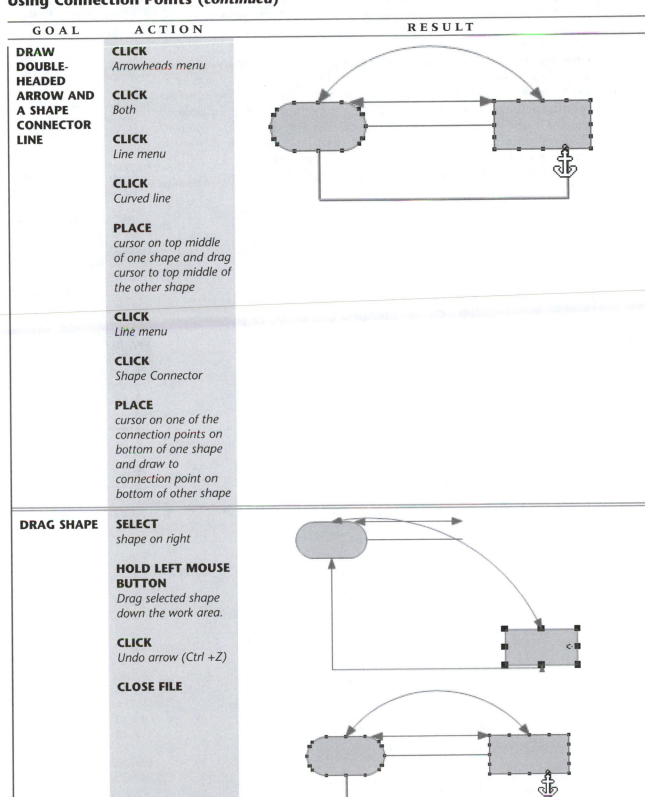
DRAG SHAPE	**SELECT** *shape on right* **HOLD LEFT MOUSE BUTTON** *Drag selected shape down the work area.* **CLICK** *Undo arrow (Ctrl +Z)* **CLOSE FILE**	

WHAT ARE CONNECTION POINTS AND ANCHORS?

Lines and arrows may be linked with objects, like shapes, to allow the shape to be moved and still retain the relationship with the connection lines and shapes or objects. Depending on the application, you may want to connect the lines or arrows at specific points on an object, like the top or bottom or a particular side. In some graphics it may be important to have a connection at a specific point, such as in an electrical diagram. The connection point option may be selected from the **Design** tab's **Connection Points menu**. Shapes may have a fixed number of points (the default setting) or additional points. Shapes that have a continuous border may be set to allow a connection at any place on the border, **Continuous** setting. Up to 16 individual points may be set using a **Custom** setting.

Connection Points Menu

GOAL	ACTION	RESULT
CONNECT SHAPES USING DEFAULT CONNECTION POINT SETTING	**CLICK** *Blank Flyer in Flyer category of Document Browser* **CLICK** *SmartDraw button* **CLICK** *Options* **CLICK** *Allow Lines to Link* **ADD** *two shapes to work area (oval and rectangle)* **CLICK** *Line menu* **CLICK** *Shape Connector* **PLACE** *cursor on connection point on bottom of one shape and draw to connection point on bottom of other shape*	

Connection Points Menu (*continued*)

GOAL	ACTION	RESULT
CONNECT SHAPE USING CONTINOUS CONNECTION POINT OPTION	**SELECT** *shape on right* **CLICK** *Design tab* **CLICK** *Connection Points menu* **CLICK** *Continuous in Select Setting area* **CLICK** *OK* **DRAW** *line between shapes, placing end point anywhere along border of shape*	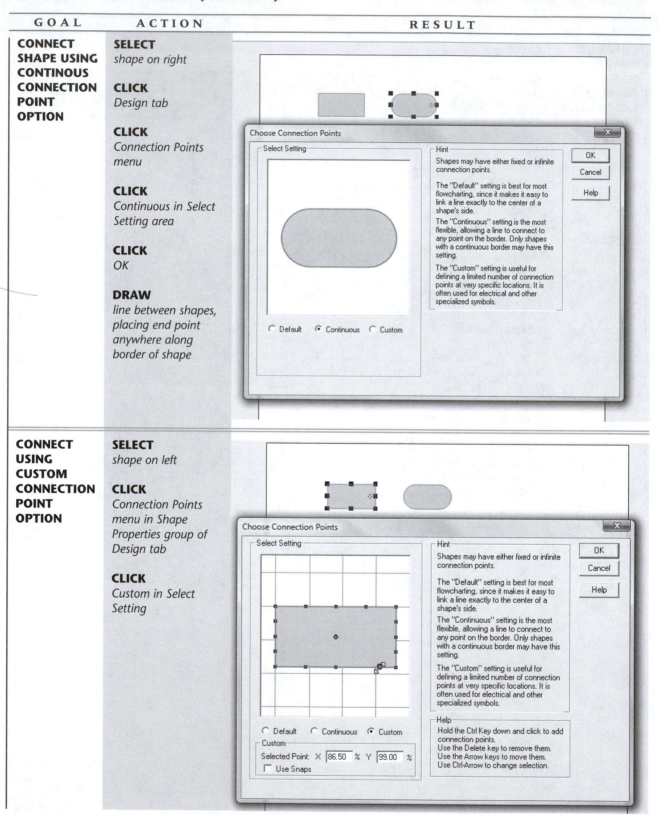
CONNECT USING CUSTOM CONNECTION POINT OPTION	**SELECT** *shape on left* **CLICK** *Connection Points menu in Shape Properties group of Design tab* **CLICK** *Custom in Select Setting*	

Connection Points Menu (*continued*)

GOAL	ACTION	RESULT
CHANGE CONNECTION POINT TO INSIDE SHAPE	**CLICK and HOLD** *cursor on connection point on bottom border* **DRAG** *cursor (now arrows) to middle right inside shape* **RELEASE** *cursor* **CLICK** *OK* **DRAW** *line between new connection point and other shape*	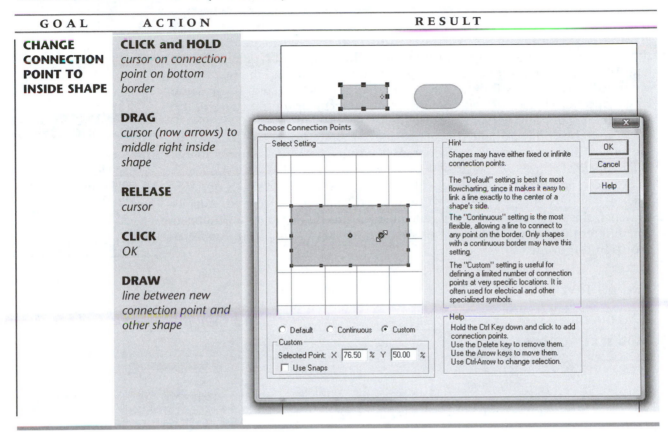

Close this file; we will not use it again.

HOW DO I ADD TEXT?

You can add text to a drawing by clicking on the **Text** button in the **Tools group** in the **Home tab**, or by clicking **Add Text box** in the SmartPanel (if shown). Place the cursor at the starting point for the text and type the desired text. When you are finished, click the mouse anywhere to end the text entering process. The text will be in a text box that may be selected in the same way that other objects are selected: by moving the cursor on the edges of the box until it is illuminated and clicking the left mouse button.

A **text box** may be added inside shapes or along lines. The location of the cursor after you select the text option determines where the text will initially appear.

You can add text as part of a text box that has the characteristics of other objects. The box may be selected (illuminated), moved, or resized, and its contents, the text, may be resized, edited, or changed. Text may be changed to a different type font, size, color, or style (e.g., bold or italic) from the **Font group** in the Home tab.

> ### N O T E
>
> Type font, size, style, and color can be selected from the Home tab-Font group or from the menu expanded by clicking the arrow in the lower right side of the Font group.

Adding Text

GOAL	ACTION	RESULT
ADD TEXT	**OPEN** *existing document or a Blank Flyer* **CLICK** *Home tab* **CLICK** *Text in the Tools group or Add Text in the SmartPanel* **PLACE** *cursor at desired beginning point, and* **TYPE** *text*	
EDIT OR ADD ADDITIONAL TEXT	**CLICK** *Text in the Tools group* **PLACE** *mouse cursor where you want to add additional text* **DOUBLE CLICK** *in existing text box at point where new text is to be added or existing text is to be edited* **CLOSE FILE**	 ADDITIONAL TEXT Place podium and microphone at front of room

Symbols
(You Mean There Is More?)

- What Are Symbols and Shapes?
- How Do I Add Symbols to a Drawing?
  - ▲ *Tutorial—Adding Symbols to a Document*
- Where Do I Find More Symbols?
  - ▲ *Tutorial—Using the Symbol Libraries*
- How Do I Rotate a Symbol?
  - ▲ *Tutorial—Rotating Symbols*
- How Do I Resize a Symbol?
  - ▲ *Tutorial—Resizing Symbols*
  - ▲ *Tutorial—Using the Shape Properties Menu*
- Can I Resize Symbols Using Dimensions?
  - ▲ *Tutorial—Resizing Symbols by Typing Dimensions*
- How Do I Add Color to a Symbol or Shape?
  - ▲ *Tutorial—Adding Color to Symbols*
- How Do I Save My Work?
  - ▲ *Tutorial—Saving a File Created in SmartDraw*
- Can I Export My Work to Another Program?
  - ▲ *Tutorial—Exporting a File*

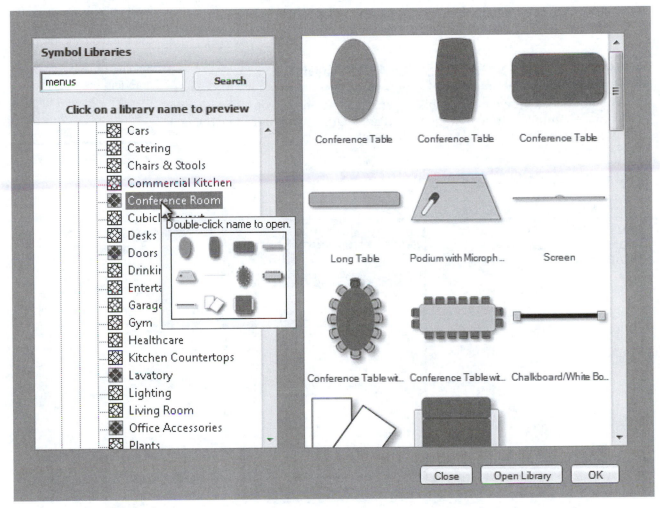

Source: SmartDraw Symbol Libraries

WHAT ARE SYMBOLS AND SHAPES?

Symbols are graphic objects that can be added to documents. SmartDraw provides an extensive library of symbols grouped by type or application, such as floor plans or maps. The symbol libraries also contain clip art, which are photolike images that can be added to documents in the same way symbols are added to documents. Most of the symbols are objects created using SmartDraw and can be edited and customized. Most of the clip art and a few symbols cannot be customized but may be resized.

Most symbols are combinations of shapes, or of shapes and lines. Therefore, they can be edited using the **Shape menu** in the Tools group in the Home tab. (This menu is similar to the menu of line and arrow styles.)

HOW DO I ADD SYMBOLS TO A DRAWING?

When you choose an example or blank template, an initial context-sensitive collection of symbols is shown in the SmartPanel. Other symbols can be opened into the SmartPanel from the Symbol Libraries.

N O T E

A symbol may be selected by a left mouse click and then placed at the desired location with another left mouse click. You can also use the drag-and-drop method (clicking and holding the mouse while dragging the cursor to a new location, and then releasing the mouse button).

Adding Symbols to a Document

GOAL	ACTION	RESULT
USE SYMBOLS FROM SMARTPANEL	**CLICK** *Blank Floor Plan in Document Browser* **CLICK** *Library tab in the SmartPanel to expand list of symbols* **CLICK** *Add Single Wall* **DRAW** *4-foot wall*	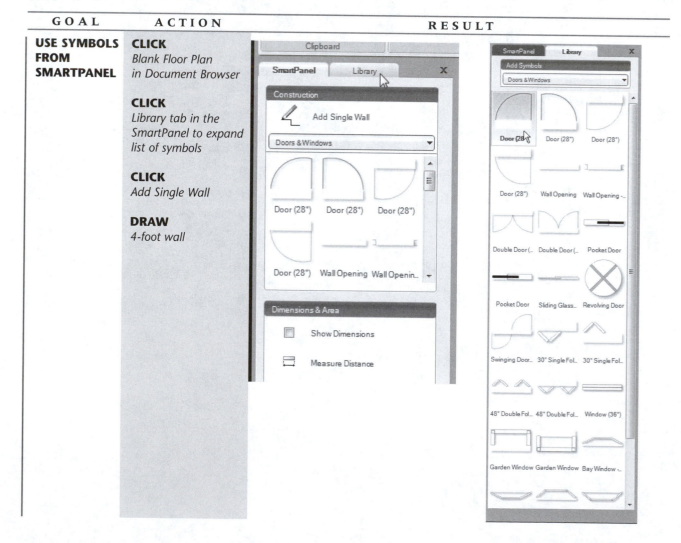

Adding Symbols to a Document (*continued*)

GOAL	ACTION	RESULT
ADD SYMBOL TO DRAWING	**CLICK** *Door (28")* **PLACE CURSOR** *at right end of wall* **CLICK** *to place door symbol*	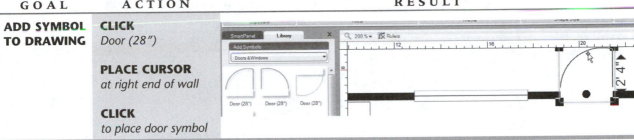

WHERE DO I FIND MORE SYMBOLS?

An initial selection of symbols is shown in the SmartPanel based on the template or example selected. SmartDraw provides thousands of additional symbols that can be added to any document from the **Symbol Libraries**. Additional symbols from any Symbol Libraries category can be added to a document. Mixing and matching symbols from different library categories sometimes provides just the exact detail you need. The full list of categories may be displayed and a new set of symbols added to the SmartPanel Library display. Once a category is selected, it is added to the list of categories in the SmartPanel pull-down category list for quick access.

The podium symbol will be used in the next five tutorials.

Using the Symbol Libraries

GOAL	ACTION	RESULT
ADD SYMBOLS FROM SYMBOL LIBRARIES	**CLICK** *More in the drop-down menu* **CLICK** *in Symbol Libraries—Floor Plans—Furniture—Conference Room* **DOUBLE CLICK** *to show symbols in SmartPanel or click OK*	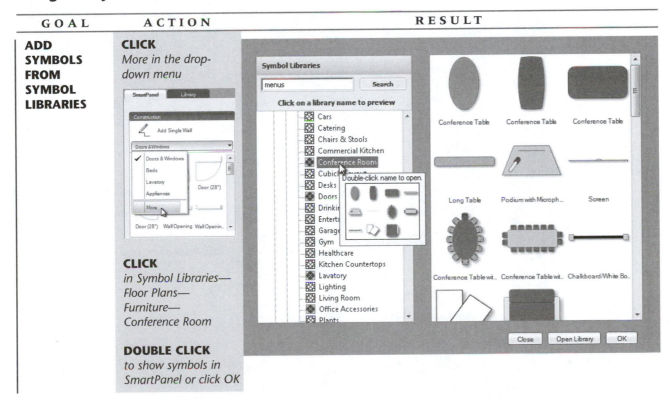

Using the Symbol Libraries (*continued*)

GOAL	ACTION	RESULT
PLACE SYMBOL IN DOCUMENT	**CLICK** *Podium with Microphone in SmartPanel* **PLACE CURSOR** *at desired location on document* **CLICK** *left mouse button*	

HOW DO I ROTATE A SYMBOL?

Most symbols and shapes can be rotated as needed. Symbols, shapes, text boxes, and other objects that can be rotated have a **rotation handle**. The rotation handle will appear when the symbol or shape is selected. You can select symbols, like other objects, by clicking the left mouse button when the cursor is on the item and it is illuminated. You can rotate the symbol around its center point by holding the left mouse button with the cursor on the rotation handle. There must be enough room in the document work area to allow the rotation to occur within the document. If you are close to the edge of the document, you may need to move the symbol away from the edge, rotate it, and put it back into its desired location.

TIP

Some symbols are so small it is hard to see the rotation handle. Resize the symbol proportionately by finding the rotation handle, rotating the symbol, and then resizing it to its original or desired size.

Rotating Symbols

GOAL	ACTION	RESULT
SELECT SYMBOL	**SELECT** *symbol* *(to show handles)*	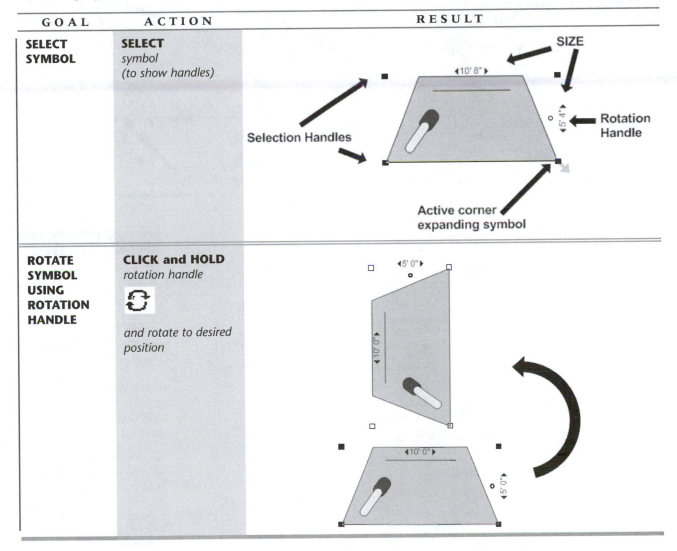
ROTATE SYMBOL USING ROTATION HANDLE	**CLICK and HOLD** *rotation handle* *and rotate to desired position*	

HOW DO I RESIZE A SYMBOL?

Most symbols may be resized the same as other objects: proportionally (retaining the ratio of length to width), or horizontally and vertically (changing the length or width, or both). The symbol must be selected so that the selection handles are visible. You can resize it by selecting a corner selection handle and moving the mouse while holding the left mouse button. Center selection handles (in the middle of the symbol) are available on most symbols and may also be used for changing the dimensions.

T I P

You can also resize symbols proportionally by holding the Shift key and the left mouse button and dragging the mouse.

Resizing Symbols

GOAL	ACTION	RESULT
CHANGING SYMBOL SIZE	**SELECT** *podium symbol to show selection handles* **CLICK and HOLD MOUSE** *on corner selection handle* **DRAG IN or OUT** *to increase or decrease size of the symbol*	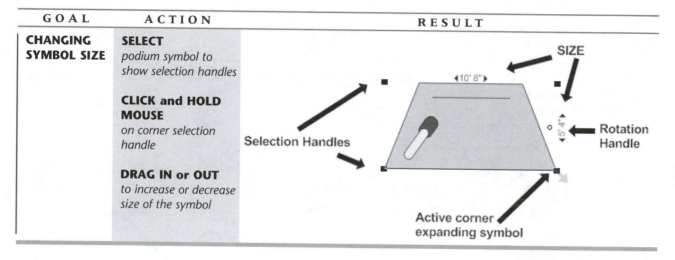

N O T E S

Most symbols will increase or decrease proportionally if the corner selection handles are used. For others, hold the Shift key and the mouse button to resize proportionally.

Some symbols are set with a default setting that only allows proportionate resizing.

Removing the restrictions in the Grow area adds additional selection handles that can be used to resize symbols using the mouse.

Using the Shape Properties Menu

GOAL	ACTION	RESULT
ACCESS SHAPE OPTIONS BY RIGHT CLICK OF MOUSE	**SELECT** *symbol* **RIGHT CLICK** *to open context-sensitive menu* **SELECT** *Shape Properties*	Add Note Delete Note Position & Size Shape Properties Lock Object Freeze Properties
SELECT SHAPE PROPERTIES FROM SHAPE PROPERTIES MENU	**CLICK** *No restrictions option in Grow area* **CLICK** *Only when selected option in Show Dimensions area* **CLICK** *OK*	**Shape Properties** Grow: ○ Proportionally ○ Horizontally only ○ Vertically only ○ No restrictions ☐ Allow sides to be independently adjusted (Applies only to certain shapes) Select the way the shape can be re-sized. Proportional growth maintains a symbol's original shape and prevents distortion. Show Dimensions: ○ Always ● Only when selected ○ Never Show Area: ☑ Always show the area of the shape Linking ☐ Allow shape to link to borders ☐ Allow shape to link to cells in table Check these boxes to allow the shape to attach to the border of another shape or to attach inside a cell in a table. ☐ Do not check spelling Checking this box turns off spelling correction for any text contained inside the shape. ☐ Print as Transparent Checking this box marks the shape as transparent so that it will print properly. ☐ Allow Image Drop Checking this box allows images to be dropped into the shape. OK Cancel Help

Using the Shape Properties Menu (*continued*)

GOAL	ACTION	RESULT
CHANGE SIZE USING MOUSE	**CLICK and HOLD** *middle selection handle and drag mouse to enlarge*	

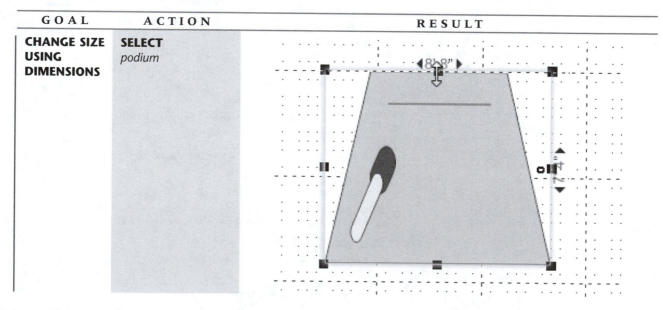

CAN I RESIZE SYMBOLS USING DIMENSIONS?

Symbols may be resized vertically, horizontally, proportionally, or in any direction. Key to resizing are the selection handles. Some symbols have only corner selection handles. This limits your ability to retain the proportionate relation of height to width when resizing. You can use the symbol's shape menu to change the properties of the symbol and add or remove selection handles.

Resizing Symbols by Typing Dimensions

GOAL	ACTION	RESULT
CHANGE SIZE USING DIMENSIONS	**SELECT** *podium*	

Resizing Symbols by Typing Dimensions (*continued*)

GOAL	ACTION	RESULT
SELECT DIMENSION TO BE CHANGED	**CLICK** *dimension numbers at top*	8'8"
ENTER NEW DIMENSION	**TYPE** *10'6"* *(new dimension)*	10'6"
RESIZE SYMBOL	**PRESS ENTER**	◀10'6"▶

HOW DO I ADD COLOR TO A SYMBOL OR SHAPE?

Shapes and most symbols may be colored or, more correctly, filled with colors or textures. A full palette of colors and a wide assortment of textures are available in the Fill menu in the Home tab—Shape Style group.

Adding Color to Symbols

GOAL	ACTION	RESULT
CHANGE COLOR OF SYMBOL (SHAPE OR OBJECT)	**SELECT** *podium* **CLICK** *Home tab* **CLICK** *Fill in the Shape Style group* **CLICK** *desired color or select one of the textures or other fill options*	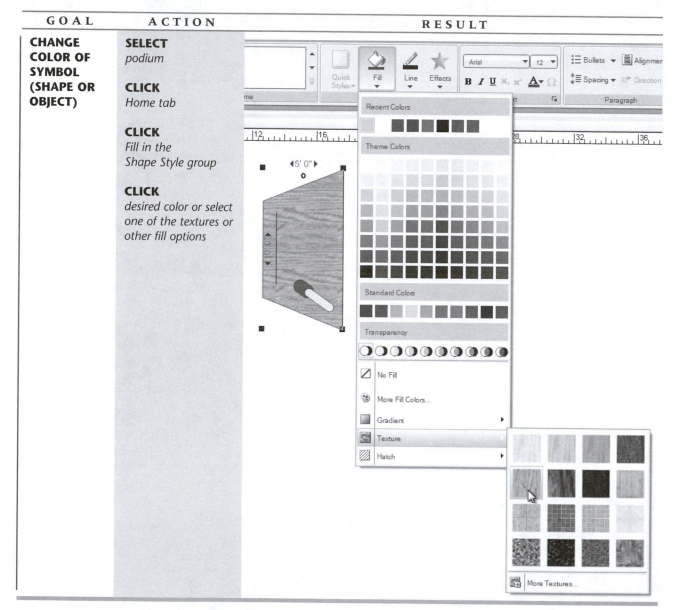

HOW DO I SAVE MY WORK?

You may save your documents in a number of different formats. A file may be saved in SmartDraw format as a document or as a template. As a document it may be opened from the Saved Documents category for further editing and customization. Saving it as a template is useful when you want to use the basic document in the future as a form, or a floor plan for a room or building. Documents saved in the SmartDraw format will appear with the extension .SDR, such as Apartment1415.SDR. You should save files in the SmartDraw file format even if you also wish to save them in another file format to allow for future use. You can access files saved as templates from the Document Browser templates in the My Templates folder. Save options are in the SmartDraw button menu. A button on the Quick Access panel also may be used to save files. A word of caution: Using the Save command or the Quick Access panel Save button will save the file with the current file name. If you are using a file that you do not want to overwrite, such as an existing file that you are using as a sample but want to retain, use the Save As option in the SmartDraw button menu. The Save As option will always prompt you for the name you want to use to save the file.

Saving a File Created in SmartDraw

GOAL	ACTION	RESULT
SAVE DOCUMENT	**CLICK** *SmartDraw Button* **CLICK** *Save As* **CLICK** *desired format*	

CAN I EXPORT MY WORK TO ANOTHER PROGRAM?

Documents can be saved in many popular graphic formats, such as PDF, JPEG, or BMP, or in compatible formats for many popular programs such as Microsoft Word or Excel. Documents saved in non-SmartDraw formats are exported in the desired format. Quick Access buttons and Export menu options permit you to save directly to other programs installed on your computer, such as Microsoft PowerPoint and LexisNexis CaseMap, by using the program icons at the top of the SmartDraw screen or from the SmartDraw Button Export menu.

Exporting a File

GOAL	ACTION	RESULT
EXPORT TO ANOTHER PROGRAM OR SAVE IN GRAPHIC FILE FORMAT	**CLICK** *SmartDraw Button* **CLICK** *desired program or file format*	**QUICK ACCESS BAR** PDF format MS Word MS Excel MS Power Point LexisNexis CaseMap

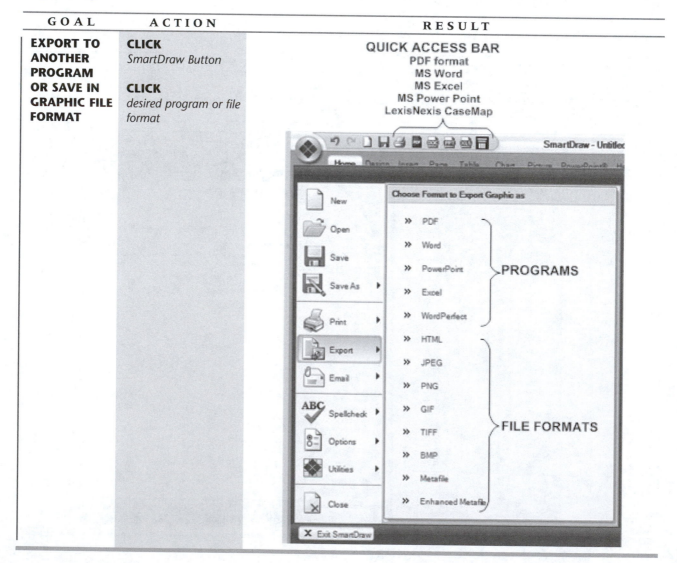

Layers
(Pictures on Top of Pictures?)

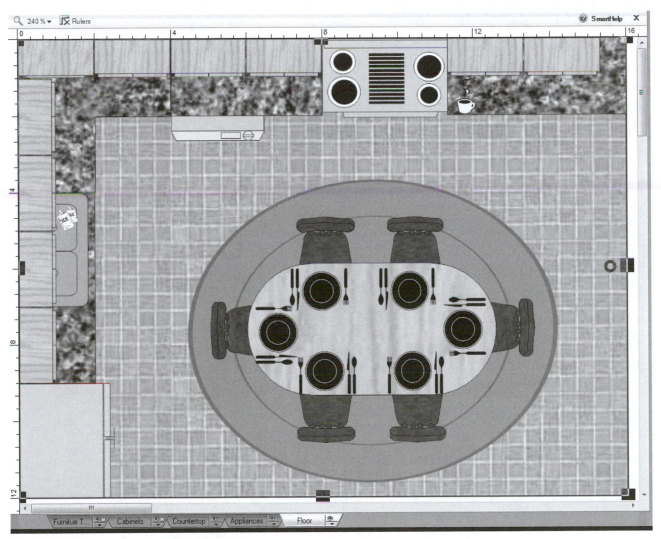

HOW DO I START A NEW DOCUMENT?

You have been creating new documents in the exercises you have completed. Every new document required the selection of a blank template or an example template from the Document Browser templates. Previously saved documents may be opened from the Saved Documents folder. All of your previous documents will be displayed in the Saved Documents folder unless you saved them on another computer or memory device. The Browse button on the Ribbon will allow you to search portable memory devices like SD memory, USB memory, or other similar storage media.

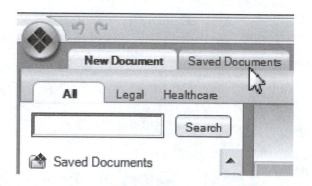

When starting a new project, try to choose a blank SmartTemplate from the category most like the document you wish to create. This will give you the maximum value from the time-saving features of the SmartPanel and the context-related help in the SmartHelp panel. For example, if you select a blank screen in Flow Chart, the SmartPanel and SmartHelp for Flow Charts will appear and not the items for Crime Scene, Floor Plan, or some other unwanted type. Yes, you can use the template anyway, but you will have to select the libraries and search for the desired help topics manually.

In the following tutorials the floor plan template is illustrated.

Creating a New Project

GOAL	ACTION	RESULT
CREATE A NEW DOCUMENT	**CLICK** *Floor Plans template Category in Document Browser* **CLICK** *Blank Floor Plan*	

This file will be used in the tutorials that follow.

LAYERS

Each item in a drawing may sit on top of another item (for example, a carpet sitting on a tiled floor). Each element, tiled floor and carpet, is a separate item that may be switched backward and forward, one on top of the other, and Sent to Back or Sent to Front. If one item is larger than the other the smaller item seems to disappear when it is behind the larger item. But in reality it is merely hidden from view behind the larger item. Switch the items and it returns to view. If the smaller item is on top, however, you can see the larger item as well. Together these items may be part of a **layer**, a transparent page that you can look through.

Drawings can be constructed with multiple layers, each containing smaller or larger items. When layers are stacked one on top of the other you can see down through them as long as a larger item does not block your view. Any object not blocked by a larger object in the same layer or in a higher layer will be visible. Just as objects may be moved from the front to the back in the same layer, layers with the objects they contain may also be moved from front to back in the drawing. The following tutorial uses a floor plan to illustrate how objects can be added to layers, and how layers are used together to create documents.

When you create layers, individual tabs are added at the bottom of the work area to allow access to the desired layers. Each layer may also be made visible or invisible using the menu on the layer's tab.

> **NOTE**
>
> Use Symbol Libraries to find desired symbols, such as rugs.

To open the Visible-Clickable menu, click the down arrow to the right of the desired layer.

Moving Objects in a Single Layer

GOAL	ACTION	RESULT
CREATE TWO OBJECTS IN A SINGLE LAYER	**CLICK** *Blank Floor Plan in Document Browser* **CLICK** *Home tab* **ADD** *12 x 16 foot floor using the rectangle in the Shape menu* **FILL** *rectangle with a tile color from Fill menu* **ADD** *oval rug symbol from Symbol Libraries*	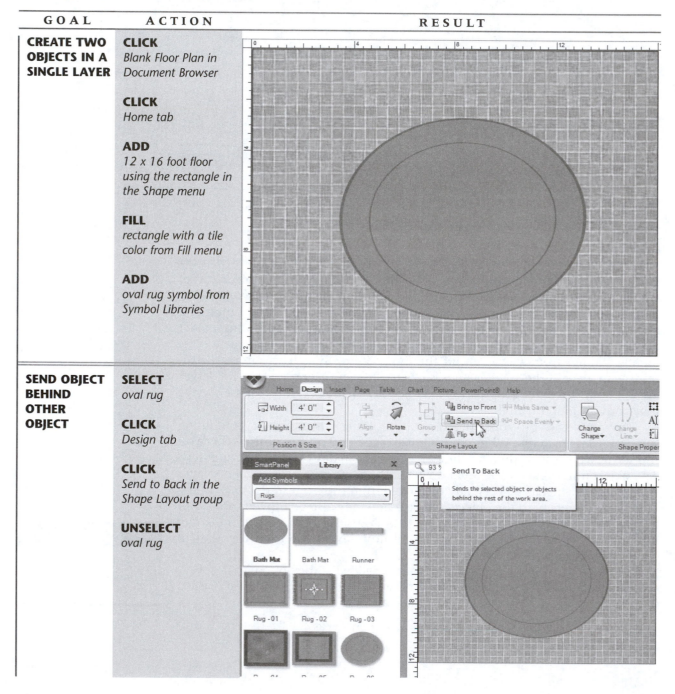
SEND OBJECT BEHIND OTHER OBJECT	**SELECT** *oval rug* **CLICK** *Design tab* **CLICK** *Send to Back in the Shape Layout group* **UNSELECT** *oval rug*	

Moving Objects in a Single Layer (*continued*)

GOAL	ACTION	RESULT
SEND TOP OBJECT BEHIND OTHER OBJECT TO SHOW ORIGINAL VIEW	**SELECT** *floor rectangle* **CLICK** *Send to Back in the Shape Layout group*	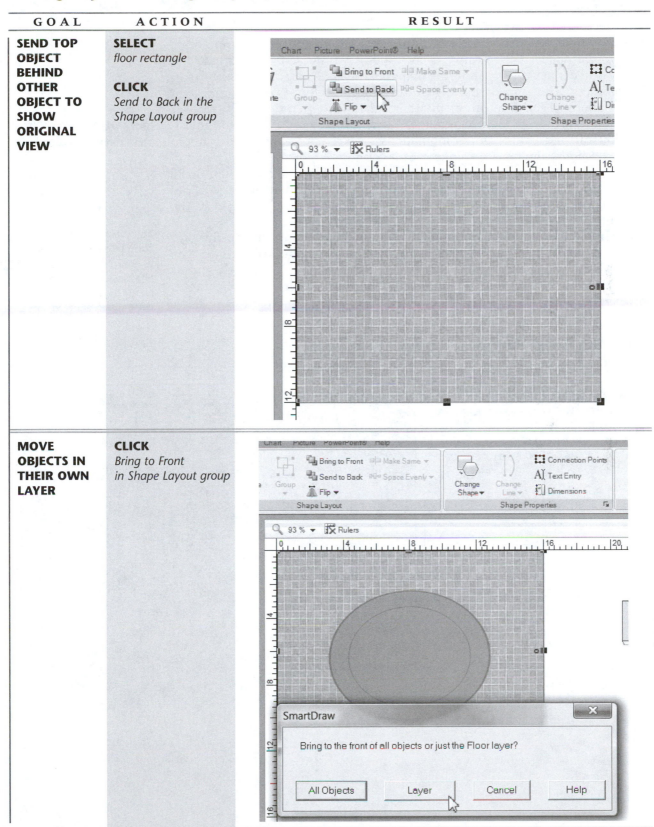
MOVE OBJECTS IN THEIR OWN LAYER	**CLICK** *Bring to Front in Shape Layout group*	

Save this file. It will be used in the next tutorial.

HOW CAN I USE LAYERS TO SEE HOW THINGS WILL LOOK?

Drawings may be created with multiple layers with each layer containing one type of object. For example, a drawing of a proposed kitchen may use separate layers to show the flooring material, the appliances, the countertops, the cabinets, and two or more furniture options. By making some layer combinations visible and others invisible, such as the tile floor, you can see how different objects look together. Because any layer can be made invisible, you can make different combinations visible. For example, you might make the floor, appliances, cabinets, and counters visible, and make one of two furniture options visible and the other invisible. Then, you could make the second furniture option visible and the first invisible. Of course, you can also make everything visible at the same time, as shown at the end of the next tutorial.

In the following tutorial, the floor and the rug drawing used in the previous tutorial is the starting point. This is the initial **default layer**. The default layer is a label used to identify the first work area document and its contents. If you select an example from the SmartTemplates, everything in the example will be part of the default layer.

Using the Layers Menu

GOAL	ACTION	RESULT
CHANGE THE NAME OF THE DEFAULT LAYER	CLICK *Page tab* CLICK *Define Layers in the Layers menu* CLICK *Edit Layer* TYPE *Floor* CLICK *OK* CLICK *OK*	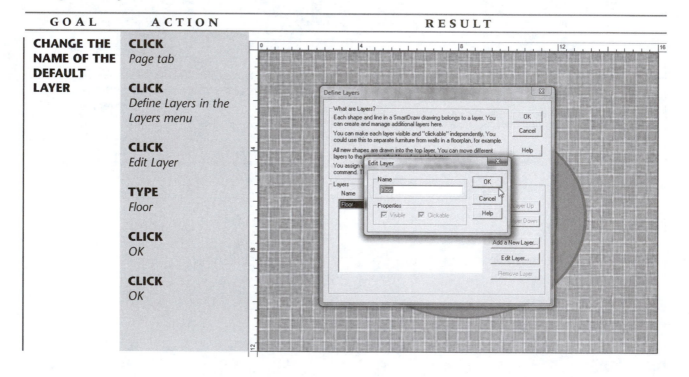

Using the Layers Menu (*continued*)

GOAL	ACTION	RESULT
CREATE A NEW LAYER (DEFINE LAYERS MENU)	**CLICK** *Add a New Layer in the Layers menu* **TYPE** *Appliances* **CLICK** *OK* **CLICK** *OK*	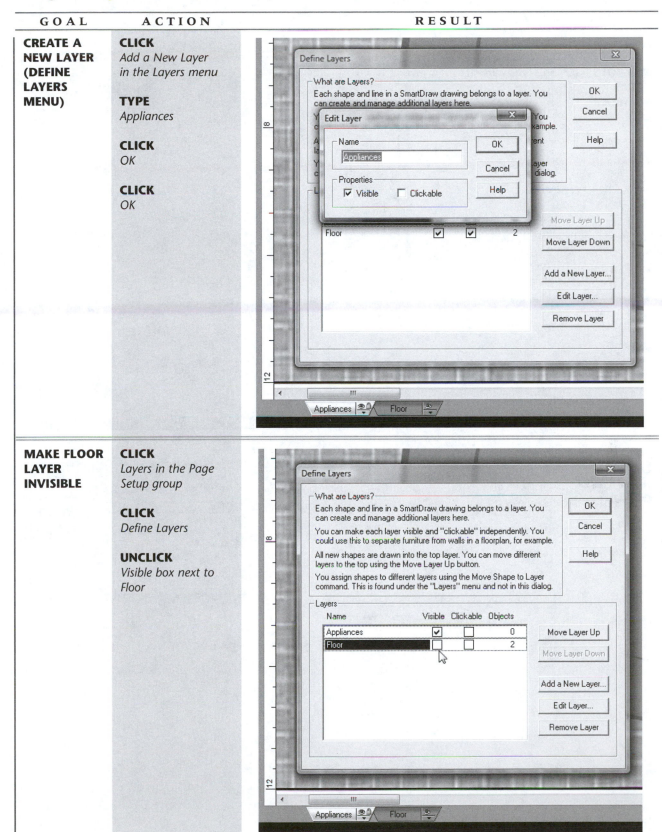
MAKE FLOOR LAYER INVISIBLE	**CLICK** *Layers in the Page Setup group* **CLICK** *Define Layers* **UNCLICK** *Visible box next to Floor*	

Using the Layers Menu (*continued*)

GOAL	ACTION	RESULT
ADD APPLIANCE SYMBOLS FROM SYMBOLS LIBRARY	**ADD** *Appliance symbols from the symbols library*	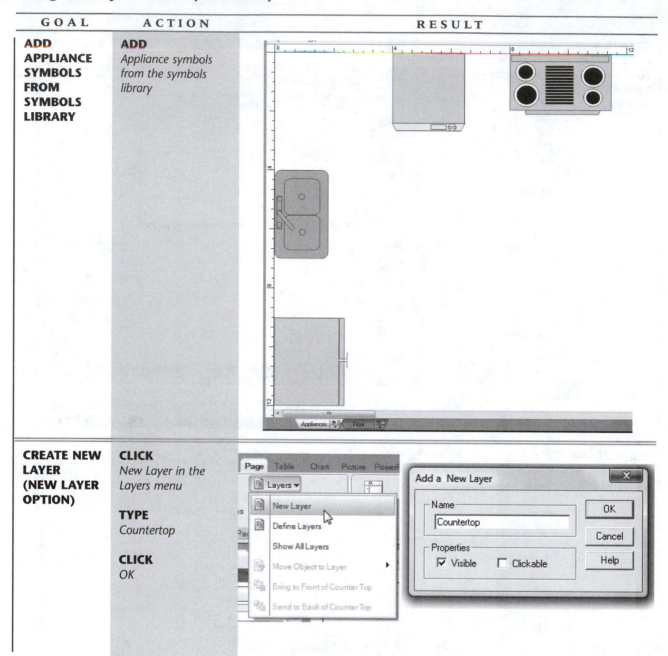
CREATE NEW LAYER (NEW LAYER OPTION)	**CLICK** *New Layer in the Layers menu* **TYPE** *Countertop* **CLICK** *OK*	

Using the Layers Menu (*continued*)

GOAL	ACTION	RESULT
ADD COUNTERTOP MAKE COUNTERTOP INVISIBLE	**ADD** *Countertop from symbols library* **RIGHT CLICK** *Countertop layer tab at bottom of work area* **UNCLICK** *Visible*	
MOVE SYMBOL FROM ONE LAYER TO ANOTHER	**CLICK** *Appliances layer tab* **CLICK** *Visible* **SELECT** *Sink* **CLICK** *Layers menu* **CLICK** *Move Object to layer* **CLICK** *Countertop*	

Using the Layers Menu (*continued*)

G O A L	A C T I O N	R E S U L T
MOVE OBJECT TO BACK OF SINGLE LAYER	**CLICK** *Countertop tab* **SELECT** *Countertop portion over sink* **CLICK** *Send to Back in the Layers menu in the Page Setup group* **UNSELECT** *Countertop*	
CREATE NEW LAYER	**CLICK** *Cabinet layer tab* **ADD** *cabinets from Symbols Libraries* **SELECT** *All cabinets (HOLD SHIFT and CLICK cabinet symbols)* **FILL** *with maple wood*	

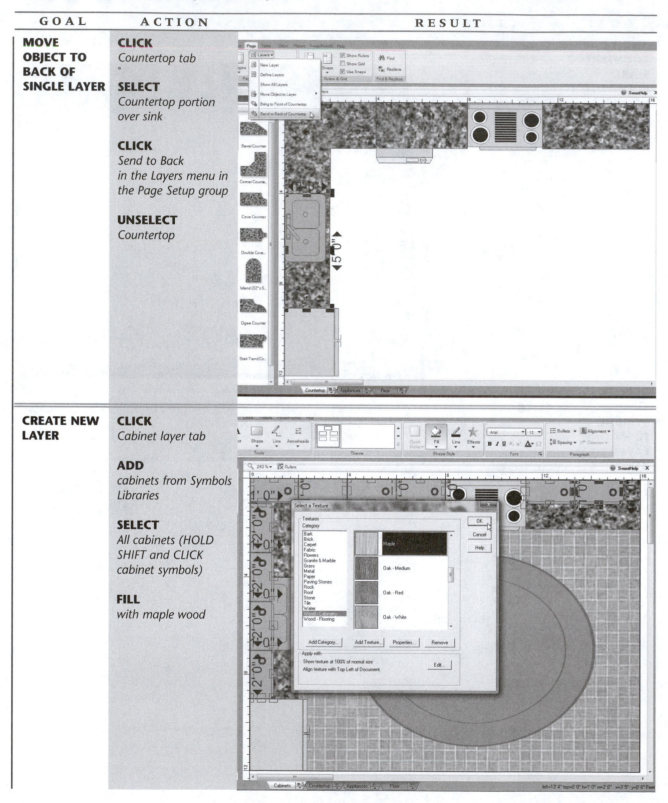

Using the Layers Menu (*continued*)

GOAL	ACTION	RESULT
CREATE LAYER WITH FIRST FURNITURE OPTION	**CLICK** *New Layer in Layers menu* **TYPE** *Furniture table setting* **ADD** *table and chairs* **Option:** *Use the Ungroup option to color the table and chairs differently.* **ADD** *table settings*	
CREATE LAYER WITH SECOND FURNITURE OPTION	**CLICK** *New Layer in Layers menu* **TYPE** *Bench and table* **FILL** *with wood color* **ENHANCE** *with table setting*	

Using the Layers Menu (*continued*)

GOAL	ACTION	RESULT
MAKE ALL LAYERS VISIBLE	**CLICK** *Visible for all layers using the Layers menu in the Page Setup group*	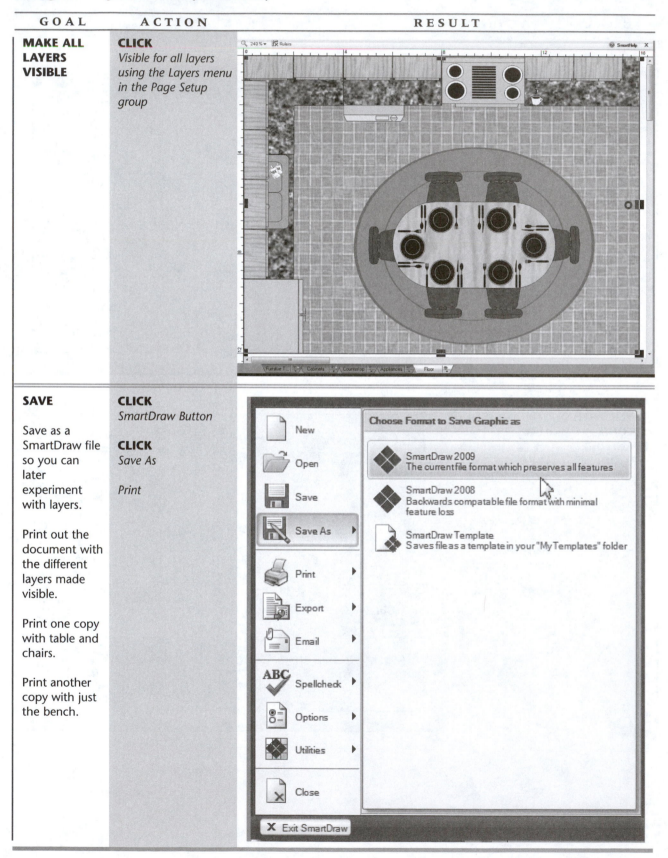
SAVE Save as a SmartDraw file so you can later experiment with layers. Print out the document with the different layers made visible. Print one copy with table and chairs. Print another copy with just the bench.	**CLICK** *SmartDraw Button* **CLICK** *Save As* *Print*	

PowerPoint® Animation
(Not Quite Animation)

- Can I Create an Animation Sequence in SmartDraw?
  - ▲ *Tutorial—Creating a PowerPoint Animation*

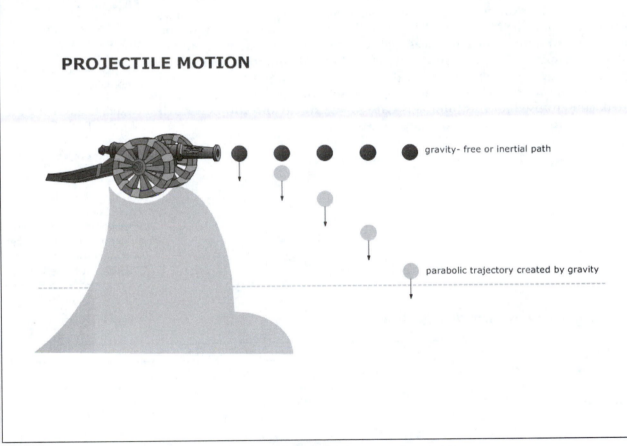

PROJECTILE MOTION

gravity- free or inertial path

parabolic trajectory created by gravity

Source: Document Browser Category: Education\Subject-Math & Physics SmartTemplates\Projectile Motion-2

CAN I CREATE AN ANIMATION SEQUENCE IN SMARTDRAW?

SmartDraw has a PowerPoint® animation creation option that allows you to show individual items in sequence in a document. Selected objects in a document may be shown in a preselected sequence appearing individually or in groups of symbols or text. You can animate previously created SmartDraw documents or SmartTemplate examples by selecting the items and assigning them to the steps in the sequence where they should appear. This is similar to the animation shown in Microsoft PowerPoint.

Complete SmartDraw documents may be exported directly to Microsoft PowerPoint for further enhancement such as the addition of sound effects. PowerPoint animation may be used with any drawing. For purposes of illustration, an example from the Education Category SmartTemplate Examples—Projectile Motion has been used. This animation has 11 animation steps. (Not all animation sequences will require this many steps.) Some of the steps require selecting a single object and others multiple objects. The procedure provides a demonstration that enables you to practice the object selection and the (equally important) object unselection process for each step. The document used for this tutorial is **Category: Education\Subject-Math & Physics SmartTemplates\Projectile Motion-2.**

T I P S

Print a copy of the document to manually mark it up with steps.

If you miss a textbox or symbol, you can edit the animation by selecting the missing items and making the step number selection.

N O T E S

Any object(s) can be shown in any order.

The first object selected is automatically set as slide 1.

Be sure to unselect object(s) from the previous step before selecting object(s) for the current step.

You must have MS PowerPoint installed on your computer to be able to export SmartDraw files and view them as PowerPoint presentations.

Creating a PowerPoint Animation

GOAL	ACTION	RESULT
DETERMINE ORDER OF DISPLAY	**CLICK** *Education Subject-Math & Physics Projectile Motion-2 in Document Browser* **DETERMINE** *sequence of object*	

Creating a PowerPoint Animation (*continued*)

GOAL	ACTION	RESULT
SELECT OBJECT FOR FIRST STEP	**CLICK** *PowerPoint tab* **SELECT** *text box Projectile Motion* **CLICK** *the Step menu of the Animation group* **CLICK** *1* **UNSELECT** *text box*	
SELECT OBJECT FOR STEP 2	**SELECT** *objects for Step 2* **CLICK** *2 in the Step menu* **UNSELECT** *object 2*	

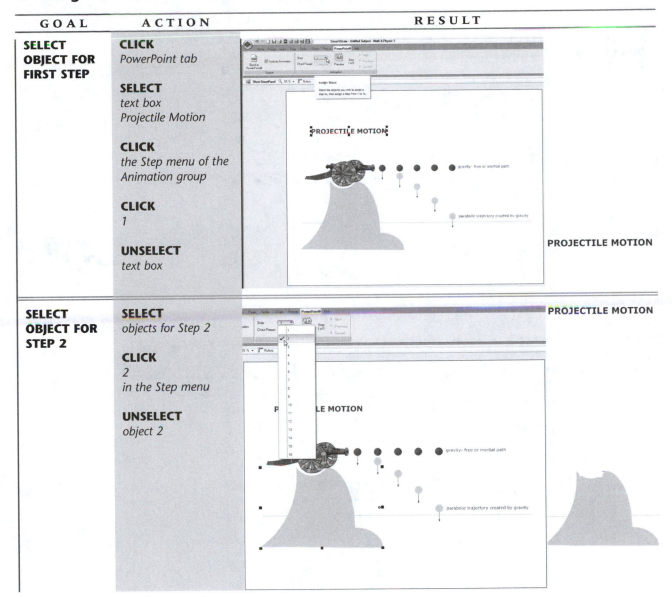

PROJECTILE MOTION

PROJECTILE MOTION

Creating a PowerPoint Animation (*continued*)

GOAL	ACTION	RESULT
SELECT OBJECT FOR STEP 3	**SELECT** *object for Step 3* **CLICK** *3* *in the Step menu* **UNSELECT** *object 3*	
SELECT MULTIPLE OBJECTS FOR STEP 4	**PRESS and HOLD SHIFT KEY** **SELECT** *objects for Step 4* **CLICK** *4* *in the Step menu* **UNSELECT** *objects for Step 4*	

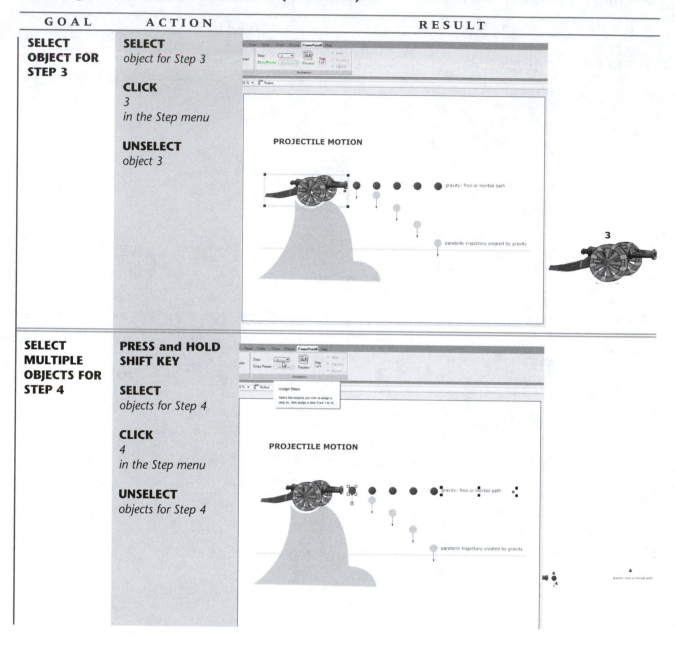

Creating a PowerPoint Animation (*continued*)

GOAL	ACTION	RESULT
SELECT OBJECT FOR STEP 5	**SELECT** object for Step 5 **CLICK** 5 in the Step menu **UNSELECT** object 5	
SELECT OBJECTS FOR STEP 6	**PRESS and HOLD SHIFT KEY** **SELECT** objects for Step 6 **CLICK** 6 in the Step menu **UNSELECT** objects for Step 6	

Creating a PowerPoint Animation (*continued*)

GOAL	ACTION	RESULT
SELECT OBJECT FOR STEP 7	**SELECT** *object for Step 7* **CLICK** *7* *in the Step menu* **UNSELECT** *object for Step 7*	
SELECT OBJECTS FOR STEP 8	**PRESS and HOLD SHIFT KEY** **SELECT** *objects for Step 8* **CLICK** *8* *in the Step menu* **UNSELECT** *all objects in Step 8*	

Creating a PowerPoint Animation (*continued*)

GOAL	ACTION	RESULT
SELECT OBJECT FOR STEP 9	**SELECT** *object for Step 9* **CLICK** 9 *in the Step menu PowerPoint® tab* **UNSELECT** *object for Step 9*	
SELECT OBJECTS FOR STEP 10	**PRESS and HOLD SHIFT KEY** **SELECT** *objects for Step 10* **CLICK** 10 *in the Step menu* **UNSELECT** *objects for Step 10*	

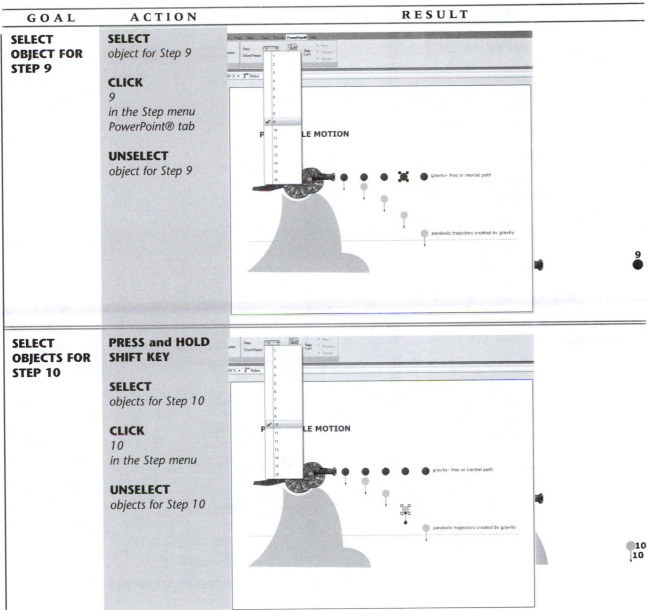

Creating a PowerPoint Animation (*continued*)

GOAL	ACTION	RESULT
SELECT OBJECTS FOR STEP 11	**PRESS and HOLD SHIFT KEY** **SELECT** *objects for Step 11* **CLICK** *11 in the Step menu* **UNSELECT** *all objects in Step 11*	
PREVIEW ANIMATION	**CLICK** *Preview in the Animation group*	

Creating a PowerPoint Animation (*continued*)

GOAL	ACTION	RESULT
SHOW NEXT STEP	**CLICK** *Next* in the Animation group	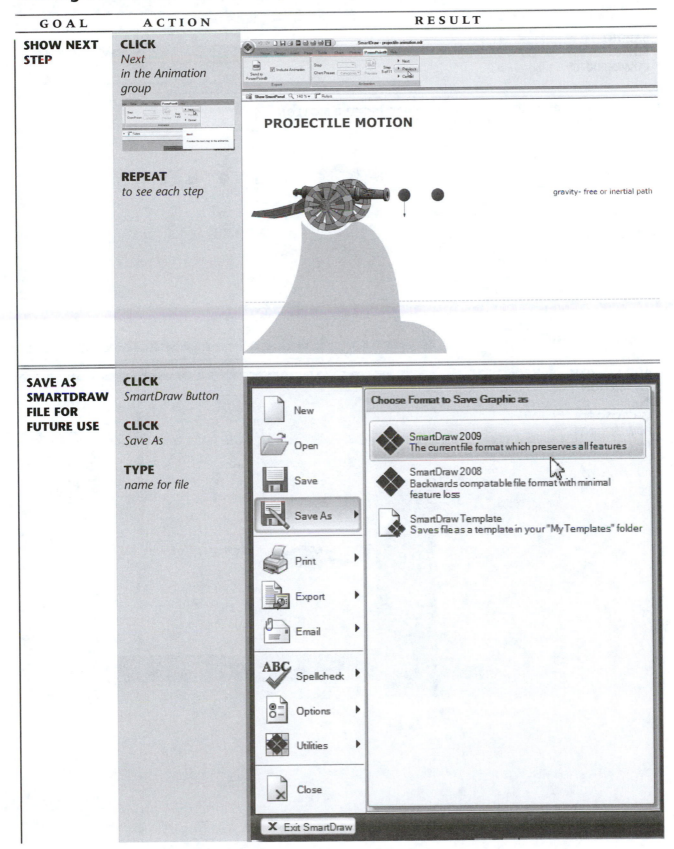
	REPEAT to see each step	
SAVE AS SMARTDRAW FILE FOR FUTURE USE	**CLICK** *SmartDraw Button* **CLICK** *Save As* **TYPE** *name for file*	

Creating a PowerPoint Animation (*continued*)

GOAL	ACTION	RESULT
EXPORT TO MICROSOFT POWERPOINT®	**CLICK** *Send to PowerPoint in Export group*	
ADD CUSTOM ANIMATION IN MICROSOFT POWERPOINT®	**SAVE** *presentation in MS PowerPoint after Export*	

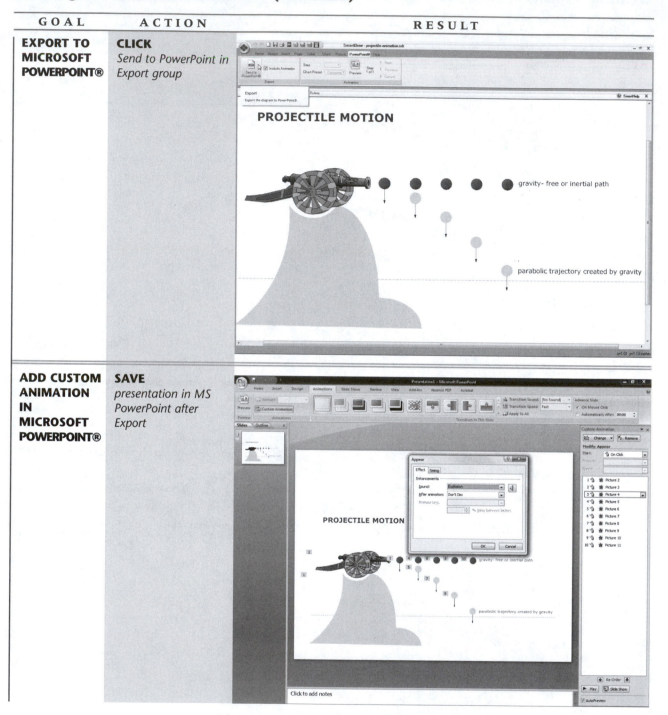

Creating a PowerPoint Animation (*continued*)

GOAL	ACTION	RESULT
RUN POWERPOINT PRESENTATION	**USE MICROSOFT POWERPOINT**	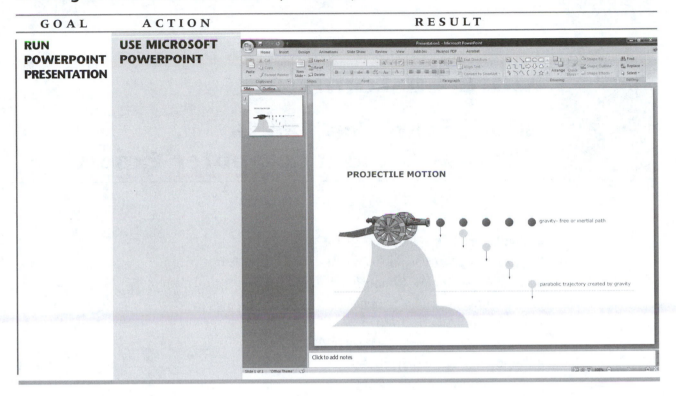

More Customizing

(More Stuff You Can Do Without Being a Computer Expert)

- Can I Edit the Symbols in the Library?
  - ▲ *Tutorial—Editing a Symbol*
- Can I Create a New Symbol?
  - ▲ *Tutorial—Grouping Elements to Create a New Symbol*
- Can I Add a Symbol to My Library?
  - ▲ *Tutorial—Saving a Symbol to the Library*
- Using New Custom Symbols
  - ▲ *Tutorial—Using New Symbols*
- Can I Add Content from the Internet?
  - ▲ *Tutorial—Adding Web Content to a Document*
- Can I Add Maps to My Documents?
  - ▲ *Tutorial—Importing Maps Using the Internet*
- Can I Insert Pictures into a Document?
  - ▲ *Tutorial—Adding Pictures to an Organization Chart*
  - ▲ *Tutorial—Adding Photographs to a Flyer*

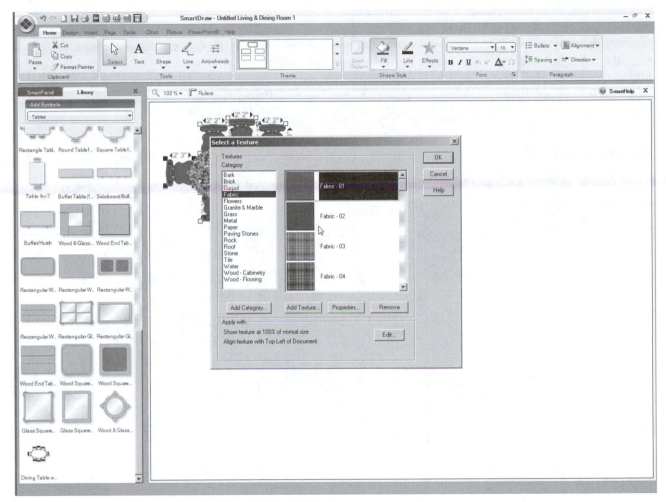

Source: Document Browser Category: Floor Plans\ Dining Room example

CAN I EDIT THE SYMBOLS IN THE LIBRARY?

Most of the symbols and a significant part of the clip art in the Symbols Libraries can be edited. The standard shapes (called **automatic shapes**) are SmartDraw symbols made up of parts (called **free form shapes**). The SmartDraw format symbols and art are made up of two or more free form shapes that have been **grouped** together to make a single object. By **ungrouping**, the individual shapes or parts can be removed, edited for size or shape, replaced, or used with other standard items from the library. In the following tutorial you will work with the table and chairs in the Dining Room example in the Document Browser Floor Plans category. You will see how the chair has been constructed of free form shapes that have been grouped together. The tutorial will show you how to ungroup and regroup objects, duplicate them, and customize them before saving them for future use. The document used for this tutorial is **Category: Floor Plans\Dining Room**.

N O T E S

For this tutorial we will use the Dining Room SmartTemplate.

To ungroup a symbol, it must be in selected mode.

Editing a Symbol

GOAL	ACTION	RESULT
UNGROUPING A SYMBOL	**CLICK** *Dining Room example in Floor Plans category in Document Browser*	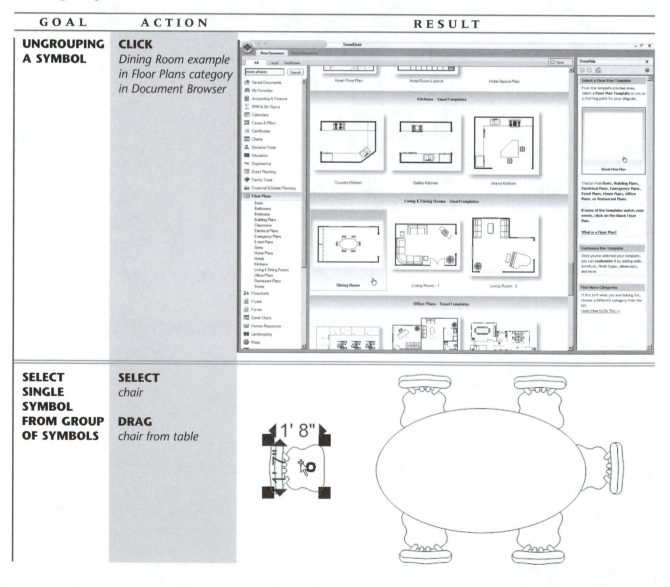
SELECT SINGLE SYMBOL FROM GROUP OF SYMBOLS	**SELECT** *chair* **DRAG** *chair from table*	

Editing a Symbol (*continued*)

GOAL	ACTION	RESULT
UNGROUP SYMBOL PARTS	**CLICK** *Design tab* **CLICK** *Ungroup Objects from the Group menu*	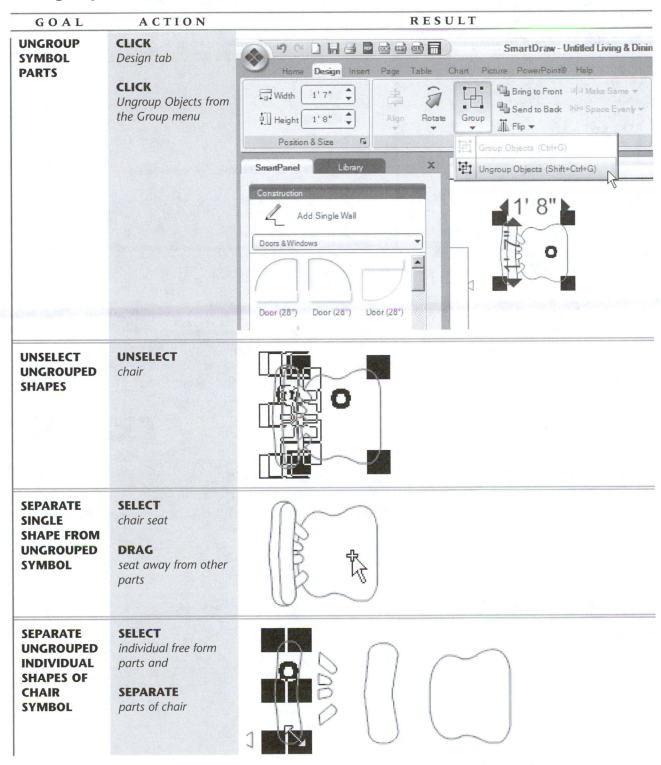
UNSELECT UNGROUPED SHAPES	**UNSELECT** *chair*	
SEPARATE SINGLE SHAPE FROM UNGROUPED SYMBOL	**SELECT** *chair seat* **DRAG** *seat away from other parts*	
SEPARATE UNGROUPED INDIVIDUAL SHAPES OF CHAIR SYMBOL	**SELECT** *individual free form parts and* **SEPARATE** *parts of chair*	

Editing a Symbol (*continued*)

GOAL	ACTION	RESULT
REGROUP SYMBOL USING THE UNDO ARROW or SHORTCUT KEYS Ctrl + Z	**CLICK** *Undo arrow as many times as necessary to reassemble chair symbol*	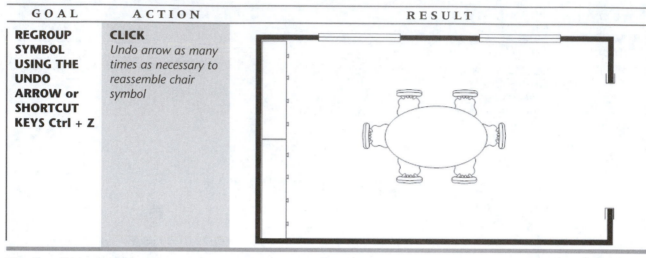

This file will be used in next tutorial.

CAN I CREATE A NEW SYMBOL?

You can create new symbols by combining other symbols or parts of other standard symbols. Any symbol can be grouped with other symbols to create a custom symbol. The following tutorial illustrates the method using the Dining Room example from the Floor Plans category. The template contains a table with six chairs. The tutorial shows how to add two chairs and make a table for eight with a custom table top and specialty fabric covering on the chairs. The individual chairs and table are grouped to create a new symbol that is added to the symbol library. The new symbol (table and eight chairs in custom fabric and colors) will have the same characteristics as a single symbol. Of course, you can ungroup the symbol, change its components, and regroup them to make the symbol a group of a table and four chairs.

Grouping Elements to Create a New Symbol

GOAL	ACTION	RESULT
CREATE A NEW SYMBOL AND ADD TO LIBRARY	**CLICK** *Dining Room example in Floor Plans category in Document Browser*	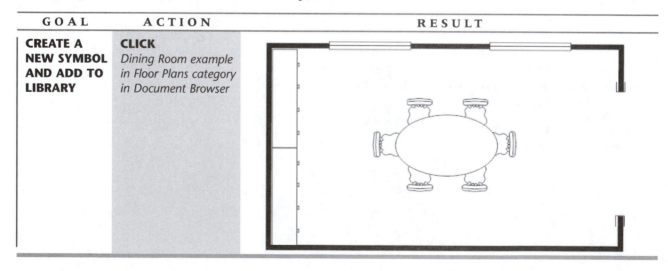

Grouping Elements to Create a New Symbol (*continued*)

GOAL	ACTION	RESULT
SELECT SYMBOL TO COPY	**SELECT** *one of the chairs*	
OPEN CONTEXT-SENSITIVE MENU	**RIGHT CLICK** **CLICK** *Copy*	

Grouping Elements to Create a New Symbol (*continued*)

GOAL	ACTION	RESULT
ADD NEW SYMBOLS	**RIGHT CLICK** **CLICK** *Paste* *from the right click menu* **REPEAT** *Paste and place second new chair*	
MOVE OBJECTS WITHIN LAYERS	**SELECT** *the two new chairs* **CLICK** *Design tab* **CLICK** *Send to Back* **OR** **SELECT** *the table and* **CLICK** *Bring to Front*	

Grouping Elements to Create a New Symbol (*continued*)

GOAL	ACTION	RESULT
CUSTOM COLOR FILL OBJECT	**SELECT** *table* **CLICK** *Home tab* **CLICK** *Fill in the Shape Style group* **CLICK** *Texture* **CLICK** *desired tabletop look* **UNSELECT** *table*	
CUSTOM COLOR FILL USING PATTERNS	**SELECT** *all the chairs* **CLICK** *Fill in the Shape Style group* **CLICK** *Texture* **CLICK** *More Textures* **CLICK** *desired fabric* **CLICK** *OK*	

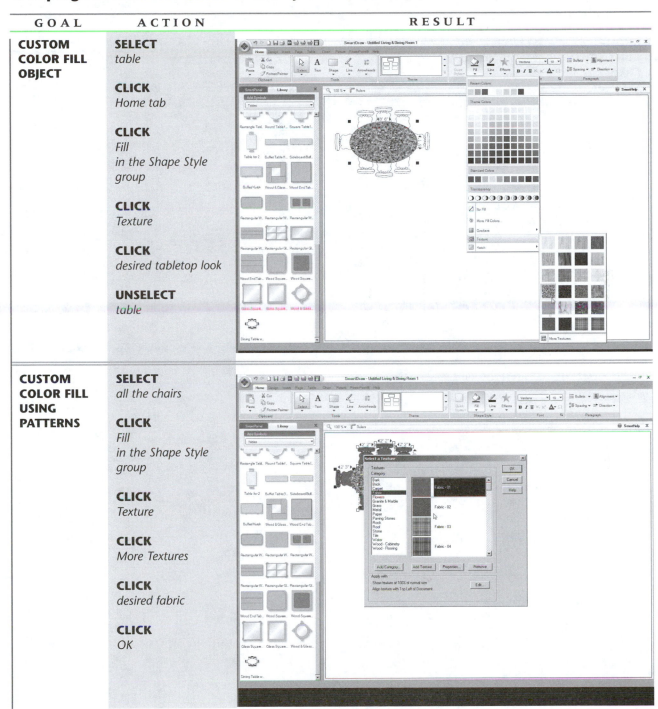

Grouping Elements to Create a New Symbol (*continued*)

GOAL	ACTION	RESULT
GROUP OBJECTS TO CREATE A SYMBOL	**SELECT** *all chairs and table* **CLICK** *Design tab* **CLICK** *Group Objects in Shape Layout group* **CLICK** *Group Objects*	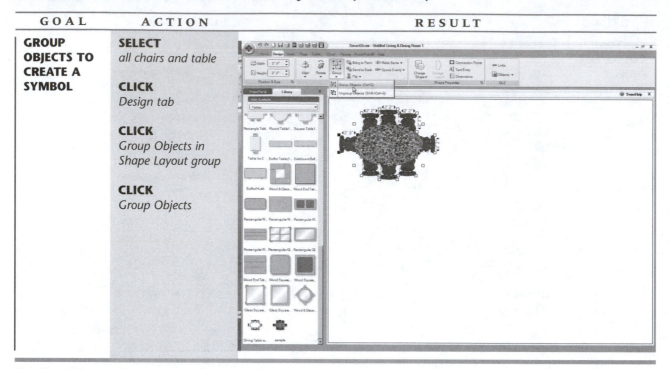

This file will be used in next tutorial.

CAN I ADD A SYMBOL TO MY LIBRARY?

New or edited symbols can be saved in the symbol library for future use. You can save time by creating your own custom library of symbols for use in future documents.

N O T E

When you drag a symbol to the symbol library, a confirmation message automatically appears.

Saving a Symbol to the Library

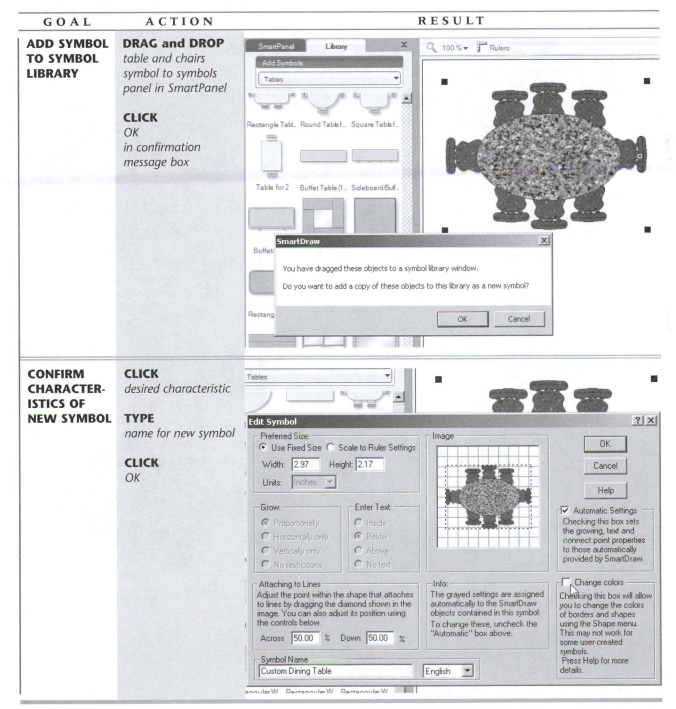

GOAL	ACTION	RESULT
ADD SYMBOL TO SYMBOL LIBRARY	**DRAG and DROP** *table and chairs symbol to symbols panel in SmartPanel* **CLICK** *OK in confirmation message box*	
CONFIRM CHARACTER-ISTICS OF NEW SYMBOL	**CLICK** *desired characteristic* **TYPE** *name for new symbol* **CLICK** *OK*	

USING NEW CUSTOM SYMBOLS

Customized symbols are saved in the symbol library in the categories that you select. As with other symbols in the library, customized symbols may be selected and stamped in documents or placed by using the drag-and-drop method.

Using New Symbols

GOAL	ACTION	RESULT
RETRIEVE NEW SYMBOL AND ADD TO DOCUMENT	**DRAG and DROP** *the new table and chairs symbol to the working space*	

CAN I ADD CONTENT FROM THE INTERNET?

You can search the Internet directly from within SmartDraw while working on a document. You can use any of the popular Internet search engines or browsers such as Yahoo or Google to find appropriate material to add to your document. You also can enter the addresses of specific websites in the Web Page browser that opens when the Insert Web Page icon is selected in SmartDraw. Inserted images may be cropped and have text and symbols added.

Adding Web Content to a Document

GOAL	ACTION	RESULT
ADD WEB IMAGES TO SMARTDRAW DOCUMENT	**CLICK** *Blank Document from Flyers category In Document Browser* **CLICK** *Insert tab* **CLICK** *Web Page in Insert group* **OR** **CLICK** *Picture tab* **CLICK** *Capture Web Image in the Get Images group*	Insert Web Page Open a web browser and navigate to a web page, then click the SmartDraw icon to insert the page into the work area. Capture Web Images Opens a special web browser for capturing screen shots of web pages.

Adding Web Content to a Document (*continued*)

GOAL	ACTION	RESULT
USE WEB BROWSER TO LOCATE DESIRED MATERIAL	**CLICK** *Web Search icon in SmartDraw Web Page Import* **OR** *enter address of web browser or specific web address*	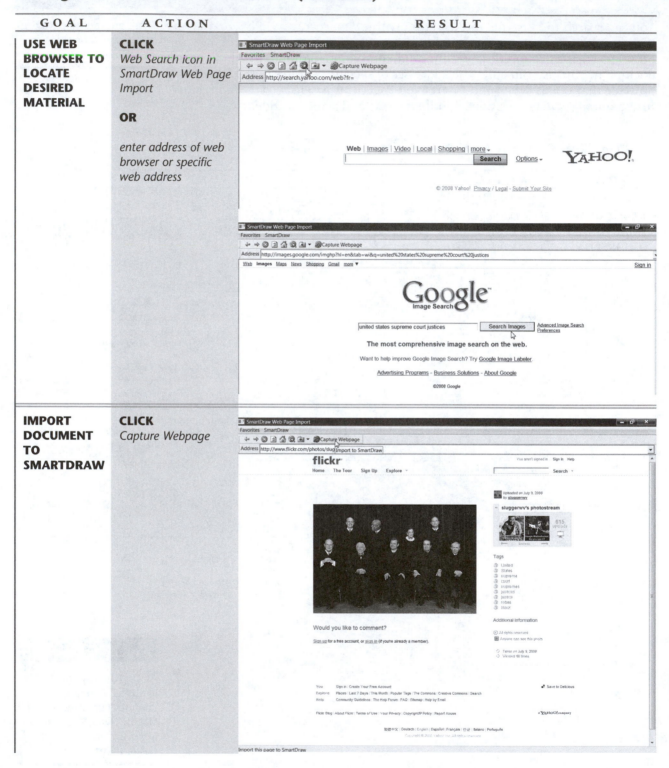
IMPORT DOCUMENT TO SMARTDRAW	**CLICK** *Capture Webpage*	

Adding Web Content to a Document (*continued*)

GOAL	ACTION	RESULT
EDIT IMAGE	**CLICK** *Picture tab* **CLICK** *Pan & Zoom in Picture group* **CLICK** *Picture Zoom tool and place cursor at starting point and drag to ending point*	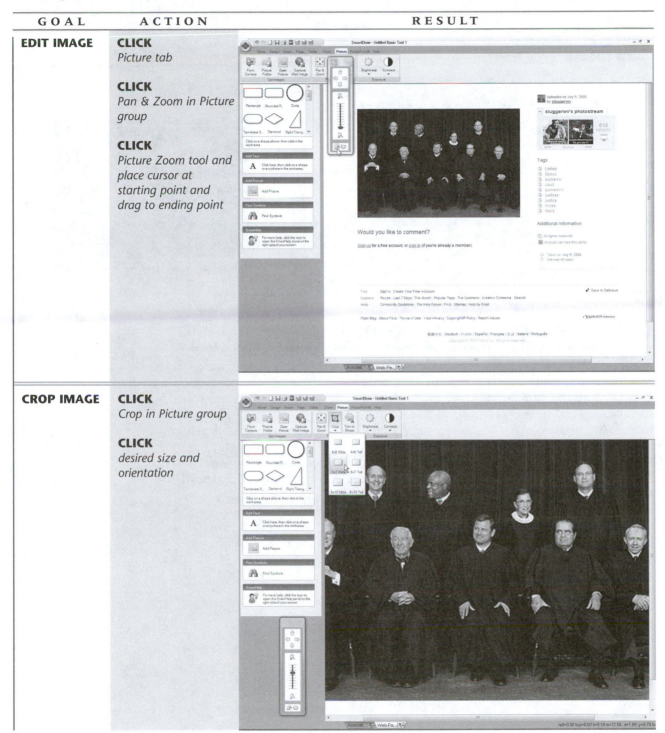
CROP IMAGE	**CLICK** *Crop in Picture group* **CLICK** *desired size and orientation*	

Adding Web Content to a Document (*continued*)

GOAL	ACTION	RESULT
ADD TEXT AND BORDER	**CLICK** *Add Text in SmartPanel* **OR** **CLICK** *Text in Home tab* **TYPE** *text* **ADD** *border from symbol library*	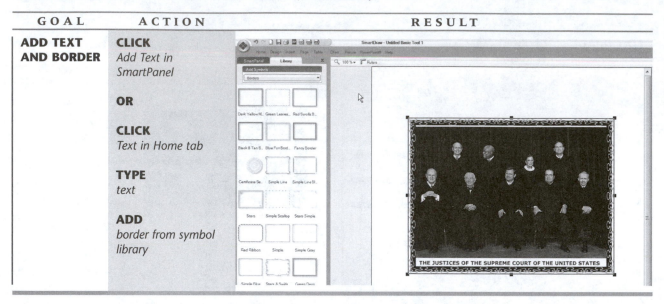

CAN I ADD MAPS TO MY DOCUMENTS?

A complete set of local, state, national, and international maps is included in the **Maps category** of the Document Browser. SmartDraw also provides a direct link to the Google map tool on the Internet in the Insert tab. (You must have an active Internet connection to use this link.) Specific map sites may be located with the Search features using street addresses, route numbers, or zip codes. The Document Browser Maps categories, USA-Live Maps and World-Live Maps, also link directly to the Google map tool on the Internet. To access the Internet maps in these categories, select a map and **double click** on it. A menu option may also be used to find maps by country, state, locality, or postal zip code.

Satellite view, road map view, or a combination of both may be imported by selecting the format option. You can also change the map size, zoom level, and other options.

Importing Maps Using the Internet

GOAL	ACTION	RESULT
IMPORT MAP	**OPEN** *Blank Interactive Map SmartTemplate in Document Browser* **CLICK** *Insert tab* **CLICK** *Map in Insert group* **OR** **CLICK** *Insert Map in SmartPanel*	
FIND DESIRED LOCATION	**TYPE** *desired location in search window* **CLICK** *desired format of map* **CLICK** *Go*	

Importing Maps Using the Internet (*continued*)

GOAL	ACTION	RESULT
IMPORT SATELLITE VIEW TO SMARTDRAW	**CLICK** *Import to SmartDraw* **ADD** *Annotation from symbols library*	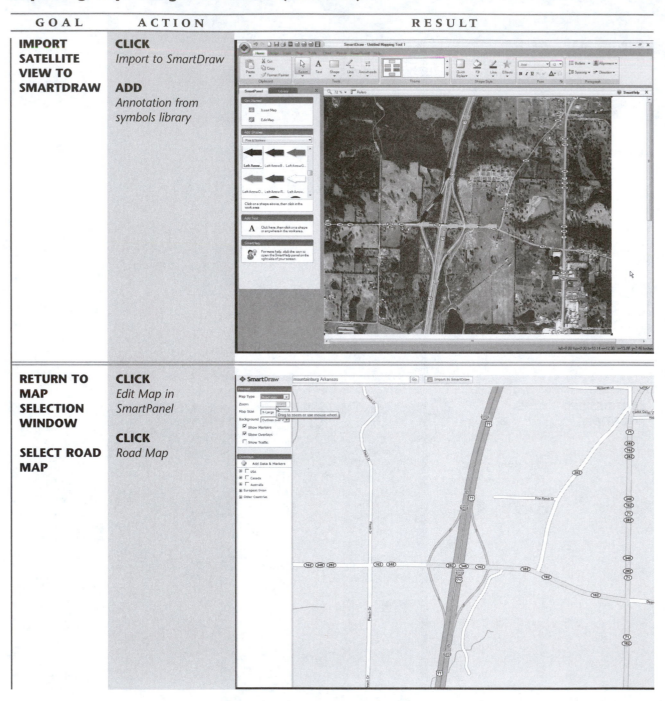
RETURN TO MAP SELECTION WINDOW **SELECT ROAD MAP**	**CLICK** *Edit Map in SmartPanel* **CLICK** *Road Map*	

Importing Maps Using the Internet (*continued*)

GOAL	ACTION	RESULT
IMPORT ROAD MAP TO SMARTDRAW	**CLICK** *Import to SmartDraw* **ADD** *symbols to customize*	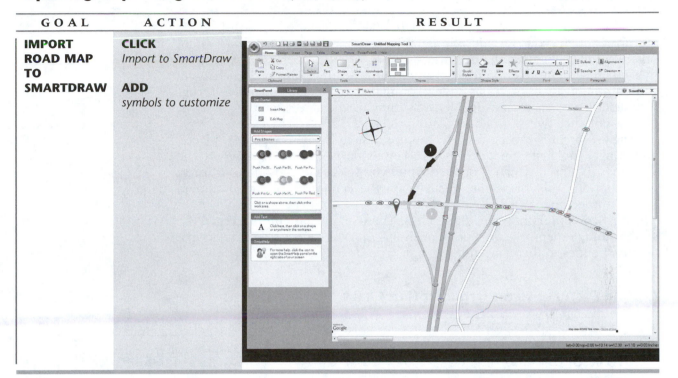

CAN I INSERT PICTURES INTO A DOCUMENT?

It has been said that a picture is worth 10,000 words. So when words alone are not enough, you can add photographs (e.g., of the people named in an organization chart, the students in a classroom, or the property in a real estate flyer) to documents to enhance communication. Seating plans with pictures of students and teachers in a classroom seating plan may help students to recognize fellow classmates or enable substitute teachers to identify students. Images enhance flyers, brochures, and posters.

Digital cameras can be used to capture desired images of people, places, and things. The digital images may be accessed for use in SmartDraw with the Windows Explorer, which is opened when you select the add photo or insert photo option. The image files may be on the computer or digital camera media storage media.

Most computers have media readers. These allow computers to read the media storage memory cards popular in most digital cameras without transferring the files to the computer.

Adding Pictures to an Organization Chart

GOAL	ACTION	RESULT
INSERT PHOTO INTO ORGANIZA-TION CHART SHAPE	**OPEN** *Blank Org chart in Org Chart category in Document Browser* **CLICK** *Home tab* **CLICK** *Select* **CLICK** *All Shapes* **CLICK** *Box Format* **CLICK** *Top Align Photo*	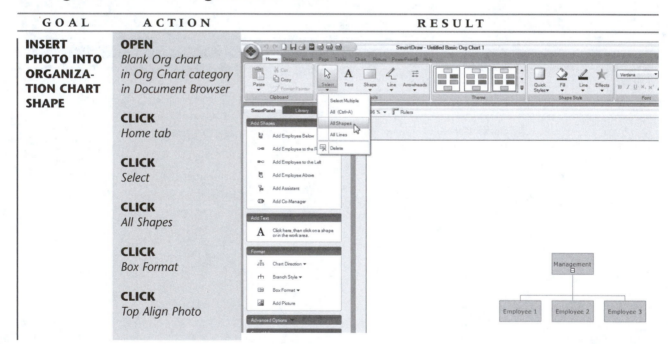

Adding Pictures to an Organization Chart (*continued*)

GOAL	ACTION	RESULT
CHANGE FORMAT TO LEFT ALIGN PHOTO BOX FORMAT	**CLICK** *Box Format* **CLICK** *Left Align Photo* **UNSELECT** *Shapes* **SELECT** *box to add photo*	
INSERT PHOTO	**CLICK** *Insert tab* **CLICK** *Picture* **CLICK** *desired photo from Insert Picture box* **CLICK** *Open*	
ADD TEXT DESCRIPTION	**SELECT** *text box* **EDIT** *text*	

Adding Photographs to a Flyer

GOAL	ACTION	RESULT
INSERT PHOTOGRAPH INTO FLYER	**CLICK** *Flyers category in Document Browser* **CLICK** *For Rent-2 in Signs* **DOUBLE CLICK TYPE** *Mountain Hideaway* **CLICK** *Insert tab* **CLICK** *Picture* **CLICK** *desired photograph* **CLICK** *Open*	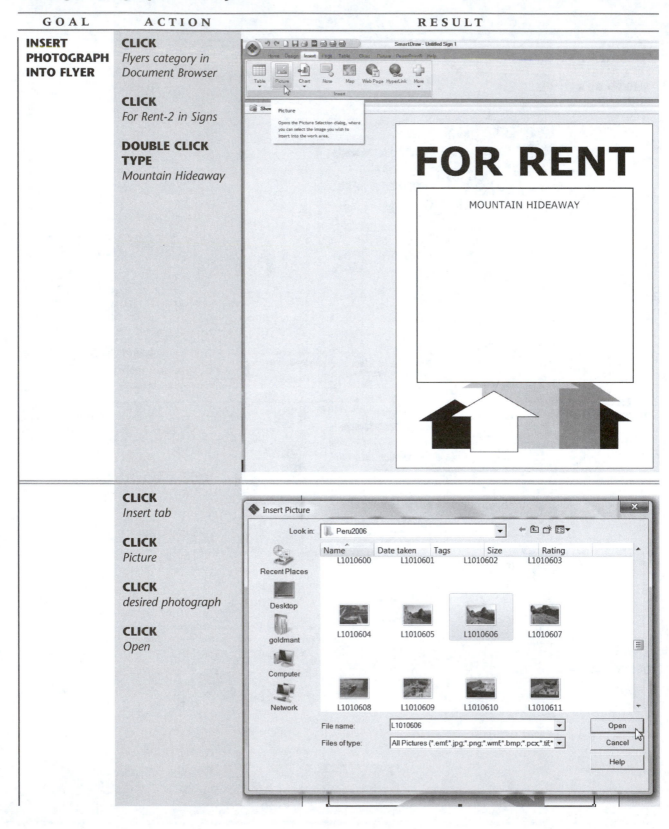

Adding Photographs to a Flyer (*continued*)

GOAL	ACTION	RESULT
REPLACE PHOTOGRAPH	**CLICK** *Insert tab* **CLICK** *Picture* **CLICK** *Replace* **REPEAT** *previous step to choose picture as shown in previous step*	**FOR RENT** MOUNTAIN HIDEAWAY
ADD ADDITIONAL PHOTOGRAPH AND CHANGE ITS SHAPE USING RIGHT CLICK MENU	**CLICK** *Insert tab* **CLICK** *Picture* **CLICK** *Add* **CHOOSE** *picture as shown in previous step* **SELECT** *new photograph* **RIGHT CLICK** **CLICK** *Change Shape* **CLICK** *desired shape*	**FOR RENT** MOUNTAIN HI

Adding Photographs to a Flyer (*continued*)

GOAL	ACTION	RESULT
SAVE AND PRINT FLYER	**CLICK** *SmartDraw Button* **CLICK** *Save As* **TYPE** *file name* **CLICK** *SmartDraw Button* **CLICK** *Print*	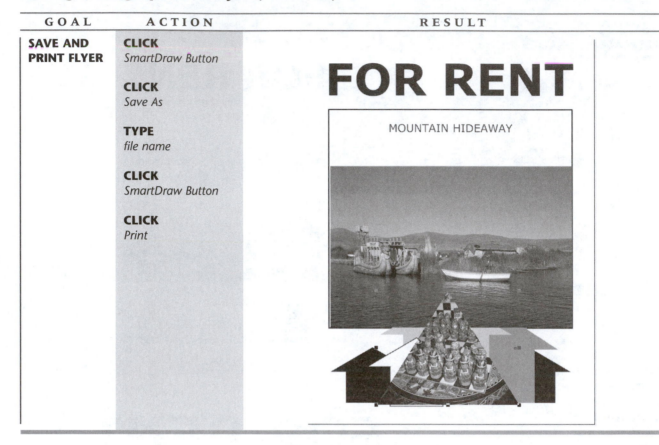

SECTION 8

Law Office Applications
(Communication Skills Win Cases)

- How Can I Create Map Exhibits?
  - ▲ *Tutorial—Creating Map Exhibits Using Live Maps*
- How Can I Create an Exhibit Showing How the Accident Happened?
  - ▲ *Tutorial—Creating Map and Photo Exhibits*
- How Can I Create a Timeline of a Case?
  - ▲ *Tutorial—Creating a Case Timeline*
- How Can I Annotate a Timeline to Make It More Dramatic?
  - ▲ *Tutorial—Adding Pictures and Maps to a Timeline*
- How Can I Change the Line Directions of Labels?
  - ▲ *Tutorial—Changing Arrow Directions and Shapes*
- How Can I Animate an Exhibit to Show What Happened?
  - ▲ *Tutorial—Animating an Accident Presentation*
- How Can I Use SmartDraw to Create a Settlement Brochure?
  - ▲ *Tutorial—Creating a Settlement Brochure*

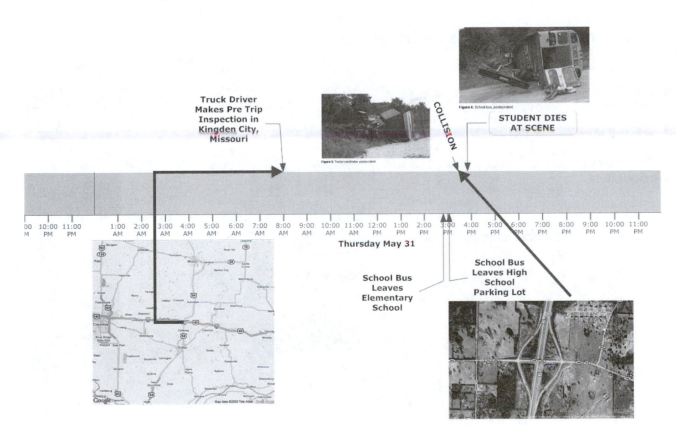

Truck Driver Makes Pre Trip Inspection in Kingden City, Missouri

Figure 5. Tractor-semitrailer, postaccident.

COLLISION

Figure 4. School bus, postaccident.

STUDENT DIES AT SCENE

Thursday May 31

School Bus Leaves Elementary School

School Bus Leaves High School Parking Lot

Source: Timeline created with SmartDraw.

HOW CAN I CREATE MAP EXHIBITS?

SmartDraw provides a full set of traditional international, national, and local maps. SmartDraw also provides direct access to Google maps through an Internet connection. The Maps category in the Document Browser has a category of Live Maps; these show a specific area, such as a state and the surrounding area. A mouse click on a highlighted area connects to the Google map for that area over the Internet. Other maps can be created using the Blank Map template and the Map tool in the Insert tab.

An actual accident case reported by the National Transportation Safety Board is used for purposes of this tutorial. The same fact pattern, dates, and location will be used in the following group of legal application tutorials.

> **N O T E**
>
> You can move around the map window with the cursor to locate and center a specific location. LEFT CLICK and HOLD the mouse and drag the map.

Creating Map Exhibits Using Live Maps

GOAL	ACTION	RESULT
OPEN MAP OPTIONS MENU IMPORT MAP TO SMARTDRAW DOCUMENT	**OPEN** *Map category in Document Browser* **CLICK** *USA-Live Map* **CLICK** *your state map* **DOUBLE CLICK** *on state map*	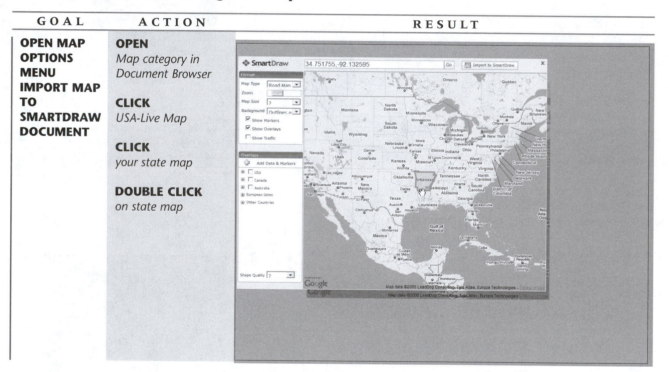

Creating Map Exhibits Using Live Maps (*continued*)

GOAL	ACTION	RESULT
SELECT SPECIFIC LOCATION BY ZOOM CONTROL	**CLICK** *Road Map option in Map Type* **ZOOM IN** *Using zoom slider to specific location* **CLICK** *Import to SmartDraw*	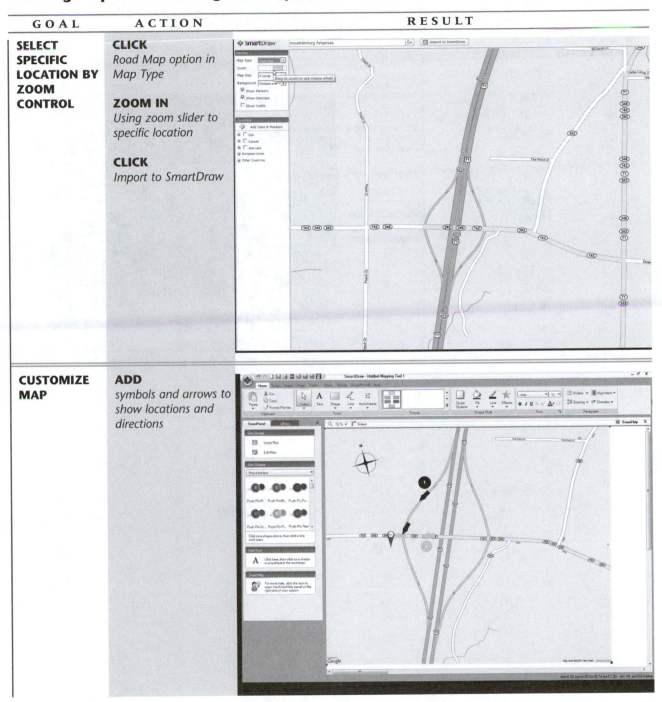
CUSTOMIZE MAP	**ADD** *symbols and arrows to show locations and directions*	

Creating Map Exhibits Using Live Maps (*continued*)

GOAL	ACTION	RESULT
IMPORT OTHER VIEWS	**CLICK** *Edit Map in SmartPanel* **CLICK** *Map Type desired (Satellite+Roads)* **CLICK** *Import to SmartDraw* **ADD** *direction arrows*	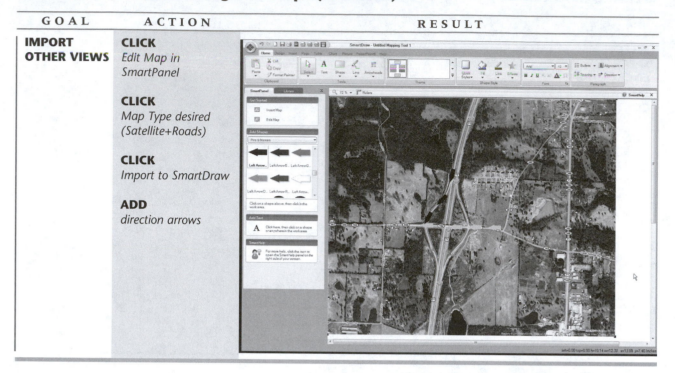

HOW CAN I CREATE AN EXHIBIT SHOWING HOW THE ACCIDENT HAPPENED?

Annotated maps and photos are frequently used as exhibits in pretrial activities and in trial. Graphic representations of how an accident occurred can be easily prepared using the SmartDraw Accident Reconstruction SmartTemplates. In many cases you will be able to find an example of a scene close enough to the one you need in the Accident Reconstruction SmartTemplates.

Creating Map and Photo Exhibits

GOAL	ACTION	RESULT
DOWNLOAD AND ANNOTATE MAP	**OPEN** *Blank Interactive Map in Document Browser* **CLICK** *Insert Map in SmartPanel*	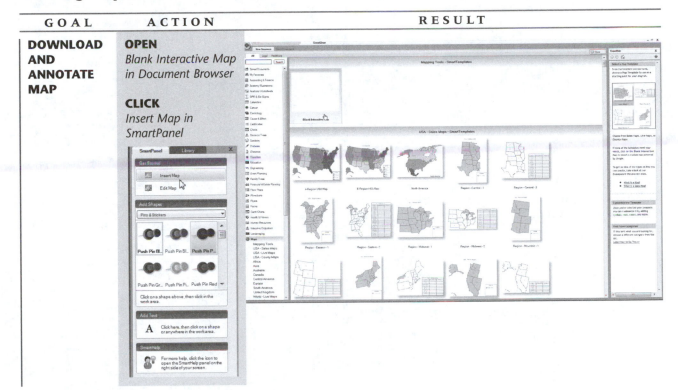

Creating Map and Photo Exhibits (*continued*)

GOAL	ACTION	RESULT
	TYPE *desired map location* **CLICK** *Map Size* **CLICK** *Map Type Desired* **CLICK** *Go* **CLICK** *Import to SmartDraw*	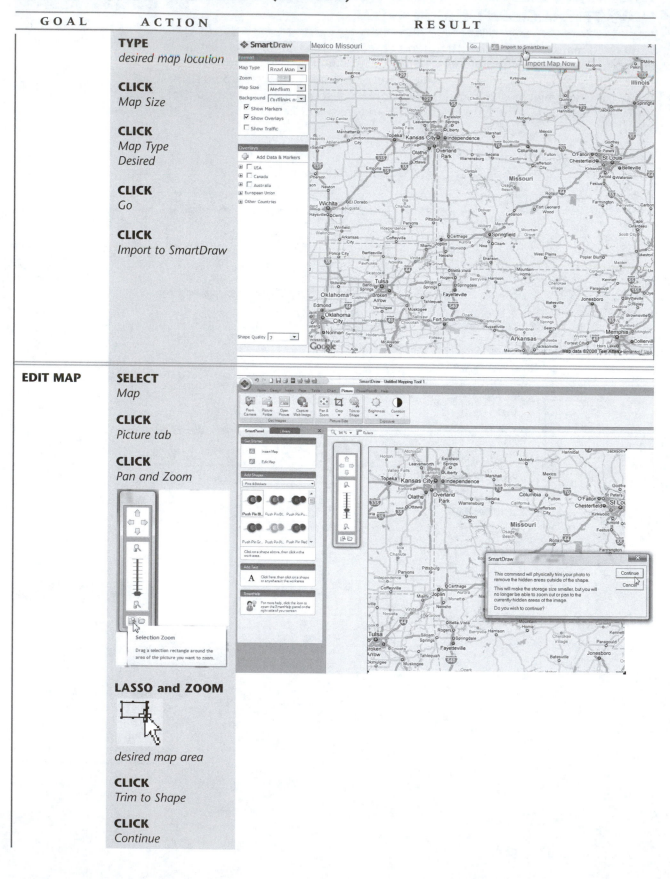
EDIT MAP	**SELECT** *Map* **CLICK** *Picture tab* **CLICK** *Pan and Zoom* **LASSO and ZOOM** *desired map area* **CLICK** *Trim to Shape* **CLICK** *Continue*	

Creating Map and Photo Exhibits (*continued*)

GOAL	ACTION	RESULT
ANNOTATE MAP	**DRAG AND DROP** *symbols from SmartPanel to annotate* **CLICK** *Add Text In SmartPanel* **TYPE** *descriptive text*	
SAVE	**CLICK** *SmartDraw Button* **CLICK** *SAVE AS SmartDraw file*	

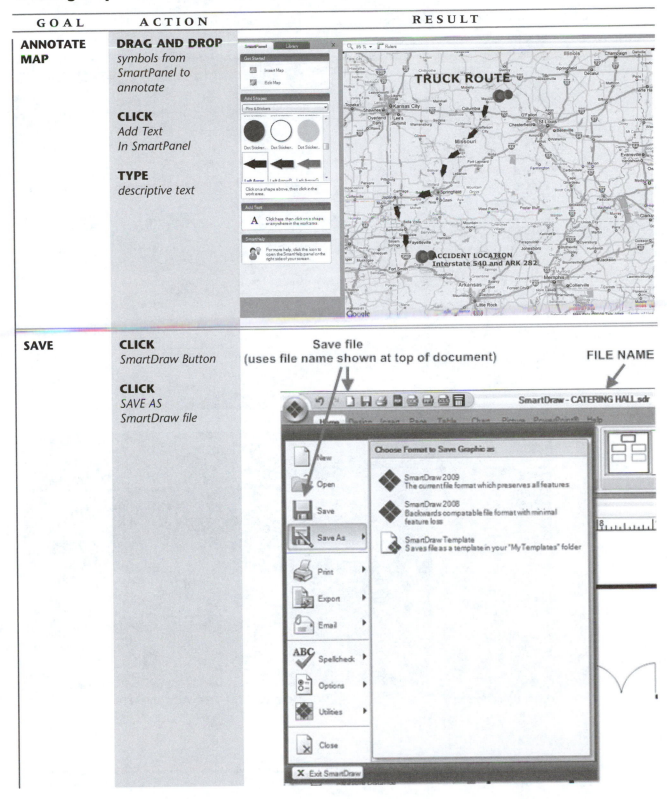

Creating Map and Photo Exhibits (*continued*)

GOAL	ACTION	RESULT
ANNOTATE PHOTO-GRAPHS	**CLICK** *Blank Flyer in Document Browser* **CLICK** *Insert tab* **CLICK** *Picture* **CLICK** *desired picture* **CLICK** *Open*	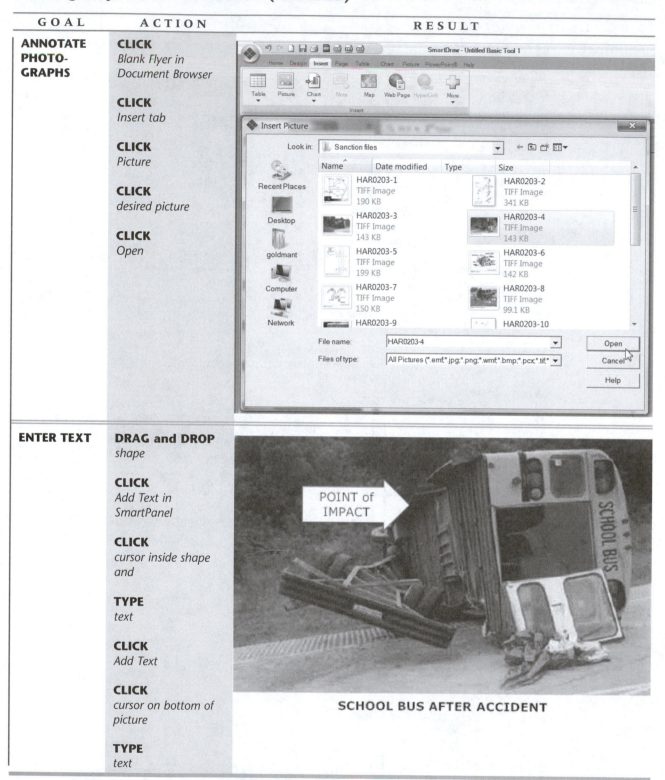
ENTER TEXT	**DRAG and DROP** *shape* **CLICK** *Add Text in SmartPanel* **CLICK** *cursor inside shape and* **TYPE** *text* **CLICK** *Add Text* **CLICK** *cursor on bottom of picture* **TYPE** *text*	

HOW CAN I CREATE A TIMELINE OF A CASE?

A timeline is a useful way to quickly present a full sequence of events. It can also be used to summarize a series of events leading to a claim for injury or death. An annotated timeline can be used to show what happened and when it happened in making an argument to a claims adjuster, arbitration panel, or jury. The SmartDraw timeline templates may be annotated with pictures and maps. As mentioned earlier, the case used to illustrate this tutorial is an actual case reported by the National Transportation Study Board.

Creating a Case Timeline

GOAL	ACTION	RESULT
CREATE TIMELINE STARTING EVENT	**CLICK** *Timeline in Document Browser* **CLICK** *Start Date for timeline in SmartPanel* **ENTER** *date*	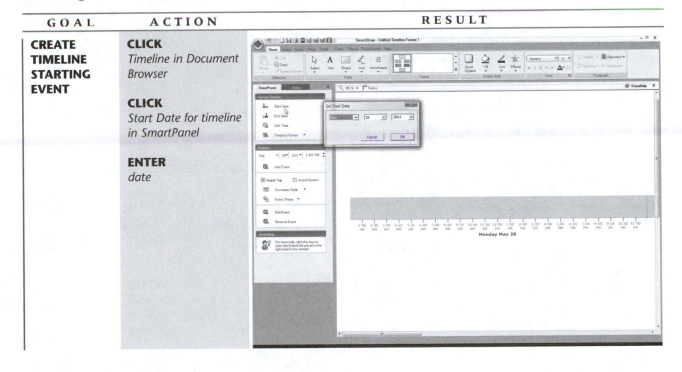

Creating a Case Timeline (*continued*)

GOAL	ACTION	RESULT
CREATE TIMELINE ENDING EVENT	**CLICK** *End Date for timeline in SmartPanel* **ENTER** *date*	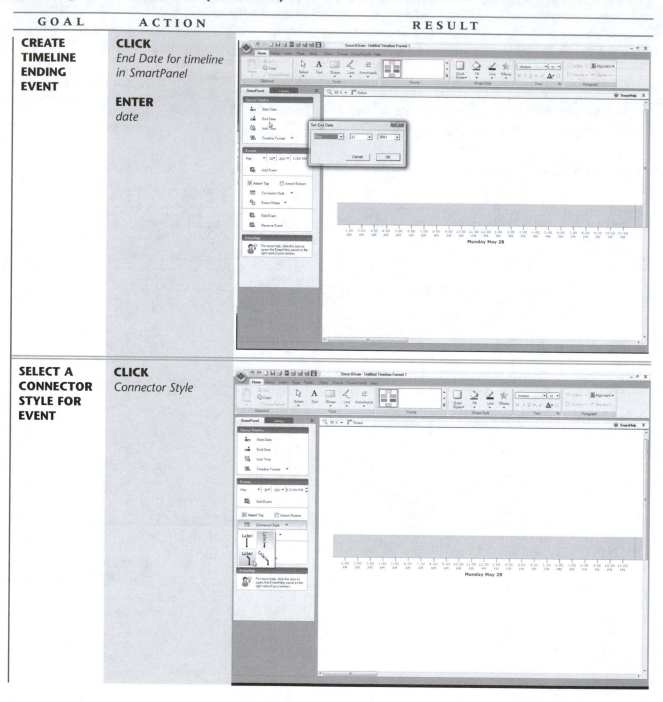
SELECT A CONNECTOR STYLE FOR EVENT	**CLICK** *Connector Style*	

Creating a Case Timeline (*continued*)

GOAL	ACTION	RESULT
SELECT THE EVENT SHAPE	**CLICK** *Event Shape*	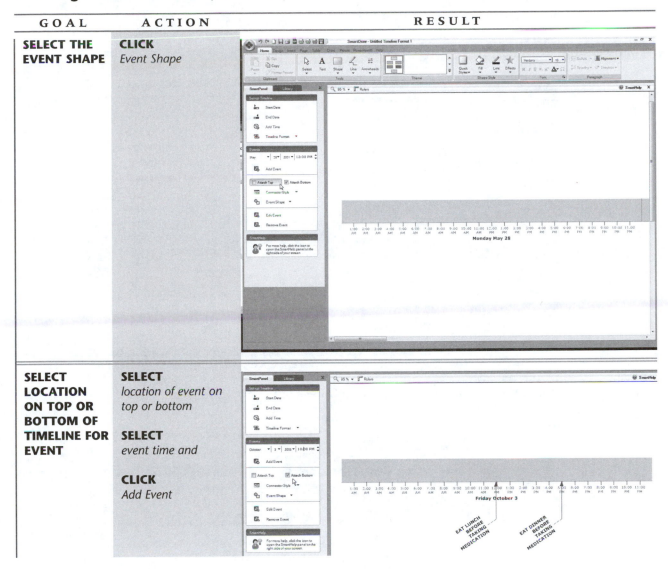
SELECT LOCATION ON TOP OR BOTTOM OF TIMELINE FOR EVENT	**SELECT** *location of event on top or bottom* **SELECT** *event time and* **CLICK** *Add Event*	

Creating a Case Timeline (*continued*)

GOAL	ACTION	RESULT
COLOR FILL EVENT SHAPE	**SELECT** *Event Shape* **CLICK** *Home tab* **CLICK** *Fill and select color to enhance significant events*	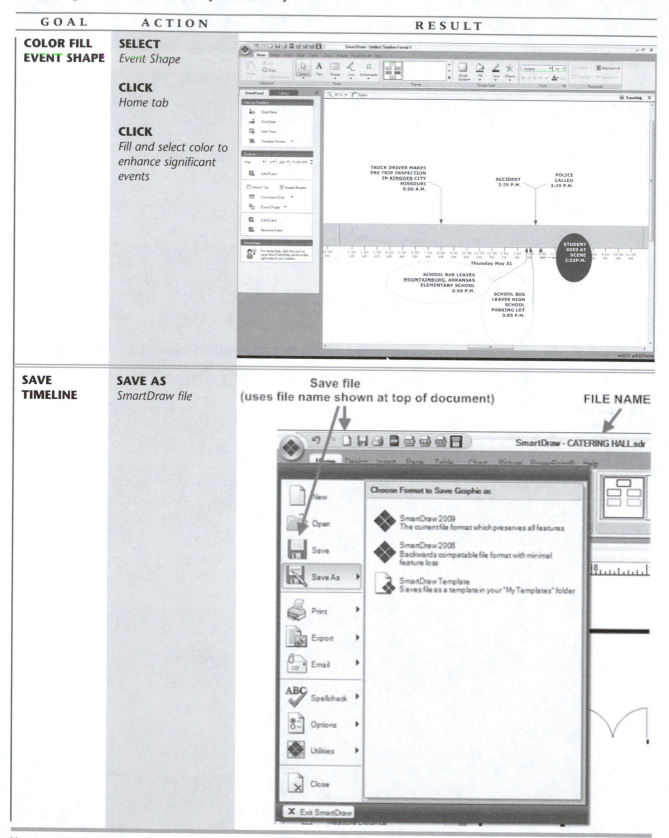
SAVE TIMELINE	**SAVE AS** *SmartDraw file*	

You may use this timeline in the next tutorial or start a new one.

HOW CAN I ANNOTATE A TIMELINE TO MAKE IT MORE DRAMATIC?

A basic timeline can be very useful in showing facts. But a timeline annotated with pictures and maps, when permitted in court or in pretrial settlement activities, can communicate the story even more effectively. The timeline used in the previous tutorial is used in the following tutorial with the addition of maps and pictures. This tutorial provides the steps to add pictures. Before you start, locate a few sample pictures on your computer that you can use to practice inserting pictures in a timeline.

Adding Pictures and Maps to a Timeline

GOAL	ACTION	RESULT
INSERT PICTURE IN TIMELINE	**CLICK** *Insert tab* **CLICK** *Picture* **CLICK** *Add a New Picture* **CLICK** *desired picture* **CLICK** *Open*	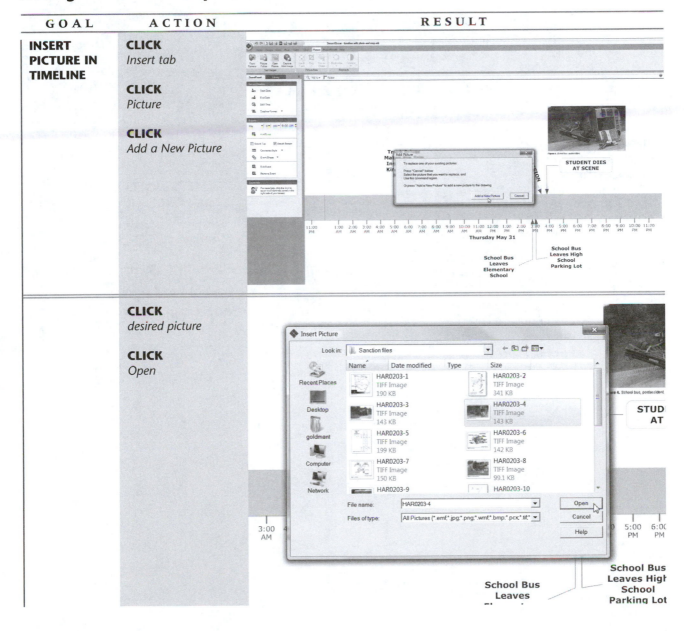

Adding Pictures and Maps to a Timeline (*continued*)

GOAL	ACTION	RESULT
DOWNLOAD AND INSERT MAP IN TIMELINE	**CLICK** *Insert tab* **CLICK** *Map* **TYPE** *desired map location* **CLICK** *Go* **CLICK** *Import to SmartDraw* **RESIZE** *and place as desired*	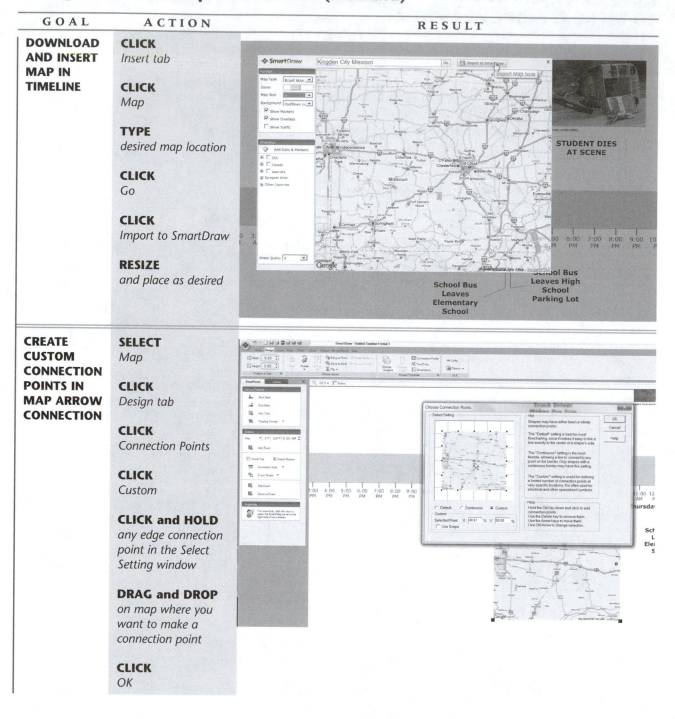
CREATE CUSTOM CONNECTION POINTS IN MAP ARROW CONNECTION	**SELECT** *Map* **CLICK** *Design tab* **CLICK** *Connection Points* **CLICK** *Custom* **CLICK and HOLD** *any edge connection point in the Select Setting window* **DRAG and DROP** *on map where you want to make a connection point* **CLICK** *OK*	

Adding Pictures and Maps to a Timeline (*continued*)

GOAL	ACTION	RESULT
DRAW LINE FROM MAP TO TIMELINE	**CLICK** *Home tab* **CLICK** *Arrowheads* **CLICK** *Right* **DRAW** *arrow from map to timeline* **SELECT** *Arrow* **RIGHT CLICK** *to open menu* **CLICK** *Color* **CLICK** *Line Thickness*	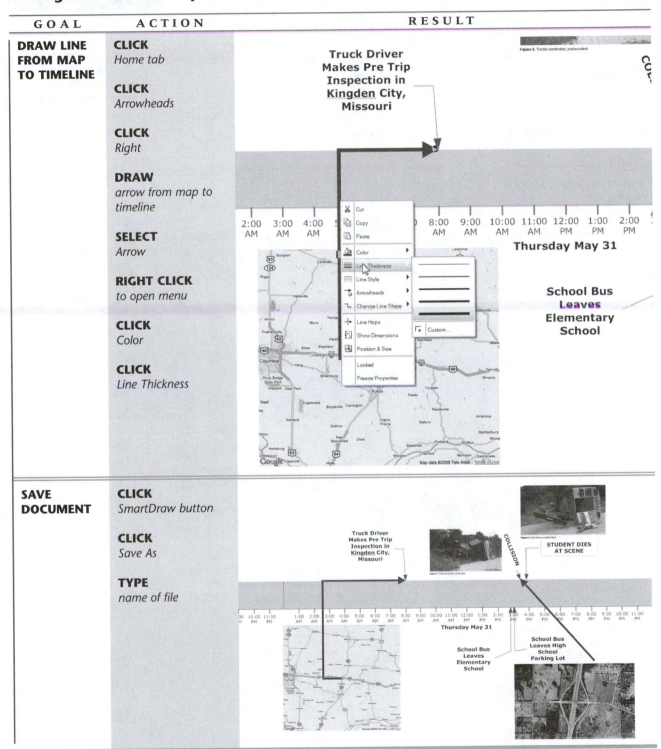
SAVE DOCUMENT	**CLICK** *SmartDraw button* **CLICK** *Save As* **TYPE** *name of file*	

HOW CAN I CHANGE THE LINE DIRECTIONS OF LABELS?

Arrows in timelines have selection handles. Depending on the type of label selected these may be fixed as a straight arrow, or have intermediate handles that can be moved to change direction or shape.

Changing Arrow Directions and Shapes

GOAL	ACTION	RESULT
EDIT LINES IN TIMELINE	**SELECT** *Arrow* **CLICK** *handles* **DRAG** *to new location*	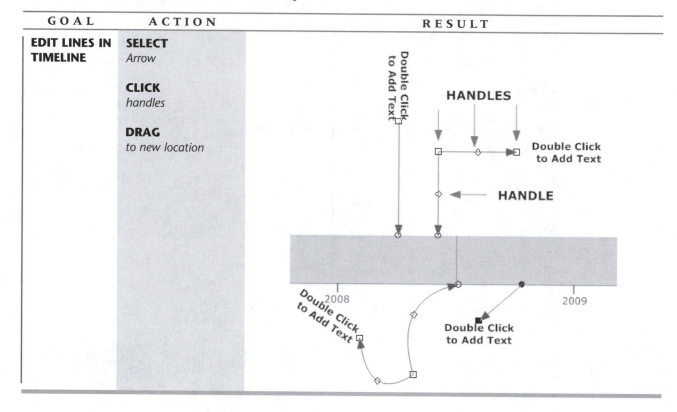

HOW CAN I ANIMATE AN EXHIBIT TO SHOW WHAT HAPPENED?

Your client says the other car struck her car while it was parked. Creating an animated recreation would be nice, but the case does not justify the cost of a full-scale animation. SmartDraw enables you to create a step-by-step presentation of the position of the vehicles based on testimony or depositions.

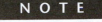

N O T E

This tutorial requires the Legal version of SmartDraw.

T I P S

Save animations in SmartDraw as well as in MS PowerPoint in case you need to modify the sequence later.

Save settlement brochure pages as SmartDraw files for future use and modification and as PDF documents for potential electronic distribution with restrictions to prevent any changes to the PDF file.

Animating an Accident Presentation

GOAL	ACTION	RESULT
CREATE ANIMATION SHOWING ACCIDENT FROM ACCIDENT SCENE GRAPHIC	**CLICK** *Legal tab* **CLICK** *Auto accident reconstruction* **CLICK** *4 way Intersection Accident* **CLICK** *PowerPoint® tab*	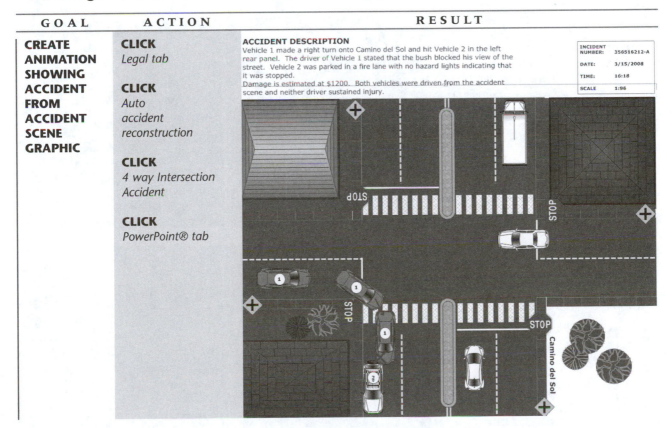

ACCIDENT DESCRIPTION
Vehicle 1 made a right turn onto Camino del Sol and hit Vehicle 2 in the left rear panel. The driver of Vehicle 1 stated that the bush blocked his view of the street. Vehicle 2 was parked in a fire lane with no hazard lights indicating that it was stopped.
Damage is estimated at $1200. Both vehicles were driven from the accident scene and neither driver sustained injury.

INCIDENT NUMBER:	356516212-A
DATE:	3/15/2008
TIME:	16:18
SCALE	1:96

Animating an Accident Presentation (*continued*)

GOAL	ACTION	RESULT
SELECT FIRST STEP GROUP OF OBJECTS TO ANIMATE	**HOLD SHIFT KEY** **SELECT** *car and number 1 symbol* **CLICK** *Step option in Animation group of PowerPoint® tab* **CLICK** *1* **UNSELECT** *car and number 1 symbol*	
SELECT SECOND STEP OBJECT TO ANIMATE	**SELECT** *arrow symbol* **CLICK** *Step option in Animation group of PowerPoint® tab* **CLICK** *2* **UNSELECT** *Arrow symbol*	
SELECT THIRD STEP GROUP OF OBJECTS TO ANIMATE	**SELECT** *car and number symbol* **CLICK** *Step option in Animation group of PowerPoint® tab* **CLICK** *3* **UNSELECT** *car and number symbol*	

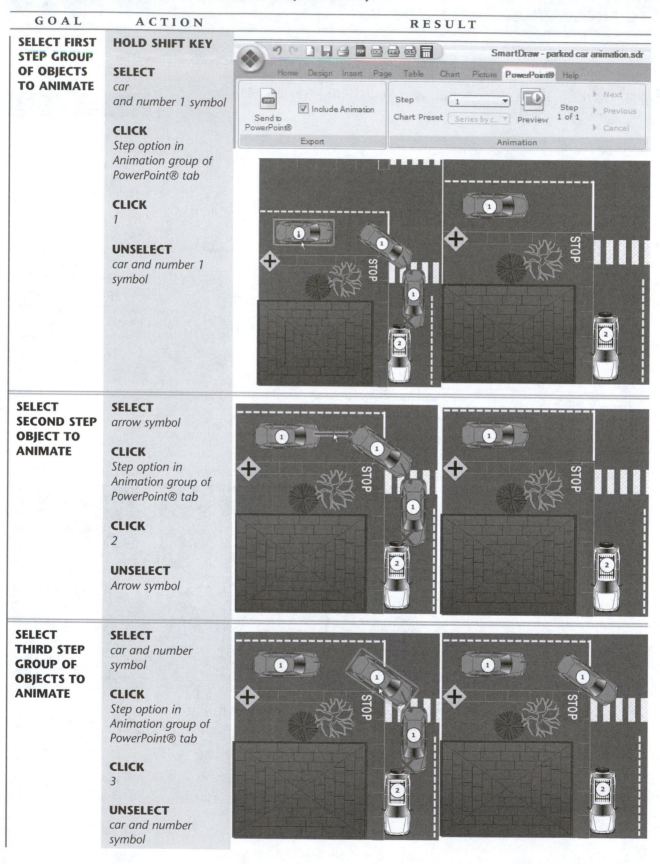

Animating an Accident Presentation (*continued*)

GOAL	ACTION	RESULT
SELECT FOURTH STEP OBJECT TO ANIMATE	**SELECT** *arrow symbol* **CLICK** *Step option in Animation group of PowerPoint tab* **CLICK** *4* **UNSELECT** *arrow symbol*	
SELECT FIFTH STEP GROUP OF OBJECTS TO ANIMATE	**SELECT** *car and number symbol* **CLICK** *Step option in Animation group of PowerPoint® tab* **CLICK** *5* **UNSELECT** *car and number symbol*	
SELECT SIXTH STEP OBJECT TO ANIMATE	**SELECT** *X symbol* **CLICK** *Step option in Animation group of PowerPoint® tab* **CLICK** *6* **UNSELECT** *X symbol*	

Animating an Accident Presentation (*continued*)

GOAL	ACTION	RESULT
PREVIEW ANIMATION SEQUENCE	**CLICK** *Preview in PowerPoint® tab* **CLICK** *Next* **REPEAT**	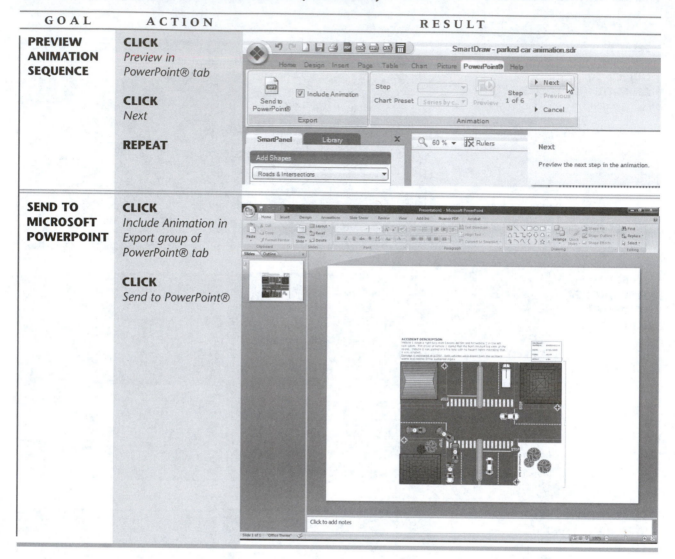
SEND TO MICROSOFT POWERPOINT	**CLICK** *Include Animation in Export group of PowerPoint® tab* **CLICK** *Send to PowerPoint®*	

HOW CAN I USE SMARTDRAW TO CREATE A SETTLEMENT BROCHURE?

A properly prepared settlement brochure can be an effective way to obtain the best possible settlement before trial. The exhibits in the brochure can also be enlarged and used as trial exhibits if the case does not settle. Photographs of injuries can show the visible signs of an injury, but not the underlying cause of the pain and suffering. An anatomically correct exhibit can show the specific body part affected by the injury, such as a spinal injury. SmartDraw Healthcare includes a wide assortment of medically accurate drawings that can be submitted in a brochure to the insurance company or opposing counsel, or enlarged for use as exhibits in trial. One of the obvious advantages of creating brochures is avoiding the cost of buying large exhibits or storing a collection.

TIPS

Exhibits in a brochure can also be printed poster size or used in electronic format in trial as exhibits.

Exhibits in brochures can also be printed poster size or used in electronic format as exhibits in trial. Local printer companies can provide the desired file format for large-scale printing.

NOTE

See page 152 for a medical exhibit from the Healthcare version.

Creating a Settlement Brochure

GOAL	ACTION	RESULT
CREATE COVER	**SELECT** *Blank Flyer template* **OR** **OPEN** *SmartDraw document* **IMPORT** *photographs and images*	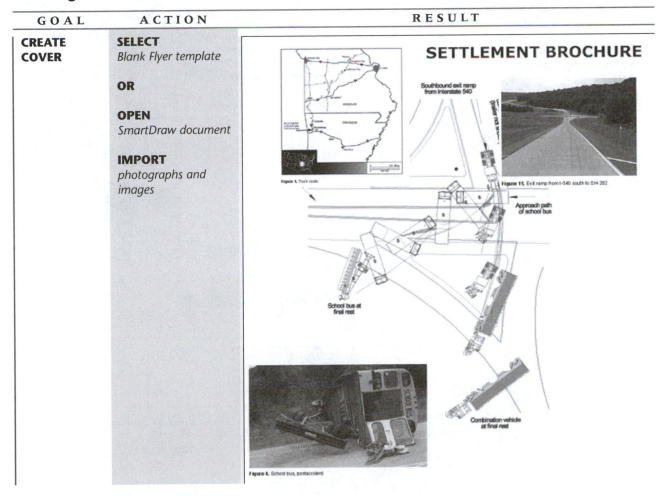

SETTLEMENT BROCHURE

Creating a Settlement Brochure (*continued*)

GOAL	ACTION	RESULT
PERSONALIZE	**ADD** *text*	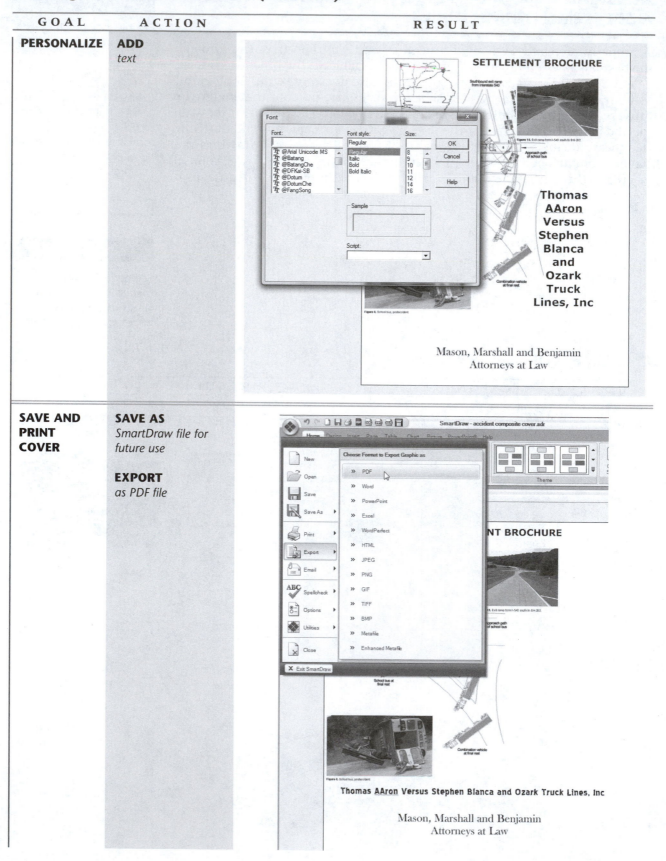
SAVE AND PRINT COVER	**SAVE AS** *SmartDraw file for future use* **EXPORT** *as PDF file*	

Creating a Settlement Brochure (*continued*)

GOAL	ACTION	RESULT
ADD PICTURES **EXPORT SMARTDRAW DOCUMENTS TO ADD TO SETTLEMENT BROCHURE**	**EXPORT** *as PDF file*	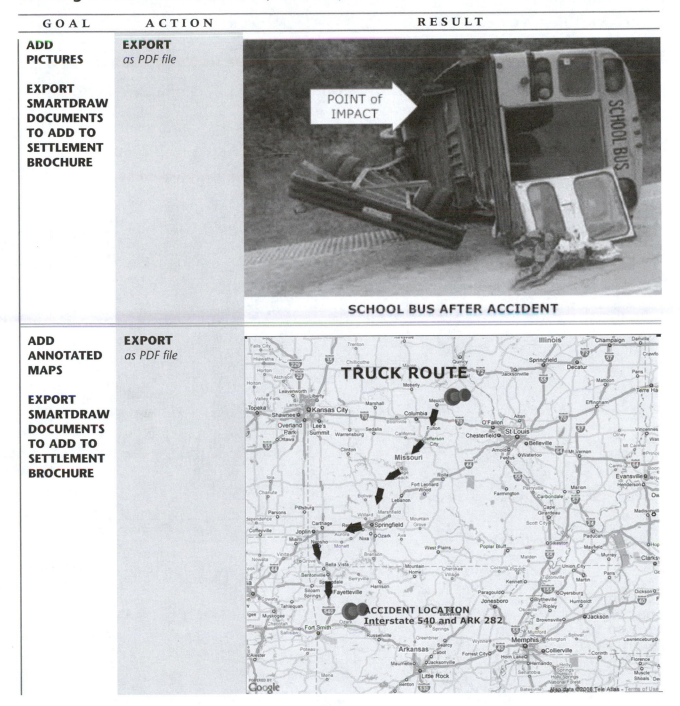
ADD ANNOTATED MAPS **EXPORT SMARTDRAW DOCUMENTS TO ADD TO SETTLEMENT BROCHURE**	**EXPORT** *as PDF file*	

Creating a Settlement Brochure (*continued*)

GOAL	ACTION	RESULT
CREATE EXHIBITS **EXPORT SMARTDRAW DOCUMENTS TO ADD TO SETTLEMENT BROCHURE**	**CLICK** *Personal Injury in Document Browser* **CLICK** *Spine* **ANNOTATE** *by adding arrow symbols and text showing area of injury*	
CREATE EXHIBITS **EXPORT SMARTDRAW DOCUMENTS TO ADD TO SETTLEMENT BROCHURE**	**ANNOTATE** *by adding arrow symbols and text showing area of injury*	

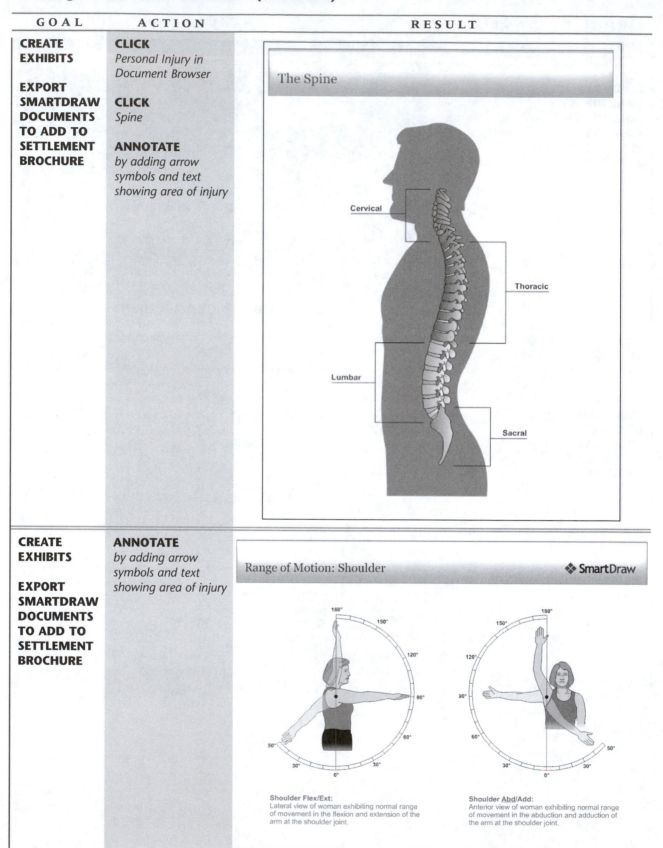

Creating a Settlement Brochure (*continued*)

GOAL	ACTION	RESULT
SEND FILES TO OUTSIDE PRINTING HOUSE TO PRINT POSTERS	**CLICK** *SmartDraw button* **CLICK** *Print* **CLICK** *Use Printing Partner*	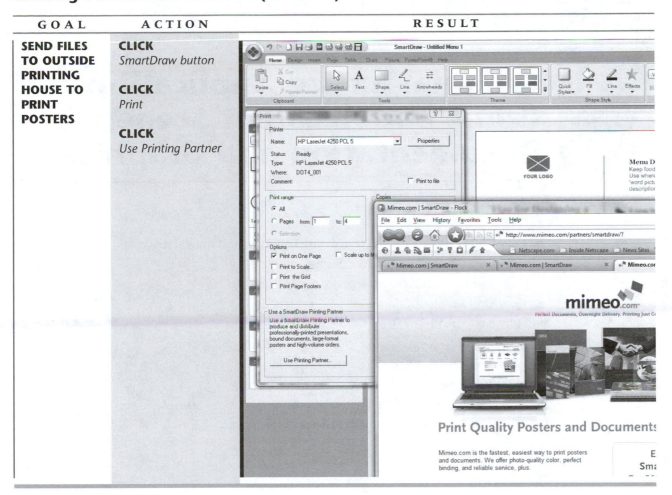

SECTION 9

Criminal Justice Applications: Crime and Accident Scene Documentation and Graphics

- How Can I Use SmartDraw to Document Crime and Accident Scenes?
- How Can I Create an Accident Scene Template?
  - ▲ *Tutorial—Creating an Accident Scene Template*
- How Do I Create a Crime Scene Reconstruction?
- How Do I Create the Basic Crime Scene Document?
  - ▲ *Tutorial—Creating a Basic Crime Scene Drawing*
- How Do I Create a Cross-Projection Drawing?
  - ▲ *Tutorial—Creating a Cross-Projection Drawing*
- How Can I Show the Sequence of Events in the Crime Scene?
  - ▲ *Tutorial—Animating the Crime Scene Document*

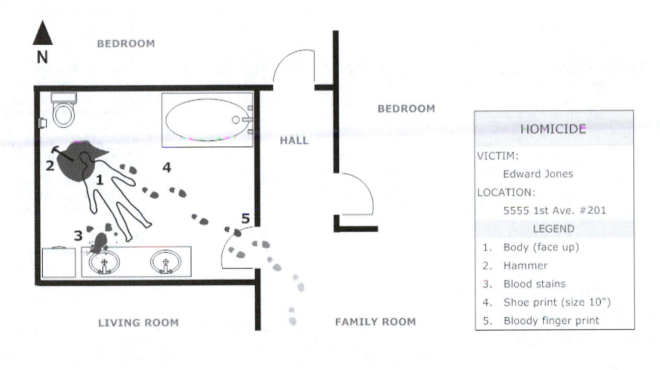

BEDROOM

N

BEDROOM

HALL

LIVING ROOM

FAMILY ROOM

HOMICIDE

VICTIM:

    Edward Jones

LOCATION:

    5555 1st Ave. #201

LEGEND

1. Body (face up)

2. Hammer

3. Blood stains

4. Shoe print (size 10")

5. Bloody finger print

CASE #:	DETECTIVE:	PHOTOGRAPHS:	DATE:
10-8002	Robert Walker	Anthony Young	3/15/2007

Source: Legal Version Document Browser Category: Crime Scene Reconstruction\Examples\Xrime Scen-Bathroom

HOW CAN I USE SMARTDRAW TO DOCUMENT CRIME AND ACCIDENT SCENES?

A standard responsibility of police and crime scene investigators is documenting the scene. Traditional methods include the paper-and-pencil rough sketch taken on the scene. Depending on departmental policy or case complexity, they may also include redrawing the sketch on an official form and, in some cases, creating a formal drawing using computer graphics for use during the investigation or at the time of trial.

The Legal version of SmartDraw provides many accident scene and crime scene examples. In addition to the graphic documentation examples, the program has numerous forms that may be used as is or modified to fit such individual needs as chain of evidence, photo logs, and other first responder needs.

HOW CAN I CREATE AN ACCIDENT SCENE TEMPLATE?

One time-saving feature of SmartDraw is its ability to create and save custom or personalized templates. In accident scene investigations a drawing is routinely prepared showing the location and dimensions of vehicles. Having a template of intersections or locations at hand that requires only the addition of the vehicles helps save time. Limiting the time needed to take measurements and walk the scene in bad weather, at night, or in heavy traffic increases the safety of the onsite responders. Accident scene investigators may also want to create a collection of road intersections or frequent accident sites during nonemergency periods for use during investigations.

The following tutorials require the Legal version of SmartDraw.

TIPS

Grid and rulers can be used to draw lines and position symbols.

Save a basic intersection document to print and use in making a rough sketch.

NOTE

After the arrowhead style is chosen, using add lines in SmartPanel will draw the arrowheads until a new style is chosen.

Creating an Accident Scene Template

GOAL	ACTION	RESULT
CREATE AND SAVE AN ACCIDENT SCENE TEMPLATE	CLICK *Legal tab* CLICK *Accident Reconstruction category in Legal version's Document Browser* CLICK *Blank Accident Diagram in Other Tools—SmartTemplates*	

Creating an Accident Scene Template (*continued*)

GOAL	ACTION	RESULT
SET UP WORK SPACE	**CLICK** *Page tab* **CLICK** *Show Grid* **CLICK** *Home tab* **CLICK** *Line* **CLICK** *Straight Line* **OR** **CLICK** *Add Lines in SmartPanel* **REPEAT** *for each line*	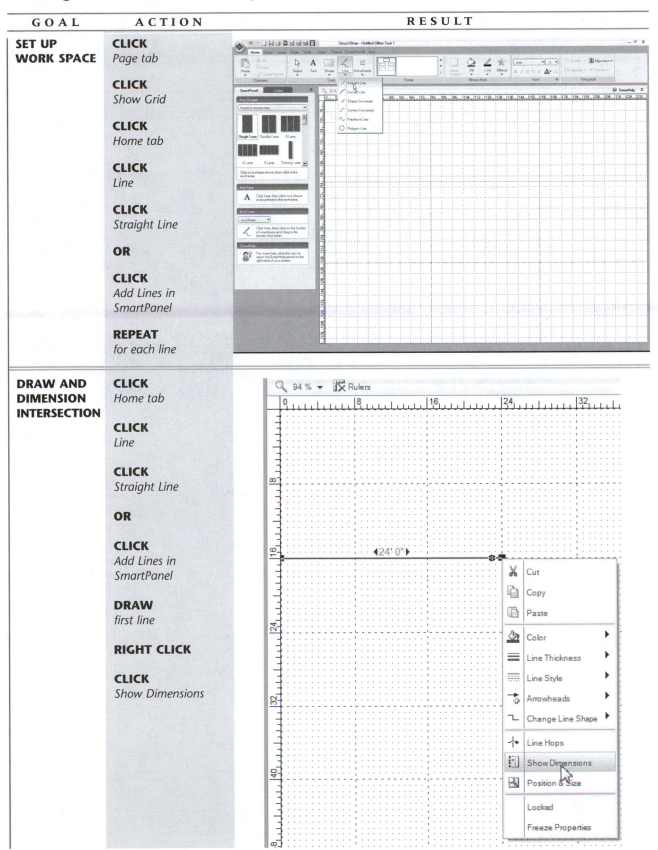
DRAW AND DIMENSION INTERSECTION	**CLICK** *Home tab* **CLICK** *Line* **CLICK** *Straight Line* **OR** **CLICK** *Add Lines in SmartPanel* **DRAW** *first line* **RIGHT CLICK** **CLICK** *Show Dimensions*	

Creating an Accident Scene Template (*continued*)

GOAL	ACTION	RESULT
TURN ON SHOW DIMENSIONS	**CLICK** *Always* **CLICK** *OK*	
ADD STREET DIMENSIONS	**CLICK** *Home tab* **CLICK** *Arrowheads* **CLICK** *Both*	

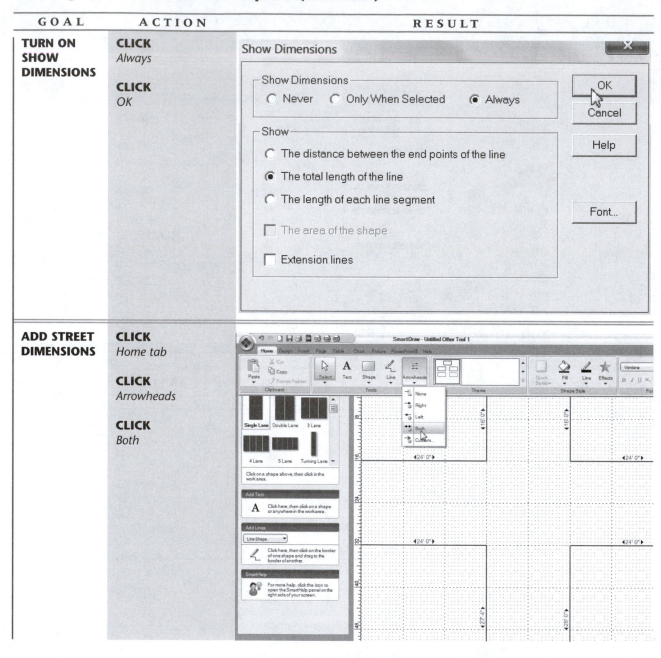

Creating an Accident Scene Template (*continued*)

GOAL	ACTION	RESULT
ADD DIMENSIONS BETWEEN CURBS	**DRAW** *line between curb lines* **REPEAT** *for other street*	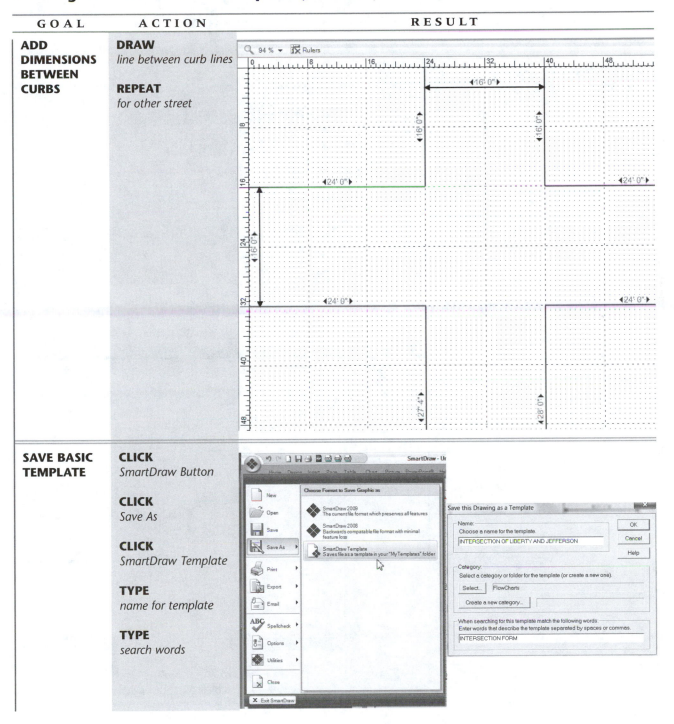
SAVE BASIC TEMPLATE	**CLICK** *SmartDraw Button* **CLICK** *Save As* **CLICK** *SmartDraw Template* **TYPE** *name for template* **TYPE** *search words*	

Creating an Accident Scene Template (*continued*)

GOAL	ACTION	RESULT
OPEN ROAD AND INTERSECTION SYMBOLS	**CLICK** *Roads & Intersections in SmartPanel* **CLICK** *More* **CLICK** *library symbol category desired*	
ADD SYMBOLS TO DRAWING	**CLICK** *symbol* **ADD** *to document*	

HOW DO I CREATE A CRIME SCENE RECONSTRUCTION?

A number of crime scene reconstruction drawings are available for modification in the SmartDraw Legal Version. You may also create a drawing using a **Blank Crime Scene Reconstruction template**. Traditionally, crime scene and accident scene reconstruction starts with carefully surveying the scene, making a sketch, taking accurate measurements of the scene, and locating objects or evidence. Digital cameras have made photographs of scenes more quickly and easily available. These photographs may be used in preparing exhibits or in constructing crime and accident scene documentation for use in the investigation. In most cases a scene, such as a typical automobile accident or street crime, will involve a street location or an interior location of a room in a building. Each of these can be drawn to exact dimensions.

The most common crime scene is the traditional view looking down on the scene. In some cases, however, a cross-projection view may be used. The cross-projection view starts with the traditional view looking down toward the floor of the room or scene. The walls are then added to the drawing to show relevant items, such as blood splatter or bullet holes. A sample of both views is shown below.

HOW DO I CREATE THE BASIC CRIME SCENE DOCUMENT?

Interior crime scene documentation typically includes the room or rooms in which the crime occurred or the evidence was found. The scene may also include a surrounding hall or rooms. The starting point is to create the walls and room access. This is the same as creating a floor plan. There are a number of examples of interior crime scenes in the Crime Scene Reconstruction category in the Legal version's Document Browser. Other potentially useful examples may be found in the Floor Plans category.

Outside or exterior crime scenes are similar to the documents created for accident reconstruction. These may be modified to include expanded areas, such as sidewalks, and exterior building components, such as porches and fences.

Individual symbols, such as the blood splatter, the victim, and the broken glass, are added to the drawing from the symbols library.

Creating a Basic Crime Scene Drawing

GOAL	ACTION	RESULT
CREATE CRIME SCENE USING TEMPLATE	**CLICK** *Crime Scene Reconstruction* **CLICK** *Bedroom in Crime Scene Areas— SmartTemplates*	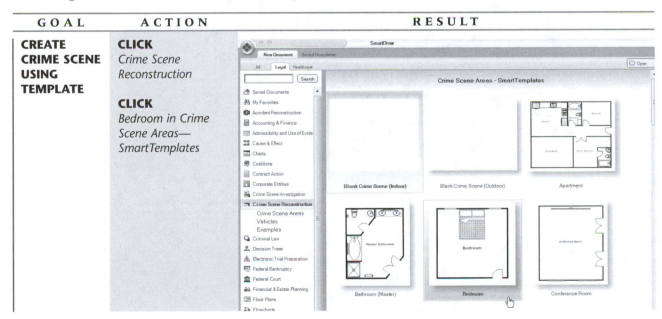

Creating a Basic Crime Scene Drawing (*continued*)

GOAL	ACTION	RESULT
RESIZE DIMENSIONS	**SELECT** *right wall* **CLICK and HOLD** **DRAG** *to desired dimension*	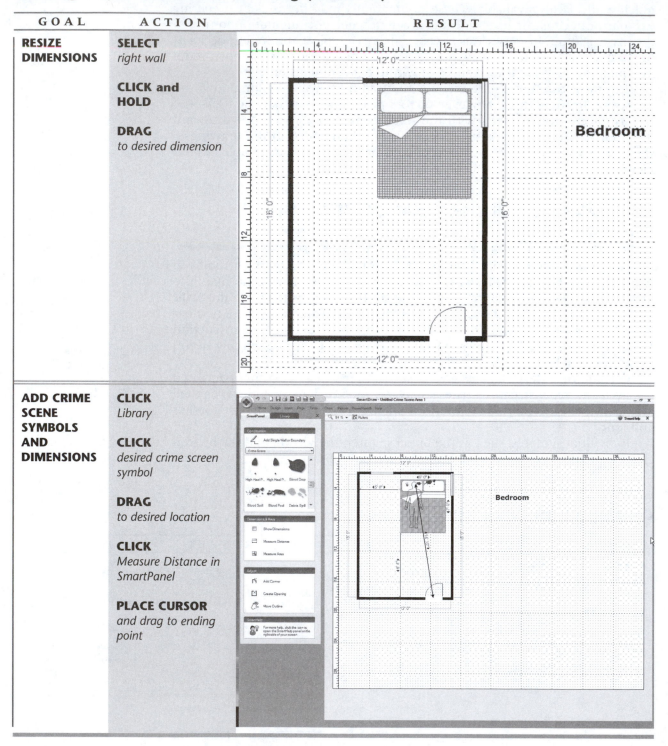
ADD CRIME SCENE SYMBOLS AND DIMENSIONS	**CLICK** *Library* **CLICK** *desired crime screen symbol* **DRAG** *to desired location* **CLICK** *Measure Distance in SmartPanel* **PLACE CURSOR** *and drag to ending point*	

HOW DO I CREATE A CROSS-PROJECTION DRAWING?

A cross-projection drawing is basically a five-panel drawing: the floor, and the east, west, north, and south walls. In most cases the opposite walls will be the same size with a uniform height, and the base dimensions the same as the floor. The doors, windows, and other openings are only shown on the appropriate walls. The easiest method is to construct the floor, leaving enough room on the working screen to add the walls. After one wall is constructed, it can be copied and pasted on the opposite side or on all four sides, if they are the same size. Once they are in position, the walls may be resized to fit the dimensions just as any other symbol may be resized.

TIP

Use lines, not walls, to create the cross-projection view and avoid the issue of the wall thickness.

NOTE

The advantage of the cross-projection is that it allows relevant markings on the wall to be added to the crime scene drawing.

Creating a Cross-Projection Drawing

GOAL	ACTION	RESULT
CREATE CROSS-PROJECTION TEMPLATE	**CLICK** *Crime Scene Reconstruction* **DRAW** *floor diagram* **DRAW** *four walls*	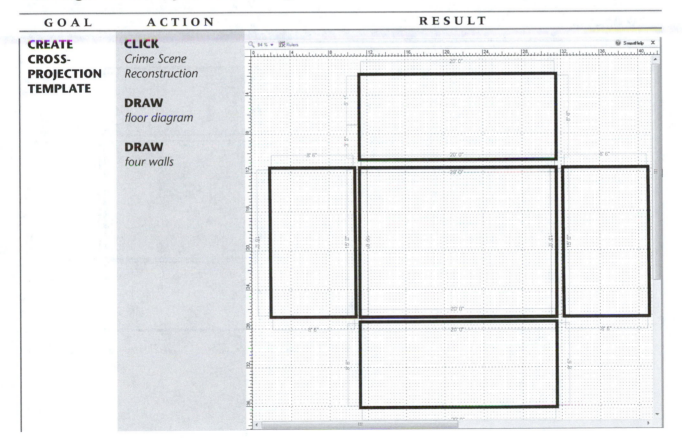

Creating a Cross-Projection Drawing (*continued*)

GOAL	ACTION	RESULT
SAVE CROSS-PROJECTION TEMPLATE	**CLICK** *SmartDraw button* **CLICK** *Save As* **CLICK** *SmartDraw Template* **TYPE** *name for template* **TYPE** *search words*	
ADD OBJECTS	**CLICK** *down arrow in Crime Scene symbols* **CLICK** *More* **CLICK** *desired symbol library* **CLICK** *desired symbol* **PASTE** *on drawing*	

Creating a Cross-Projection Drawing (*continued*)

GOAL	ACTION	RESULT
ADD WINDOWS AND DOORS TO WALLS	**CLICK** *Home tab* **CLICK** *Shape* **CLICK** *Rectangle*	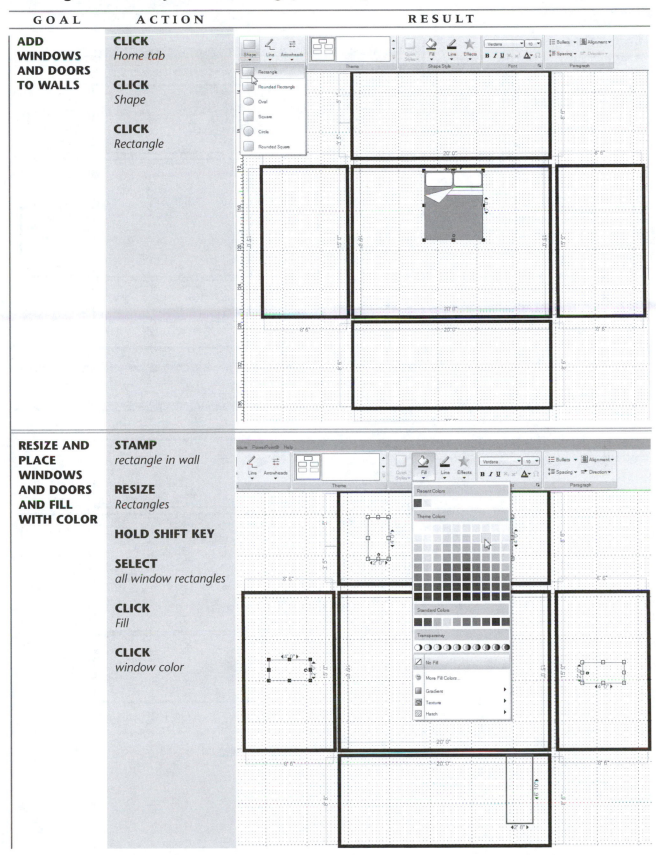
RESIZE AND PLACE WINDOWS AND DOORS AND FILL WITH COLOR	**STAMP** *rectangle in wall* **RESIZE** *Rectangles* **HOLD SHIFT KEY** **SELECT** *all window rectangles* **CLICK** *Fill* **CLICK** *window color*	

Creating a Cross-Projection Drawing (*continued*)

GOAL	ACTION	RESULT
ADD VICTIM AND RESIZE TO ACTUAL HEIGHT AND WIDTH	**CLICK** *Crime Scene symbol library* **CLICK** *victim profile and* **STAMP** *victim profile in place on drawing* **SELECT** *victim symbol* **RESIZE**	
ADD BLOOD SPLATTER TO SCENE	**CLICK** *blood splatter from Crime Scene symbols library* **STAMP** *splatter as needed*	

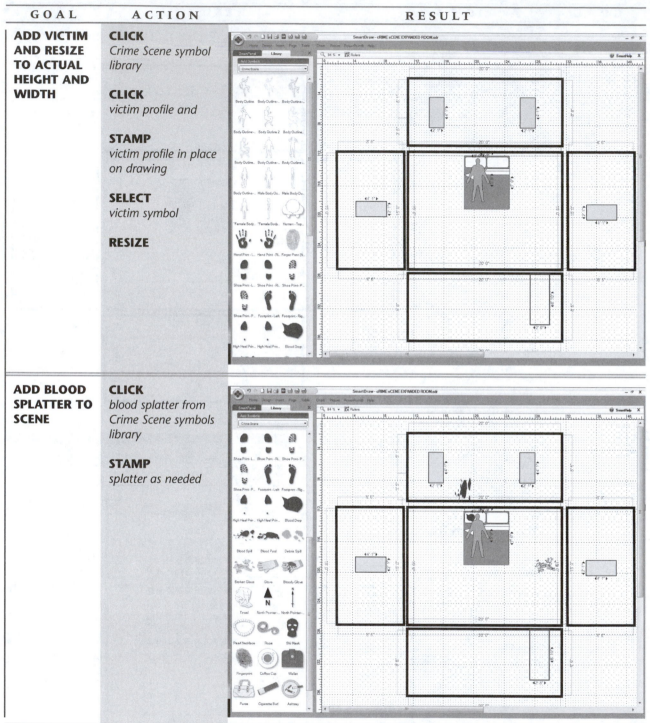

HOW CAN I SHOW THE SEQUENCE OF EVENTS IN THE CRIME SCENE?

A graphic representation of a crime scene that displays the events as they are alleged to have occurred can be an important investigatory tool. Looking at the sequence may make it clear that the physical evidence does not support the assumed facts. For example, the first responders may have moved the victim or other physical evidence in treating the victim's injuries. A step-by-step sequence may help to put things in a proper time and location sequence.

TIP

To select multiple items, hold down the control (Ctrl) key on the keyboard as you select the items. All selected items will be treated the same way. This procedure may also be used in other situations where you want to apply the same treatment to multiple symbols (such as deleting them or filling them with color).

Animating the Crime Scene Document

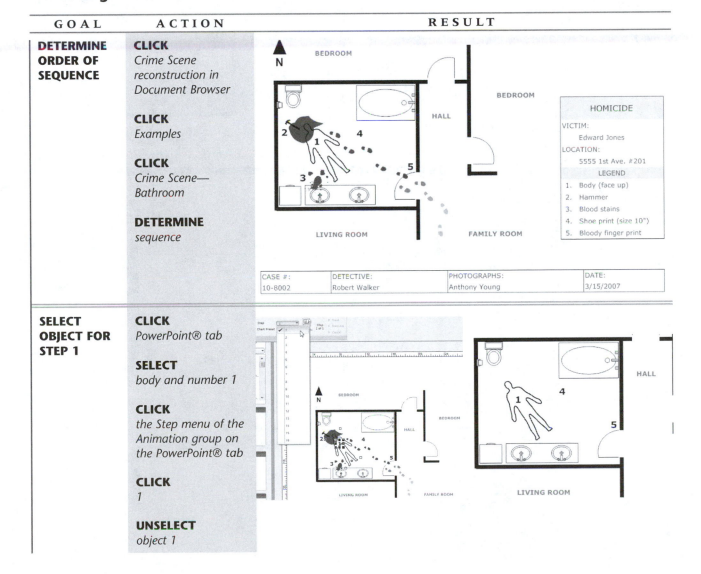

GOAL	ACTION	RESULT
DETERMINE ORDER OF SEQUENCE	**CLICK** *Crime Scene reconstruction in Document Browser* **CLICK** *Examples* **CLICK** *Crime Scene— Bathroom* **DETERMINE** *sequence*	
SELECT OBJECT FOR STEP 1	**CLICK** *PowerPoint® tab* **SELECT** *body and number 1* **CLICK** *the Step menu of the Animation group on the PowerPoint® tab* **CLICK** *1* **UNSELECT** *object 1*	

Animating the Crime Scene Document (*continued*)

GOAL	ACTION	RESULT
SELECT OBJECT FOR STEP 2	**SELECT** *Step 2 object (hammer)* **CLICK** 2 *in the Step menu* **UNSELECT** *object 2*	
SELECT OBJECT FOR STEP 3	**SELECT** *Step 3 object (blood splatter)* **CLICK** 3 *in the Step menu* **UNSELECT** *object 3*	
SELECT OBJECT FOR STEP 4	**SELECT** *Step 4 objects (bloody footprints)* **CLICK** 4 *in the Step menu* **UNSELECT** *object 4*	

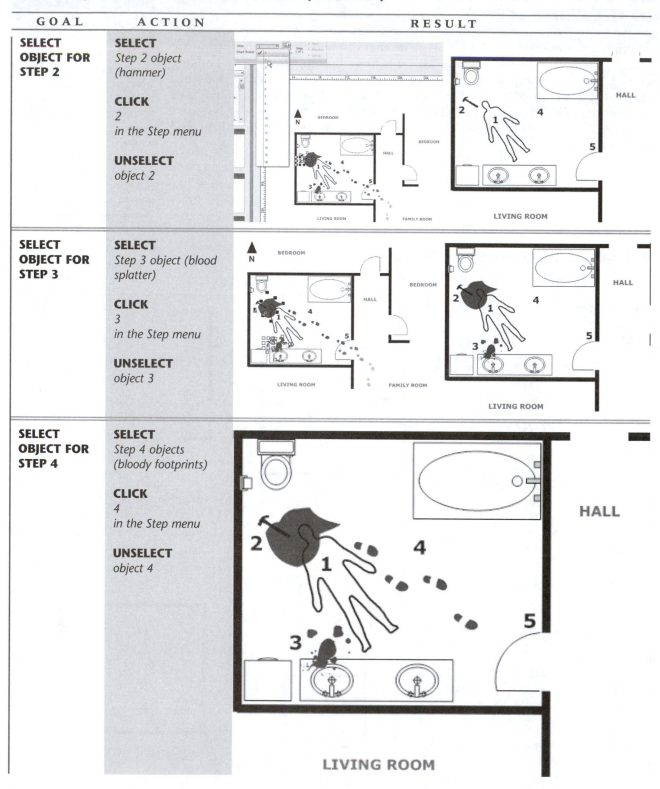

Animating the Crime Scene Document (*continued*)

GOAL	ACTION	RESULT
SELECT OBJECT FOR STEP 5	**SELECT** *Step 5 object (rest of footprints)* **CLICK** *5* *in the Step menu* **UNSELECT** *object 5*	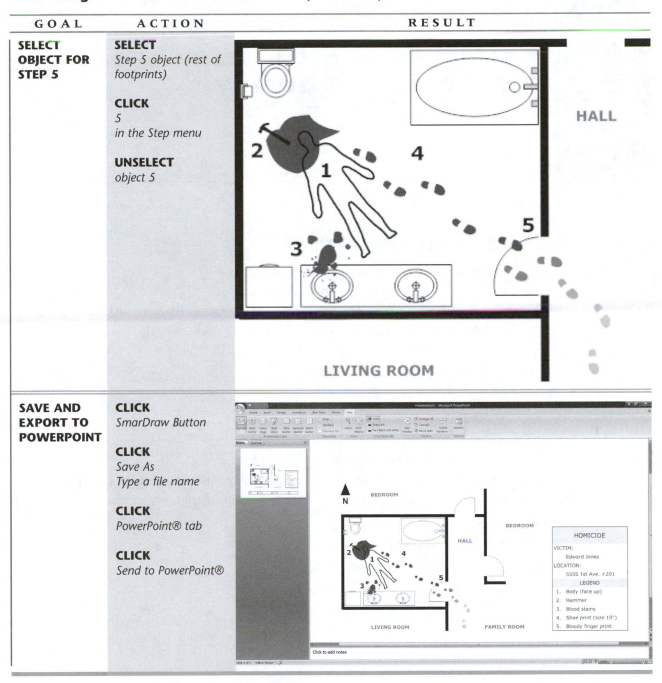
SAVE AND EXPORT TO POWERPOINT	**CLICK** *SmarDraw Button* **CLICK** *Save As* *Type a file name* **CLICK** *PowerPoint® tab* **CLICK** *Send to PowerPoint®*	

Hospitality Industry

HOTEL-MOTEL APPLICATIONS

- How Can I Create and Try out New Room Designs?
  - ▲ *Tutorial—Creating a Room Template and Layout*
- How Can I Create an Emergency Exit Drawing to Post in Every Room?
  - ▲ *Tutorial—Creating a Temporary Emergency Exit Plan*

RESTAURANT APPLICATIONS

- How Can I Create Menus?
  - ▲ *Tutorial—Creating a Menu Template*
- How Can I See If the New Equipment Will Fit?
  - ▲ *Tutorial—Creating a Commercial Kitchen Layout*
- Can I Create a Layout Showing Wait Staff Assignments or Seating Arrangements?
  - ▲ *Tutorial—Adding Seating Charts and Wait Staff Assignments*

EVENT PLANNING

- How Can I Create a Facility Floor Plan?
  - ▲ *Tutorial—Creating a Facility Floor Plan*
  - ▲ *Tutorial—Creating a Layout for a Wedding*

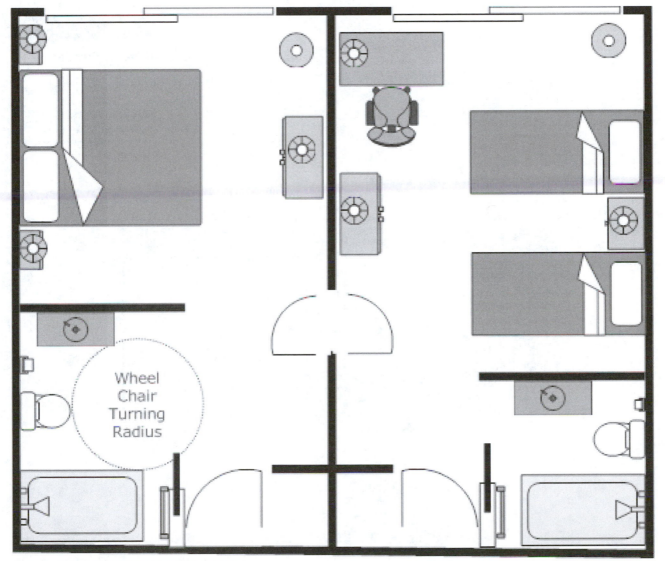

Wheel Chair Turning Radius

Source: Created using SmartDraw Floor Plan template

HOW CAN I CREATE AND TRY OUT NEW ROOM DESIGNS?

Basic room floor plans with or without furniture and other details can be created and saved as templates. These templates can then be used to try out different combinations of interior layout. Renovations to rooms, such as making a room handicap-accessible, can be tried and retried without incurring the usual cost for professionally drawn and certified prints.

<table>
<tr><td>

T I P

When measuring, interior dimensions are to the inside of walls. Building dimension may be calculated to the center of walls.

</td></tr>
<tr><td>

N O T E S

Resize the doors to comply with local building codes for public spaces.

Handicap access may require redesign of rooms.

</td></tr>
</table>

Creating a Room Template and Layout

GOAL	ACTION	RESULT
CREATE BASIC ROOM TEMPLATE	**CLICK** *Floor Plan in Document Browser* **CLICK** *Blank Floor Plan* **CLICK** *Add Single Wall in SmartPanel* **DRAW** *room outline*	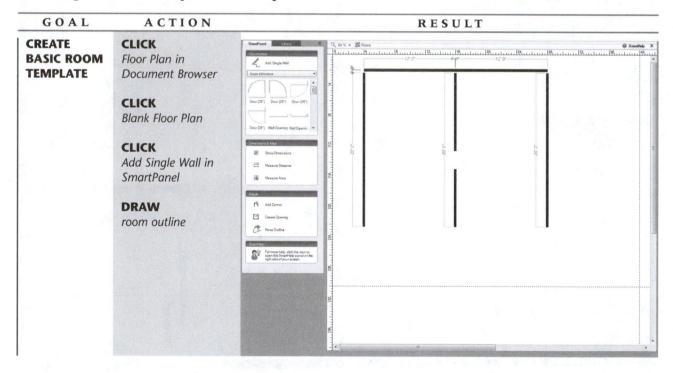

Creating a Room Template and Layout (*continued*)

GOAL	ACTION	RESULT
ADD OPENINGS AND DOORS	**CLICK** *desired doors and openings in Doors & Windows symbol library in SmartPanel* **PLACE** *selected doors and openings* **RESIZE** *doors and openings to correct sizes*	
SAVE LAYOUT AS TEMPLATE	**CLICK** *SmartDraw button* **CLICK** *Save As* **CLICK** *SmartDraw Template* **TYPE** *name for template* **TYPE** *search words*	

Creating a Room Template and Layout (*continued*)

GOAL	ACTION	RESULT
ADD BATHROOM ELEMENTS	**CLICK** *down arrow in Doors & Windows* **CLICK** *More* **CLICK** *required symbols from symbol library* **CLICK** *desired item* **PLACE** *in drawing*	
ADD FURNITURE	**CLICK** *down arrow in Lavatory* **CLICK** *More* **CLICK** *desired symbol library* **CLICK** *desired symbol* **PLACE** *in drawing* **REPEAT** *other items*	

Creating a Room Template and Layout (*continued*)

GOAL	ACTION	RESULT
SAVE DRAWING	**CLICK** *Smart Button* **CLICK** *Save As* **CLICK** *SmartDraw 2009* **TYPE** *file name*	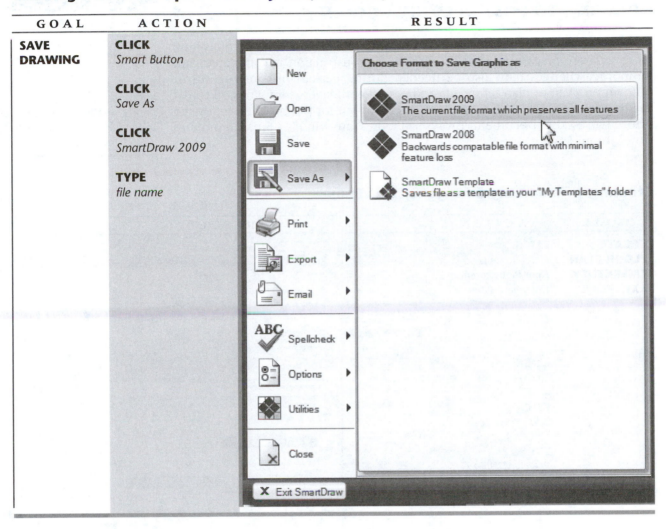

HOW CAN I CREATE AN EMERGENCY EXIT DRAWING TO POST IN EVERY ROOM?

Emergency exit plans are required in most public places like hotels and motels. These plans may change when new construction is completed, but temporary changes may also be needed during periods of construction or renovation. A floor plan template can be used with layers (drawings on top of the drawing) to show the changes and printed out for posting. The following tutorial uses the Document Browser Floor Plans Hotels—SmartTemplates Hotel Room Layout.

Creating a Temporary Emergency Exit Plan

GOAL	ACTION	RESULT
CREATE FLOOR PLAN EMERGENCY EXIT PLAN	**CLICK** *Hotel Room Layout in Floor Plans category in Document Browser* **CLICK** *Page tab* **CLICK** *Layers* **CLICK** *Add a New Layer* **TYPE** *RENOVATION EXITS* **CLICK** *OK* **REPEAT** *for other layers*	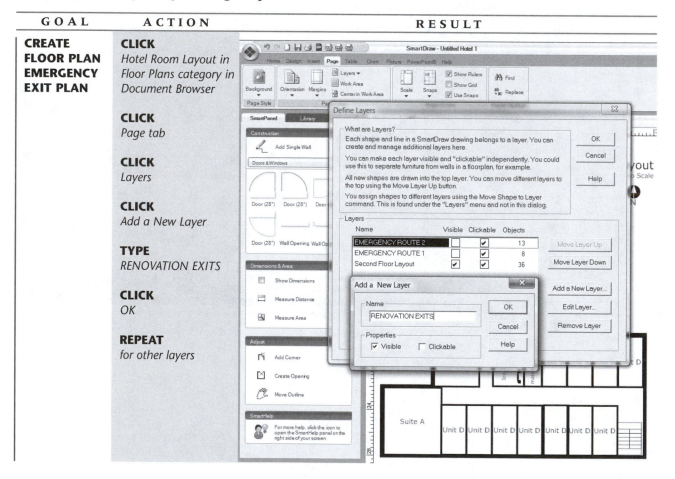

Creating a Temporary Emergency Exit Plan (*continued*)

GOAL	ACTION	RESULT
CREATE NEW LAYER FOR EMERGENCY ROUTE 1	**CLICK** *Add a Layer* **TYPE** *Emergency Route 1* **CLICK** *Layer tab at bottom of work space for Emergency Route 1* **CLICK** *Arrowheads* **DRAW** *arrows as needed* **CLICK** *Lines* **DRAW** *as needed*	
CREATE NEW LAYER FOR EMERGENCY ROUTE 2	**CLICK** *Add a Layer* **TYPE** *Emergency Route 2* **CLICK** *Layer tab at bottom of work space for Emergency Route 2* **CLICK** *Arrowheads* **DRAW** *arrows as needed* **CLICK** *Lines* **DRAW** *as needed*	

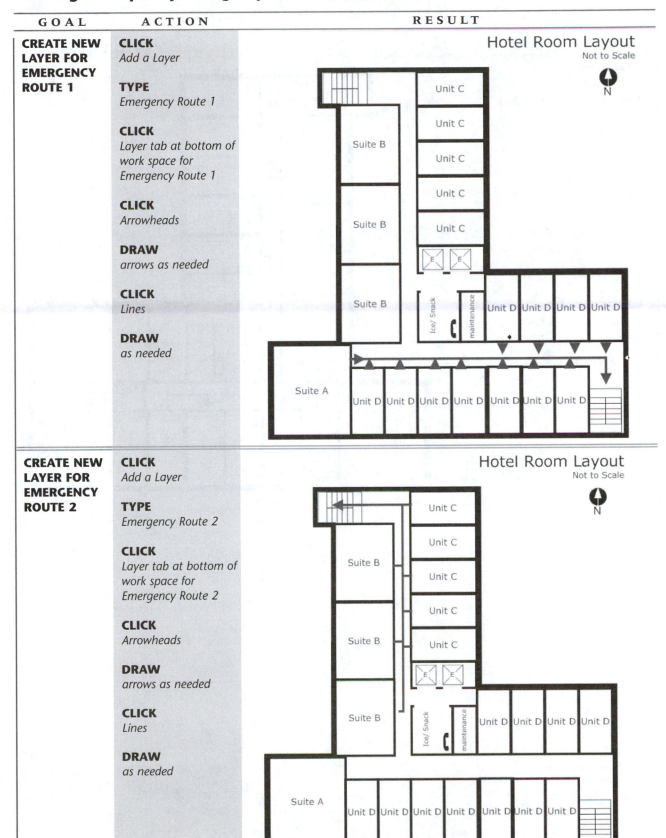

Creating a Temporary Emergency Exit Plan (*continued*)

GOAL	ACTION	RESULT
CREATE LAYER FOR ALTERNATE EMERGENCY ROUTE	**CLICK** *Add a Layer* **TYPE** *Alternate Emergency route* **CLICK** *Layer tab at bottom of work space for Alternate Emergency Route* **CLICK** *Arrowheads* **DRAW** *arrows as needed* **CLICK** *Lines* **DRAW** *as needed* **CLICK** *Add Text* **TYPE** *as needed*	Hotel Room Layout Not to Scale N

Hotel Room Layout (Not to Scale):
- Suite B, Suite B, Suite B, Suite A
- Unit C (x5)
- Unit D (multiple)
- Ice/ Snack, maintenance
- E, E (elevators)
- CLOSED FOR RENOVATIONS

Creating a Temporary Emergency Exit Plan (*continued*)

GOAL	ACTION	RESULT
PRINT DOCUMENT FOR POSTING	**CLICK** *Smart Button* **CLICK** *Print Preview* **CLICK** *Print*	

Hotel Room Layout
Not to Scale

HOW CAN I CREATE MENUS?

Exciting, up-to-date menus are critical to the success of restaurants. Customers need to be induced to purchase high-profit items. A well-designed menu that accomplishes this goal can translate into increased sales. Much of the research about the physiology of menu design shows that an attractive menu that describes items without unduly emphasizing the price does increase sales. Frequent fluctuations in pricing of ingredients requires the ability to change menu prices to reflect market conditions. SmartDraw can help you create visually appealing menus that reflect daily specials and seasonal items in house, which saves money by eliminating outside printing charges. SmartDraw also includes sample menus that provide helpful suggestions on designing menus to maximize customer purchasing. Standard menu layouts into which daily specials may be inserted can be saved. These may be printed on high-quality colored paper using in-house color printers.

Creating a Menu Template

GOAL	ACTION	RESULT
PERSONALIZE MENU SIGN	**CLICK** *Flyers in Document Browser* **CLICK** *Menus* **CLICK** *Menu 1*	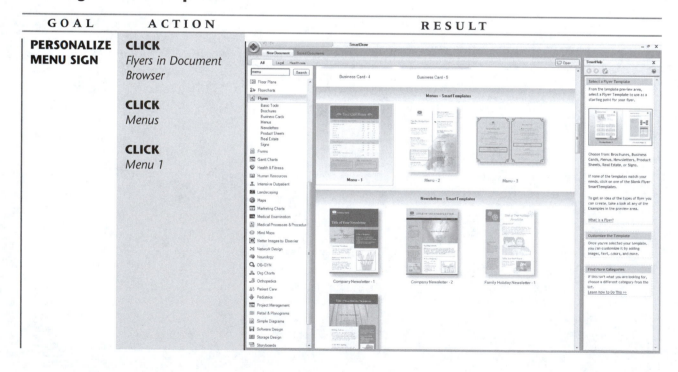

Creating a Menu Template (*continued*)

GOAL	ACTION	RESULT
CUSTOMIZE MENU	**DOUBLE CLICK** *textbox Your Café Menu* **TYPE** *Marty's Cafe*	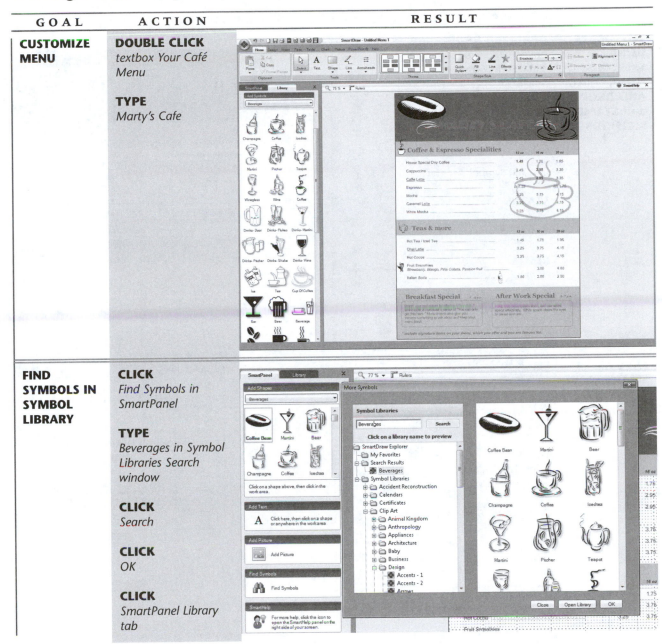
FIND SYMBOLS IN SYMBOL LIBRARY	**CLICK** *Find Symbols in SmartPanel* **TYPE** *Beverages in Symbol Libraries Search window* **CLICK** *Search* **CLICK** *OK* **CLICK** *SmartPanel Library tab*	

Creating a Menu Template (*continued*)

GOAL	ACTION	RESULT
CUSTOMIZE USING SYMBOLS USING DRAG AND DROP and STAMP METHODS	**DRAG and DROP** *Coffee symbol in SmartPanel Library to Mocha line* **RESIZE** *to fit* **CLICK** *Iced tea symbol* **STAMP** *in front of Fruit Smoothies* **RESIZE** *to fit*	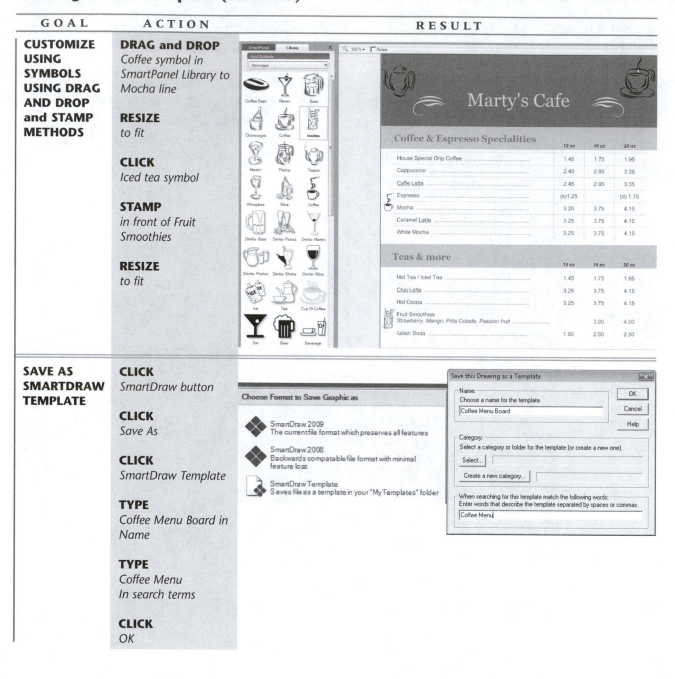
SAVE AS SMARTDRAW TEMPLATE	**CLICK** *SmartDraw button* **CLICK** *Save As* **CLICK** *SmartDraw Template* **TYPE** *Coffee Menu Board in Name* **TYPE** *Coffee Menu In search terms* **CLICK** *OK*	

Creating a Menu Template (*continued*)

GOAL	ACTION	RESULT
PRINT MENU	**CLICK** *SmartDraw button* **CLICK** *Print* **CLOSE** *drawing*	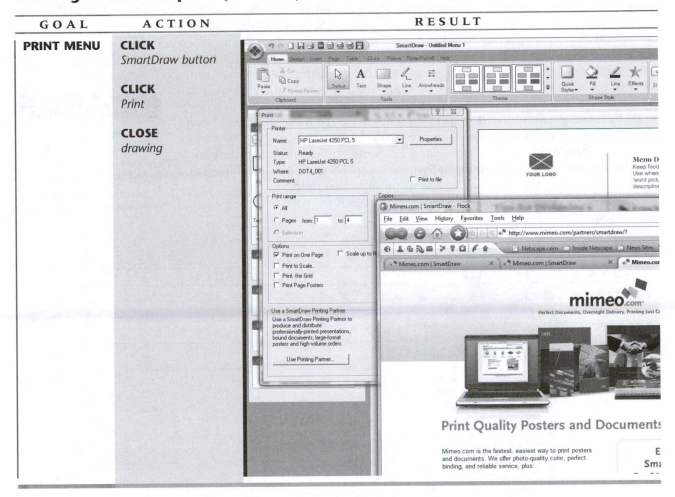

HOW CAN I SEE IF THE NEW EQUIPMENT WILL FIT?

SmartDraw enables you to try out different room layouts without moving tables and chairs, which is an obvious time and labor saver. Trying out different layouts for a kitchen without actually buying and installing equipment is an even bigger time and money saver. Moreover, using layouts has other advantages in addition to the more obvious ones. A proper paper layout can be used to ensure that needed water, utility, and sanitation lines are available. Scaled drawings can be used to obtain preapproval from building and health inspection services. In a previous exercise you designed a home kitchen using layers for the different elements of the kitchen. In a commercial kitchen, it may be advantageous to prepare individual layers for each of the utilities, and separate layers for the on-floor and wall-mounted equipment.

In the following exercise, use the facility layout from above.

> **N O T E**
>
> Displaying all the dimensions may simplify the process of doing a layout and resizing elements like work areas.

Creating a Commercial Kitchen Layout

GOAL	ACTION	RESULT
CREATE NEW LAYER FOR KITCHEN EQUIPMENT	**CLICK** *Page tab* **CLICK** *Layers* **CLICK** *Define Layers* **CLICK** *Add a New Layer* **TYPE** *Kitchen* **CLICK** *Kitchen layer tab* **CLICK** *OK*	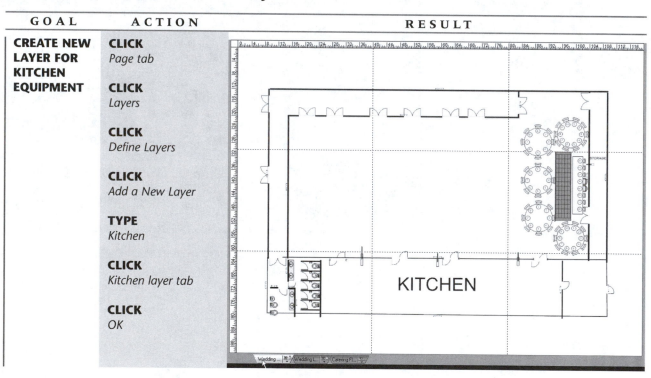

Creating a Commercial Kitchen Layout (*continued*)

GOAL	ACTION	RESULT
OPEN COMMERCIAL KITCHEN SYMBOL LIBARY	**CLICK** *More in Symbols to open Symbol Libraries* **TYPE** *Commercial Kitchen* **CLICK** *Search* **CLICK** *OK*	
SHOW DIMENSIONS OF SYMBOLS	**CLICK** *Design tab* **CLICK** *Dimensions in the Shape Properties group* **CLICK** *Always in Show Dimensions area* **CLICK** *OK*	

Creating a Commercial Kitchen Layout (*continued*)

GOAL	ACTION	RESULT
PLACE EQUIPMENT	**DRAG AND DROP** *equipment* **SAVE and CLOSE** *when finished*	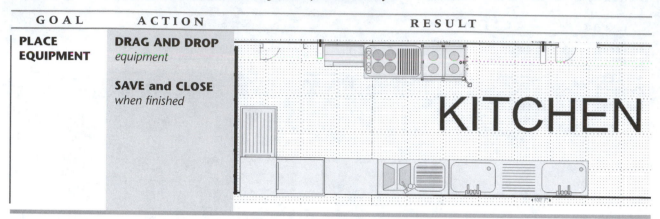

CAN I CREATE A LAYOUT SHOWING WAIT STAFF ASSIGNMENTS OR SEATING ARRANGEMENTS?

You can modify seating charts and room layouts to add charts showing seating arrangements or staff assignments. You will use a SmartTemplate as an example for this exercise.

Adding Seating Charts and Wait Staff Assignments

GOAL	ACTION	RESULT
OPEN SEATING PLAN	**CLICK** *Floor Plans in Document Browser* **CLICK** *Event Plans* **CLICK** *Wedding Seating Plan*	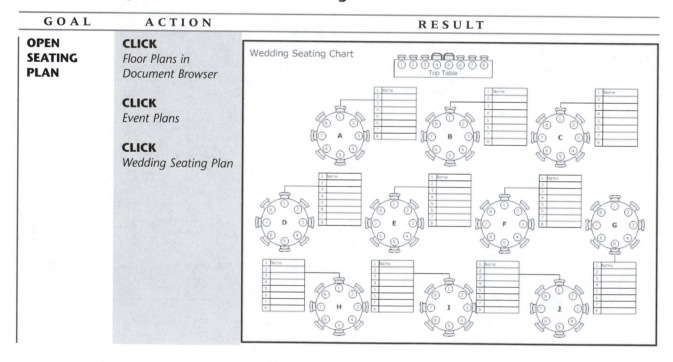

Adding Seating Charts and Wait Staff Assignments (*continued*)

GOAL	ACTION	RESULT
ADD SEATING PLAN CHART	**CLICK** *Insert tab* **CLICK** *Table* **TYPE** *8 (rows)* *2 (columns)* **CLICK** *OK* **TYPE** *numbers and labels* **RESIZE** *By moving column line*	
ADD WAIT STAFF ASSIGNMENTS	**INSERT** *3x2 table* **TYPE** *titles and names as shown* **CLOSE** *This will not be used again*	

Wedding Seating Chart

Add New Table

Select a Table Format

- Simple Rows
- Headings with Grid
- Headings with Columns
- Columns 1
- Columns 2
- Left Align Photo
- Top Align Photo
- Basic Split Box

Preview

OK
Cancel
Help

Parameters

Number of Rows: 8   Number of Columns: 2

☐ Resize the table to fit inside the selected shape (if possible)

☐ Do not include any of the text shown when applying this format.

1	
2	
3	
4	BRIDE
5	GROOM
6	
7	
8	

Captain	Ariel
Waiter	Marshall
Bus person	Ethan

1	Name
2	
3	
4	
5	
6	
7	
8	

A

HOW CAN I CREATE A FACILITY FLOOR PLAN?

An accurate facility floor plan is a very useful tool. It can be used to show prospective customers the space available and possible ways to use it for specific occasions such as meetings, exhibits, dinners, and weddings. You can use SmartDraw to create a template of the outline of the space, access points, and fixed and removable walls.

The basic template can serve as the base level of a set of layouts with layers that show different combinations of space utilization. For example, you can show a space for a wedding being converted to a dinner seating while the reception is going on in a different area. Performing multiple functions at the same time allows you to plan the layouts without actually moving heavy items like tables and chairs. The finished layouts can be printed and posted so members of the staff can make the change over as needed.

For this exercise review the exercises on creating a room template and layout in the Hotel-Motel Design section. Use the techniques presented there to create an outline drawing of the facility shown in the opening of this section as shown on the following page.

NOTES

If you do not select all the chairs, use the Ungroup option and reselect and group objects.

Use Shape to create the white runner between seats in the aisle. Add other shapes, such as flowers, to enhance the drawing.

Create a separate layer for each room setup, such as the middle room and left room in this drawing.

TIP

Each room setup can be saved as a custom symbol (e.g., the wedding chairs).

Creating a Facility Floor Plan

G O A L	A C T I O N	R E S U L T
CREATE A FLOOR PLAN OF FACILITY	**CLICK** *Floor Plan in the Document Browser* **CLICK** *Blank Floor Plan*	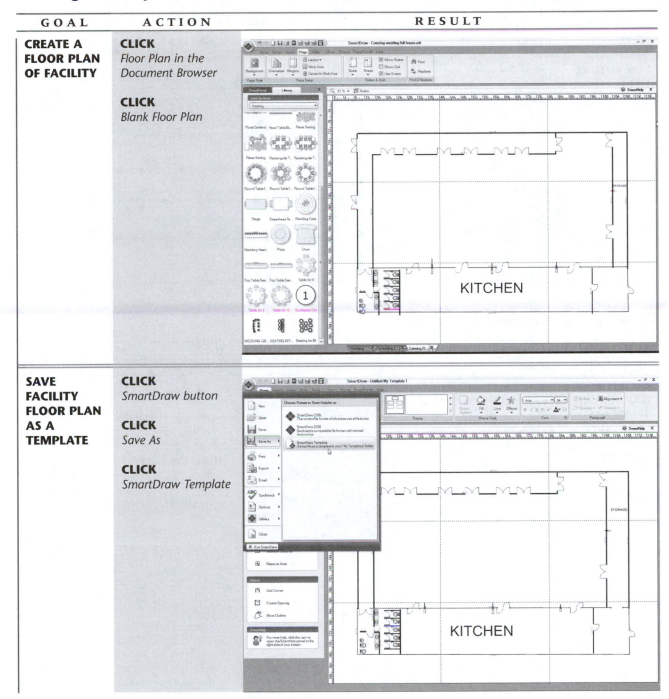
SAVE FACILITY FLOOR PLAN AS A TEMPLATE	**CLICK** *SmartDraw button* **CLICK** *Save As* **CLICK** *SmartDraw Template*	

Creating a Facility Floor Plan (*continued*)

GOAL	ACTION	RESULT
NAME TEMPLATE FOR FUTURE USE	**TYPE** *Facility Floor Plan in Name line* **TYPE** *Catering Floor Plan Template in search term field* **CLOSE** *template*	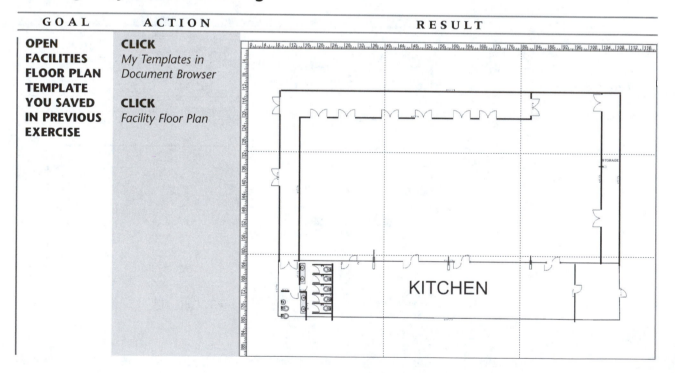

Save this Drawing as a Template

Name:
Choose a name for the template.
Facility Floor Plan

OK
Cancel
Help

Category:
Select a category or folder for the template (or create a new one).
Select...
Create a new category...

When searching for this template match the following words:
Enter words that describe the template separated by spaces or commas.
Catering Floor Plan Template

Creating a Layout for a Wedding

GOAL	ACTION	RESULT
OPEN FACILITIES FLOOR PLAN TEMPLATE YOU SAVED IN PREVIOUS EXERCISE	**CLICK** *My Templates in Document Browser* **CLICK** *Facility Floor Plan*	KITCHEN

Creating a Layout for a Wedding (*continued*)

GOAL	ACTION	RESULT
SET FLOOR PLAN AS DEFAULT LAYER AND CREATE NEW LAYER	**CLICK** *Page tab* **CLICK** *Layers* *In Page Setup group* **CLICK** *Edit Layer* **TYPE** *Floor Plan* **CLICK** *Add a New Layer* **TYPE** *Wedding setup* **CLICK** *OK*	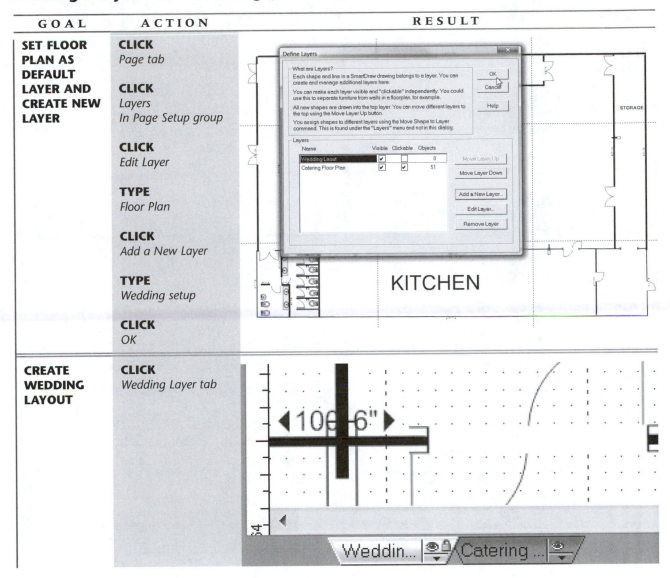
CREATE WEDDING LAYOUT	**CLICK** *Wedding Layer tab*	

Creating a Layout for a Wedding (*continued*)

GOAL	ACTION	RESULT
CREATE SEATING SYMBOL	**CLICK** *More in SmartPanel Symbols* **CLICK** *Chairs & Stools in Symbols Library* **CLICK** *OK* **CLICK** *Library tab in SmartPanel* **HOLD SHIFT KEY and CLICK** *White Folding Chair* **STAMP** *eight chairs as shown in next panel*	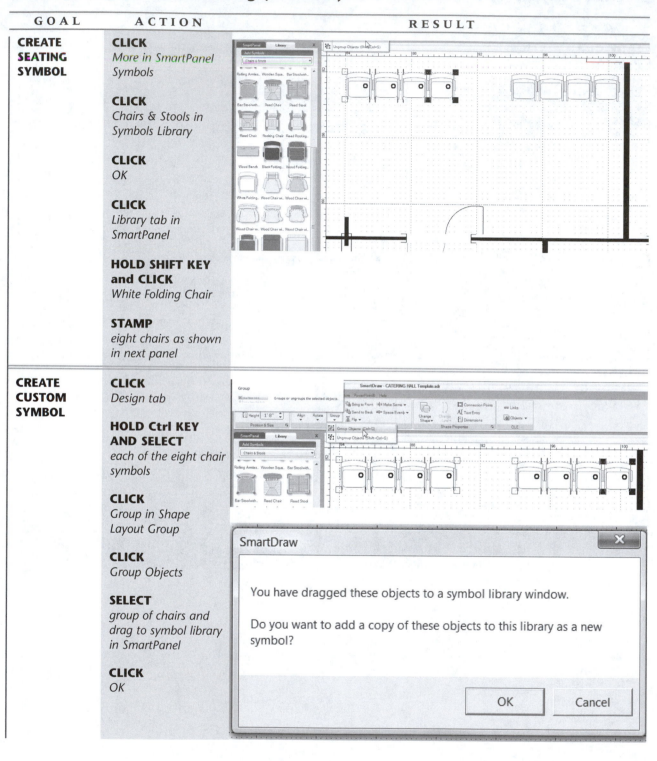
CREATE CUSTOM SYMBOL	**CLICK** *Design tab* **HOLD Ctrl KEY AND SELECT** *each of the eight chair symbols* **CLICK** *Group in Shape Layout Group* **CLICK** *Group Objects* **SELECT** *group of chairs and drag to symbol library in SmartPanel* **CLICK** *OK*	

SmartDraw

You have dragged these objects to a symbol library window.

Do you want to add a copy of these objects to this library as a new symbol?

OK   Cancel

Creating a Layout for a Wedding (*continued*)

GOAL	ACTION	RESULT
SELECT CUSTOM SETTINGS	**TYPE** *8 seats as Symbol Name* **UNCLICK** *Automatic Settings* **CLICK** *OK*	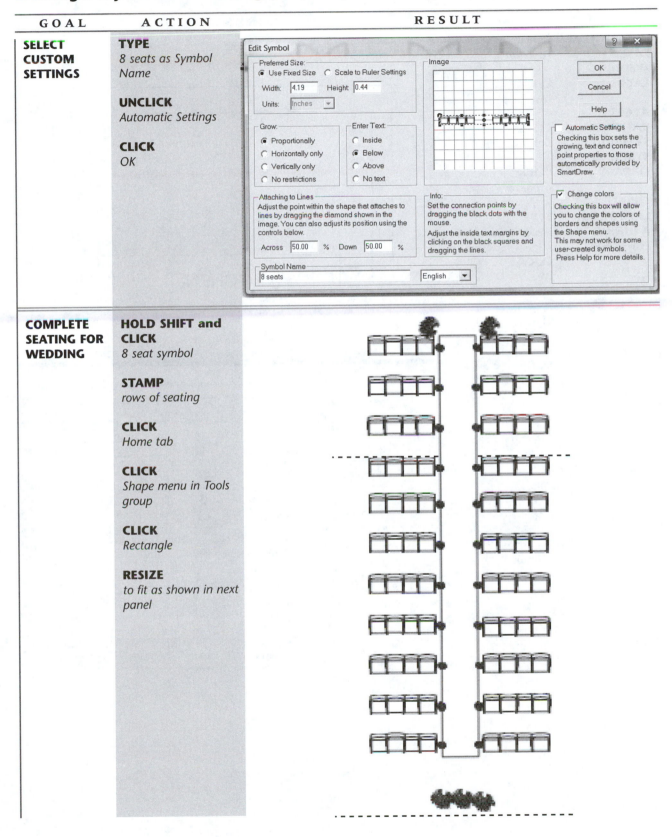
COMPLETE SEATING FOR WEDDING	**HOLD SHIFT and CLICK** *8 seat symbol* **STAMP** *rows of seating* **CLICK** *Home tab* **CLICK** *Shape menu in Tools group* **CLICK** *Rectangle* **RESIZE** *to fit as shown in next panel*	

Creating a Layout for a Wedding (*continued*)

GOAL	ACTION	RESULT
CREATE NEW LAYER FOR WEDDING LAYOUT **ACCESS CATERING SYMBOLS IN SYMBOLS LIBRARY** **CREATE LAYOUT FOR A DINING FUNCTION**	**CLICK** *Page tab* **CLICK** *Layers* **CLICK** *Define Layers* **CLICK** *Add a New Layer* **TYPE** *Wedding Dinner* **CLICK** *Wedding Dinner Layer tab* **CLICK** *OK* **CLICK** *More in Symbols to open Symbol Libraries* **CLICK** *Catering* **CLICK** *OK* **DRAG AND DROP** *Tables, Dance Floor, and Wedding Head Table symbols*	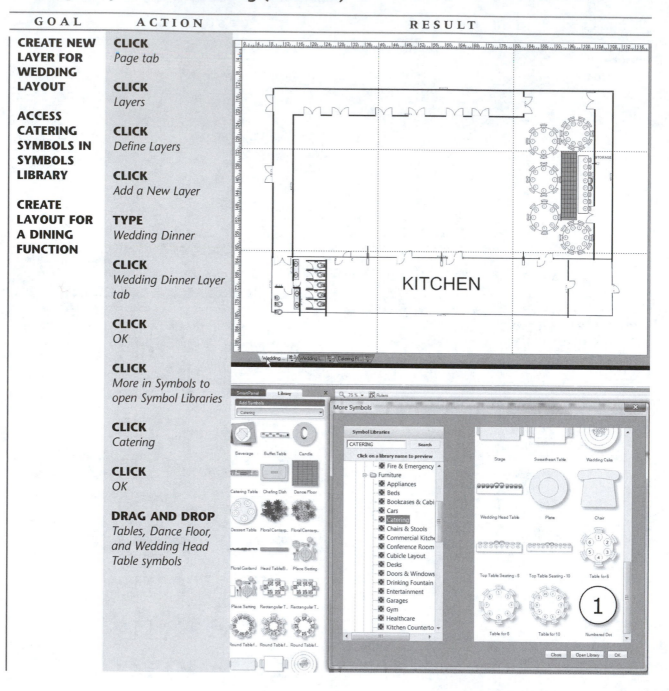

Creating a Layout for a Wedding (*continued*)

GOAL	ACTION	RESULT
SAVE DRAWING	**CLICK** *SmartDraw Button* **CLICK** *Save As* **CLICK** *SmartDraw 2009* **TYPE** *Wedding layouts*	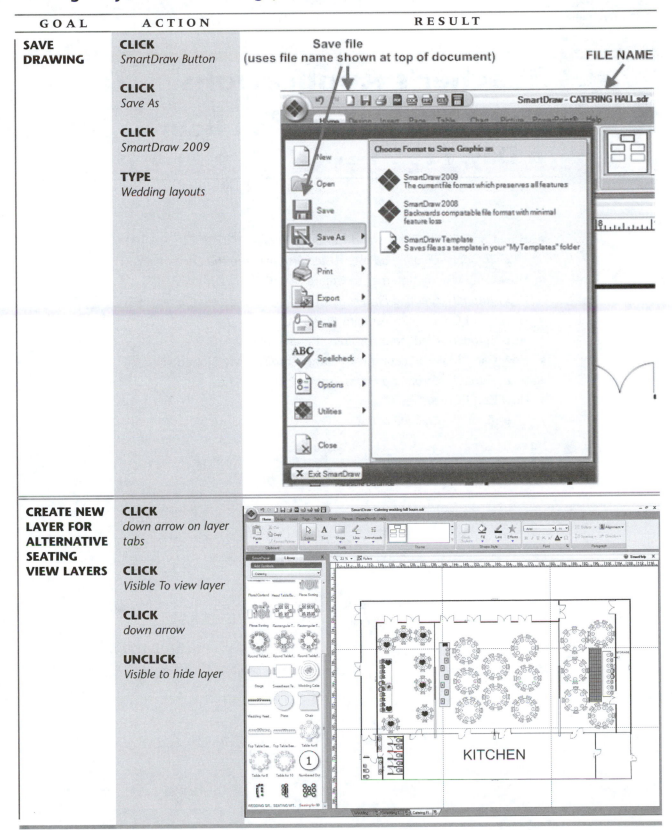
CREATE NEW LAYER FOR ALTERNATIVE SEATING VIEW LAYERS	**CLICK** *down arrow on layer tabs* **CLICK** *Visible To view layer* **CLICK** *down arrow* **UNCLICK** *Visible to hide layer*	

Teacher's Applications
(If I Could Just Save an Hour a Day, I . . .)

- How Can I Create Posters and Handouts?
  - ▲ *Tutorial—Creating a Poster Using Pictures from the Computer*
- How Can I Use the Internet to Create Material?
  - ▲ *Tutorial—Creating Posters and Handouts Using Web Content*
- How Can I Create a PowerPoint Presentation?
  - ▲ *Tutorial—Creating a PowerPoint Presentation*
- How Can I Make a Seating Plan with Pictures of My Students?
  - ▲ *Tutorial—Creating a Photo Seating Plan of a Class*
- How Can I Create Tests?
  - ▲ *Tutorial—Creating a Test*

FIELD TRIP PERMISSION SLIP

Where: _____

When: _____

Transportation: _____

Cost: _____

Make checks payable to: _____

Additional comments: _____

_____

_____

Please return permission slip by _____

I give my child, _____, permission to attend the field trip to _____

on _____ from _____ to _____.

I enclose _____ to cover the cost of the trip.

In case of an emergency, please contact _____ at _____

_____   _____

Parent's Signature   Date

HOW CAN I CREATE POSTERS AND HANDOUTS?

Graphics are a good way to communicate new concepts and ideas to students. Creating handouts, wall charts, and lecture presentations requires a full set of graphic images and the ability to add material from other sources. In addition to the clip art available in the symbols library, you can use photographs from your computer or digital camera.

In the following tutorial ancient Rome and the Coliseum are used to illustrate the subject of a geography class. Photos are used as well as images from the web.

Creating a Poster Using Pictures from the Computer

GOAL	ACTION	RESULT
INSERT PICTURES	**CLICK** Blank form in Education category in Document Browser	
	CLICK Insert tab	
	CLICK Picture	
	CLICK desired photograph in Insert Picture menu	
	CLICK Open on Insert Picture menu	
	REPEAT to insert all desired photographs	
	CLICK Home tab	
	CLICK Text	
	TYPE title	

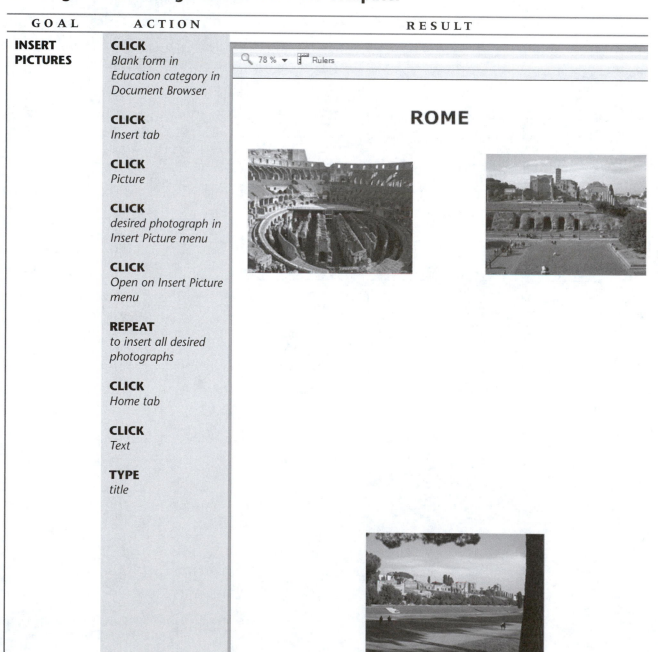

Creating a Poster Using Pictures from the Computer (*continued*)

GOAL	ACTION	RESULT
FIND AND INSERT MAP	**CLICK** *Insert tab* **CLICK** *Map* **TYPE** *location* **CLICK** *Satellite* *Map Type* *Zoom in using zoom bar* *Choose* *Map Size* **CLICK** *Go*	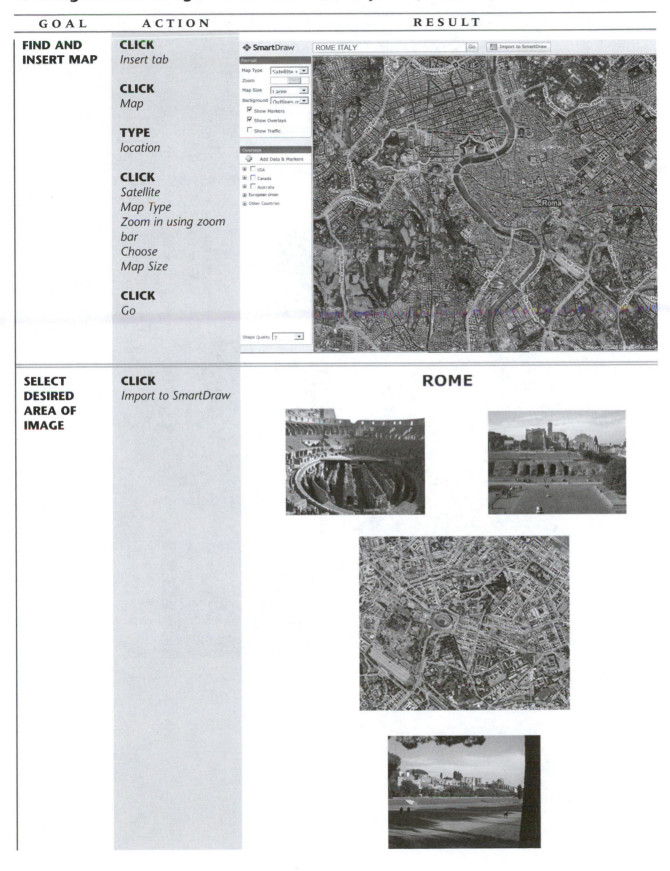
SELECT DESIRED AREA OF IMAGE	**CLICK** *Import to SmartDraw*	

Creating a Poster Using Pictures from the Computer (*continued*)

GOAL	ACTION	RESULT
CHANGE SHAPE OF IMAGE	**SELECT** *image to change* **RIGHT CLICK** *Open menu* **CLICK** *desired shape*	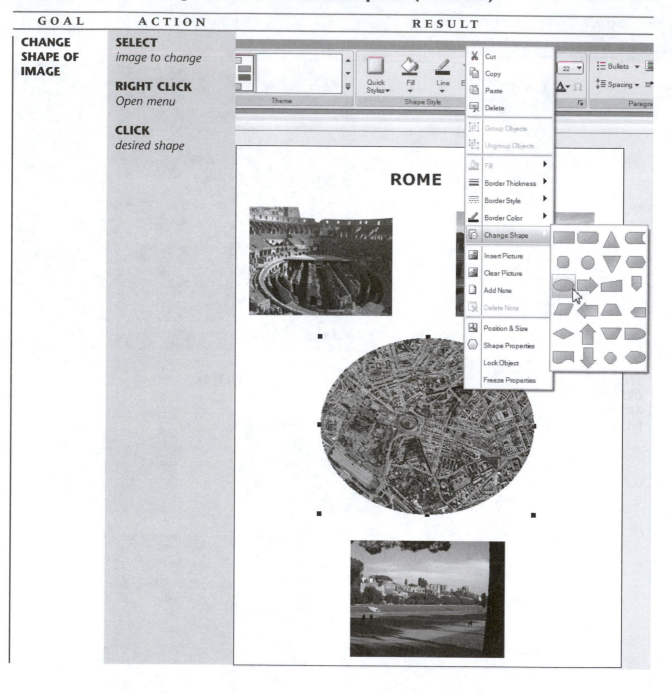

Creating a Poster Using Pictures from the Computer (*continued*)

GOAL	ACTION	RESULT
ADD ARROWS TO SHOW LOCATION	**CLICK** *Home tab* **CLICK** *Arrowheads* **CLICK** *Right Arrow* **DRAW** *arrow*	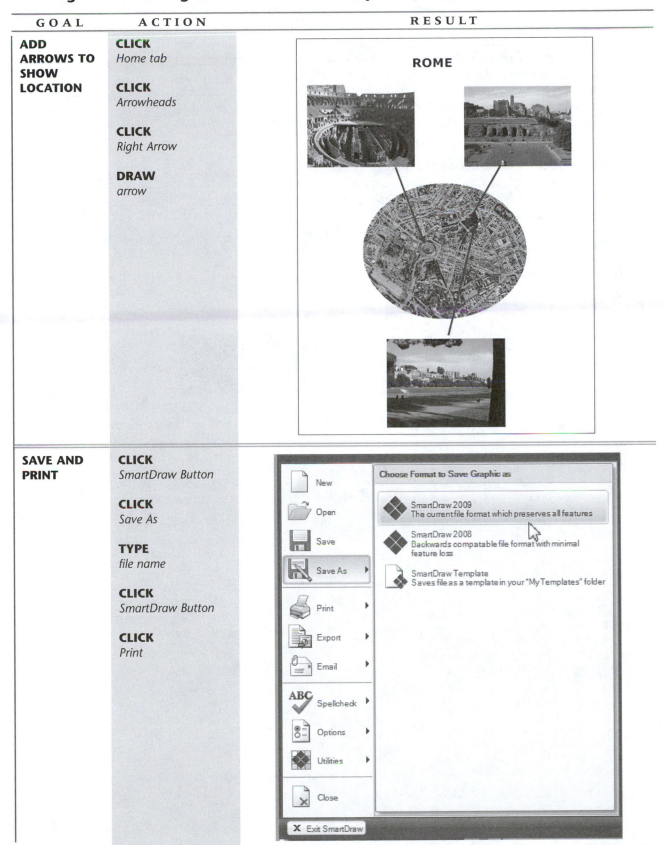
SAVE AND PRINT	**CLICK** *SmartDraw Button* **CLICK** *Save As* **TYPE** *file name* **CLICK** *SmartDraw Button* **CLICK** *Print*	

HOW CAN I USE THE INTERNET TO CREATE MATERIAL?

The availability of current and historical information and images on the Internet has made creating posters and handouts on almost any subject or topic easier. With an Internet connection and SmartDraw you can capture images, including photographs, drawings, and maps, and quickly prepare material for class. Breaking news that is the subject of a class or lecture can be captured and prepared in printed form up to minutes before a class, or as part of a class with students creating the material for presentation and discussion.

Creating Posters and Handouts Using Web Content

GOAL	ACTION	RESULT
ADD WEB IMAGES TO DOCUMENT	**CLICK** *Blank form in Education category in Document Browser*	Favorites SmartDraw Capture Webpage Address http://search.yahoo.com/web?fr=
	CLICK *Insert tab*	
	CLICK *Web Pages*	Web | Images | Video | Local | Shopping | more ▾ **Rome Italy** Search Options ▾ YAHOO! rome italy weather hotels in rome italy map of rome italy pictures of rome italy flights to rome italy
	CLICK *Search the Internet icon*	
	TYPE *desired information*	© 2008 Yahoo! Privacy / Legal · Submit Your Site
	CLICK *Images*	
	CLICK *Search*	

Creating Posters and Handouts Using Web Content *(continued)*

GOAL	ACTION	RESULT
	CLICK *desired image* **CLICK** *Capture Webpage*	
IMPORT, SELECT, AND RESIZE WEB IMAGES	**CLICK** *Trim & Shape* **CLICK** **DRAG** *lasso cursor around desired area* **CLICK** *Trim to Shape* **CLICK** *Continue* **RESIZE** *for your document*	

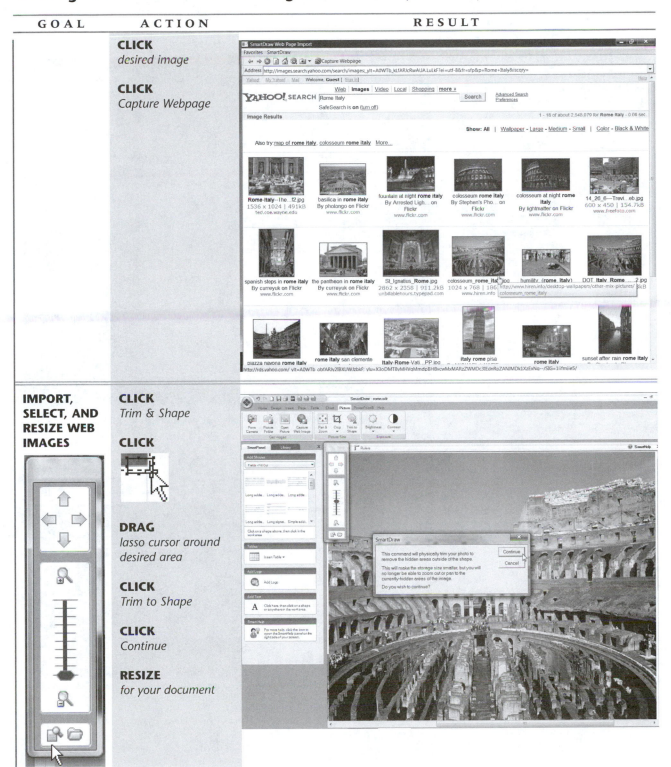

Creating Posters and Handouts Using Web Content (*continued*)

GOAL	ACTION	RESULT
ADD ADDITIONAL IMAGES AND TEXT, SAVE, AND PRINT	**ADD** *additional images as shown above* **ADD** *text* **CLICK** *SmartDraw Button* **CLICK** *Save As* **TYPE** *file name* **PRINT**	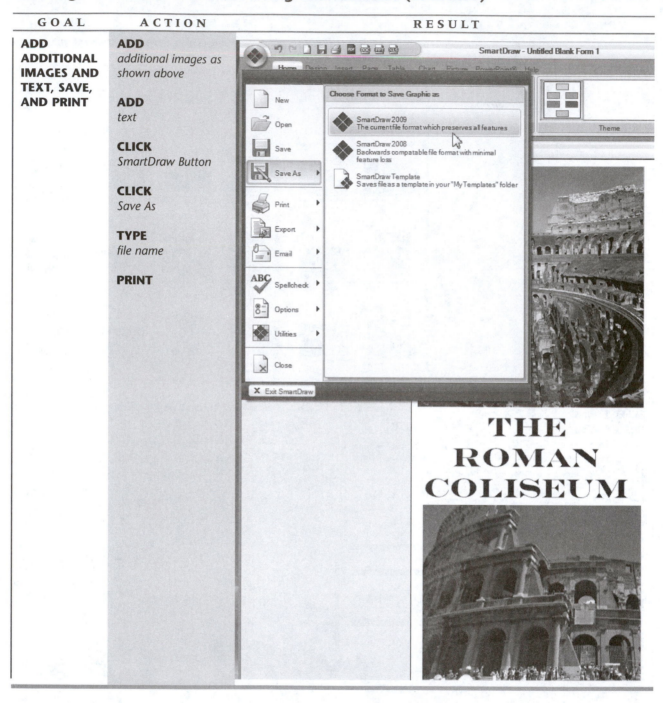

HOW CAN I CREATE A POWERPOINT® PRESENTATION?

Individual objects in a SmartDraw drawing, such as text, images, and symbols, can be sequenced or animated using the PowerPoint® feature in SmartDraw. The final animation then can be exported for use in the Microsoft PowerPoint® program. For purposes of illustration the Rome document from the previous tutorial is used in the following tutorial.

N O T E S

The first object selected is automatically set as slide 1.

Be sure to unselect object(s) from the previous step before selecting object(s) for the current step.

Creating a PowerPoint Presentation

GOAL	ACTION	RESULT
DETERMINE ORDER OF DISPLAY	**OPEN** *saved document* **DETERMINE** *sequence*	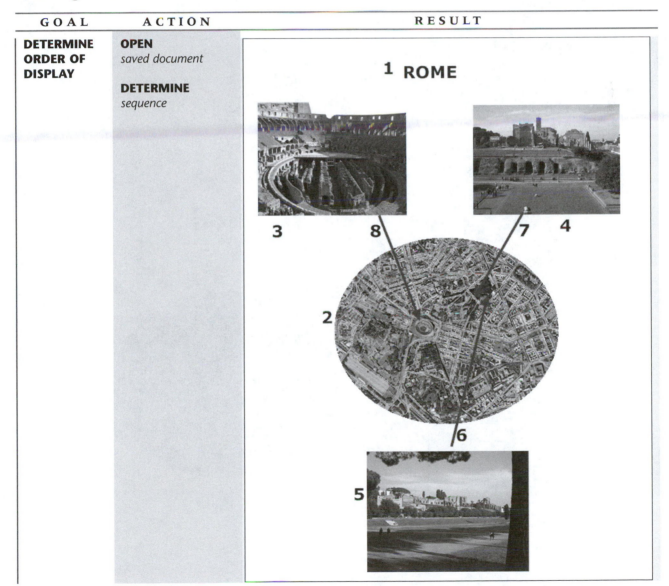

Creating a PowerPoint Presentation (*continued*)

GOAL	ACTION	RESULT
SELECT FIRST STEP	**CLICK** *PowerPoint® tab* **SELECT** *text box* *ROME* **CLICK** *the Step menu* **CLICK** *1* **UNSELECT** *text box*	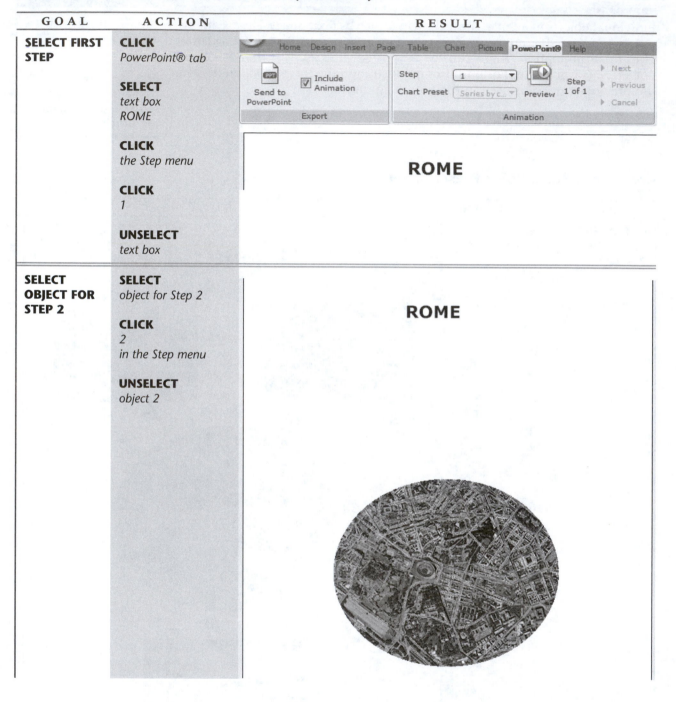
SELECT OBJECT FOR STEP 2	**SELECT** *object for Step 2* **CLICK** *2* *in the Step menu* **UNSELECT** *object 2*	

Creating a PowerPoint Presentation (*continued*)

GOAL	ACTION	RESULT
SELECT OBJECT FOR STEP 3	**SELECT** *object for Step 3* **CLICK** 3 *in the Step menu* **UNSELECT** *object 3*	
SELECT OBJECT FOR STEP 4	**SELECT** *object for Step 4* **CLICK** 4 *in the Step menu* **UNSELECT** *object for Step 4*	

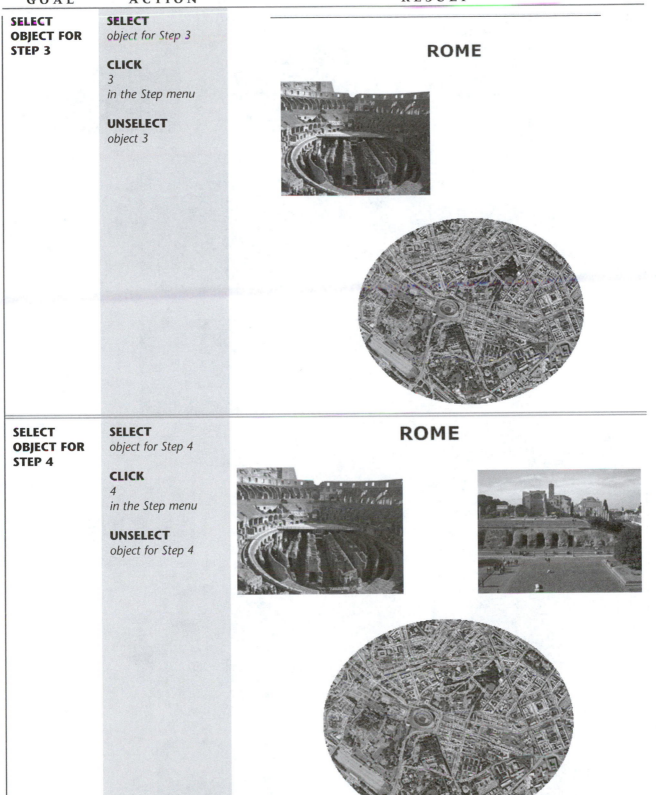

Creating a PowerPoint Presentation (*continued*)

GOAL	ACTION	RESULT
SELECT OBJECT FOR STEP 5	**SELECT** *object for Step 5* **CLICK** *5* *in the Step menu* **UNSELECT** *object 5*	
SELECT OBJECT FOR STEP 6	**SELECT** *objects for Step 6* **CLICK** *6* *in the Step menu* **UNSELECT** *object for Step 6*	

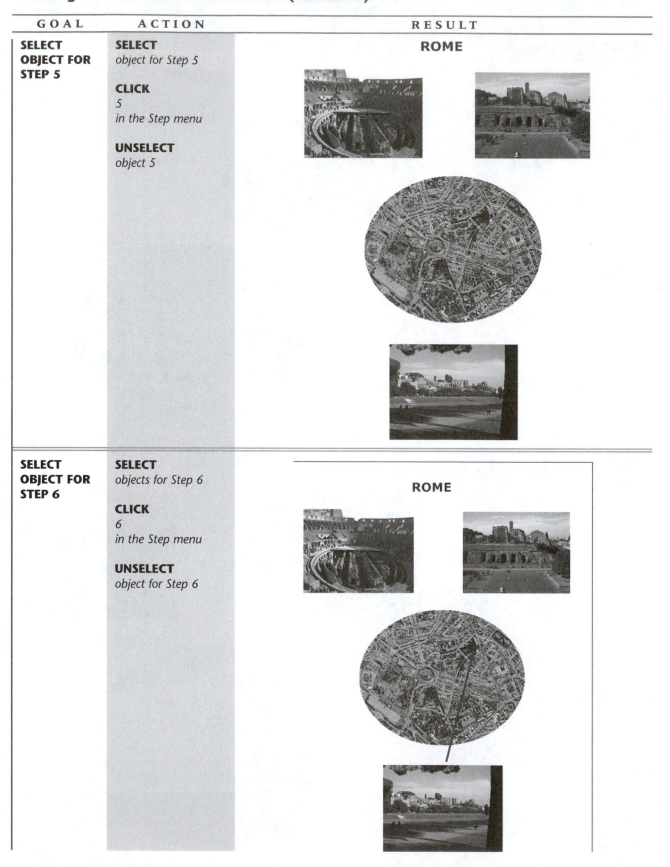

Creating a PowerPoint Presentation (*continued*)

GOAL	ACTION	RESULT
SELECT OBJECT FOR STEP 7	**SELECT** *object for Step 7* **CLICK** 7 *in the Step menu* **UNSELECT** *object 7*	ROME
SELECT OBJECT FOR STEP 8	**SELECT** *object for Step 8* **CLICK** 8 *in the Step menu* **UNSELECT** *object 8*	ROME

Creating a PowerPoint Presentation (*continued*)

GOAL	ACTION	RESULT
EXPORT TO MICROSOFT POWERPOINT®	**CLICK** *Send to PowerPoint®*	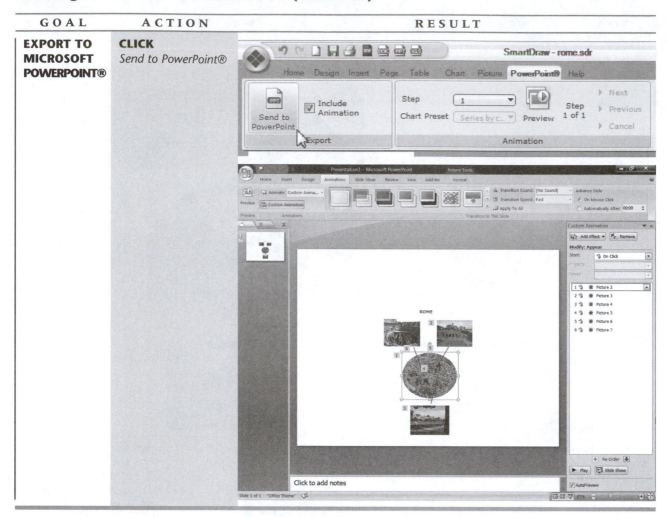

HOW CAN I MAKE A SEATING PLAN WITH PICTURES OF MY STUDENTS?

A classroom or school bus seating plan with pictures is a helpful way to introduce students to each other and to substitute or student teachers who have only limited contact with the class. Seating charts for school bus routes and for extended class trips are a useful way for bus drivers, regular and temporary, and chaperones to identify students and their assigned seats. Pictures for the seating plan can be taken with a digital camera and saved to the computer. Digital pictures are available instantly, and the seating plan can be completed quickly using a previously created and saved seating plan template with specialty shapes for pictures and text.

Creating a Photo Seating Plan of a Class

GOAL	ACTION	RESULT
USE ORGANIZA-TION CHART SMART-TEMPLATE TO CREATE A PHOTO SEATING PLAN	**OPEN** *Blank Organization Chart in Document Browser* **CLICK** *Page tab* **CLICK** *Show Grid*	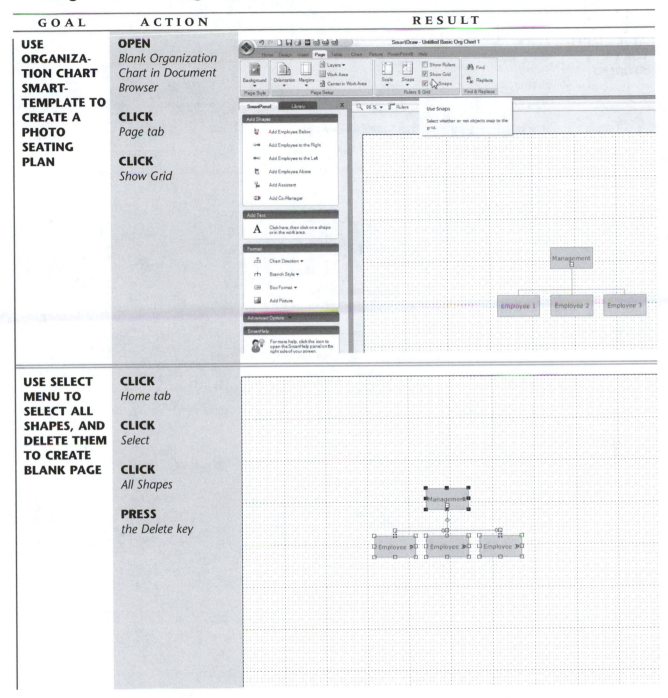
USE SELECT MENU TO SELECT ALL SHAPES, AND DELETE THEM TO CREATE BLANK PAGE	**CLICK** *Home tab* **CLICK** *Select* **CLICK** *All Shapes* **PRESS** *the Delete key*	

Creating a Photo Seating Plan of a Class (*continued*)

GOAL	ACTION	RESULT
ADD SHAPES FOR EACH STUDENT	**CLICK** *Home tab* **CLICK** *Shape menu* **HOLD SHIFT KEY** **CLICK** *Rectangle* **STAMP** *rectangles*	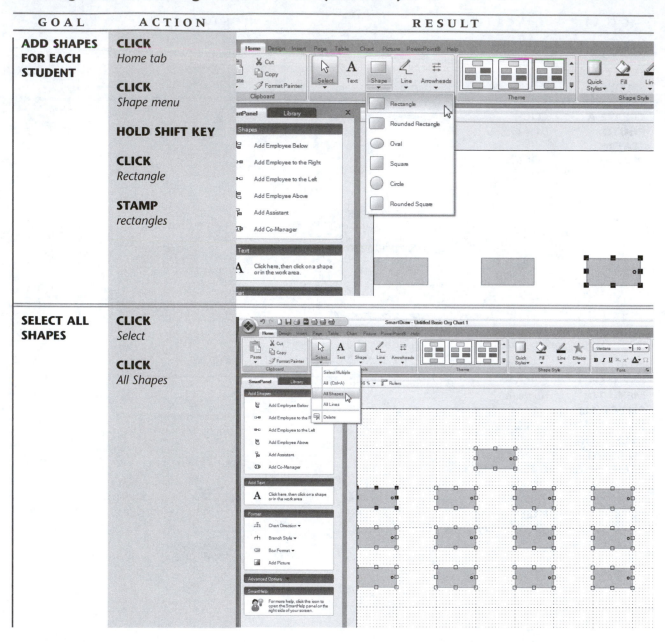
SELECT ALL SHAPES	**CLICK** *Select* **CLICK** *All Shapes*	

Creating a Photo Seating Plan of a Class (*continued*)

GOAL	ACTION	RESULT
REPLACE SHAPES WITH PHOTO BOXES	**CLICK** *Box Format in SmartPanel* **CLICK** *Left Align Photo* **CLICK** *Select (to unselect all shapes)*	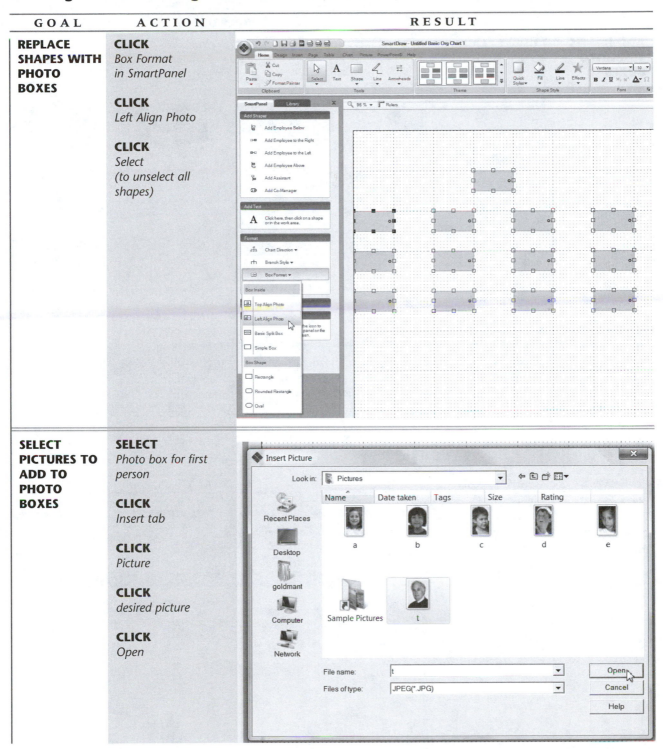
SELECT PICTURES TO ADD TO PHOTO BOXES	**SELECT** *Photo box for first person* **CLICK** *Insert tab* **CLICK** *Picture* **CLICK** *desired picture* **CLICK** *Open*	

Creating a Photo Seating Plan of a Class (*continued*)

GOAL	ACTION	RESULT
ADD NAMES TO PHOTO BOXES	**DOUBLE CLICK** *in right side of shape to enter text* **TYPE** *name* **REPEAT** *for each student*	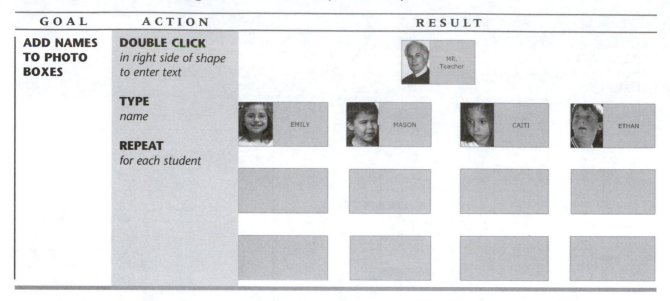

HOW CAN I CREATE TESTS?

One method of creating a test is to use a poster or handout with key terms or formulas removed. SmartDraw has an extensive collection of teacher materials that can be used as handouts or homework and then, with the information removed, used as tests, as shown in the following tutorial.

Creating a Test

GOAL	ACTION	RESULT
SELECT SMART-TEMPLATE EXAMPLE	**CLICK** *education category* **CLICK** *Volumes and Areas*	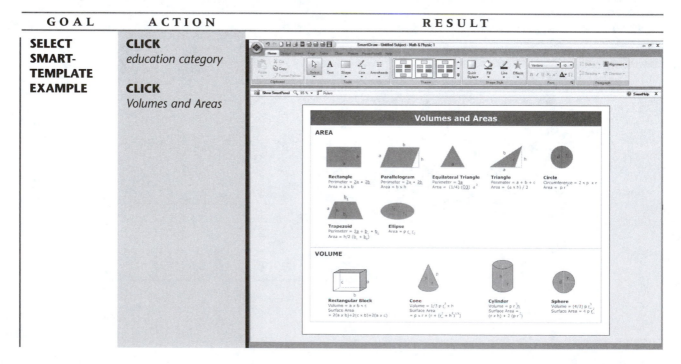

Creating a Test (*continued*)

GOAL	ACTION	RESULT
EDIT TEXT BOX TO REMOVE LABELS OR FORMULA ELEMENTS	**SELECT** *text box* **EDIT** *Insert line* **SAVE** **PRINT**	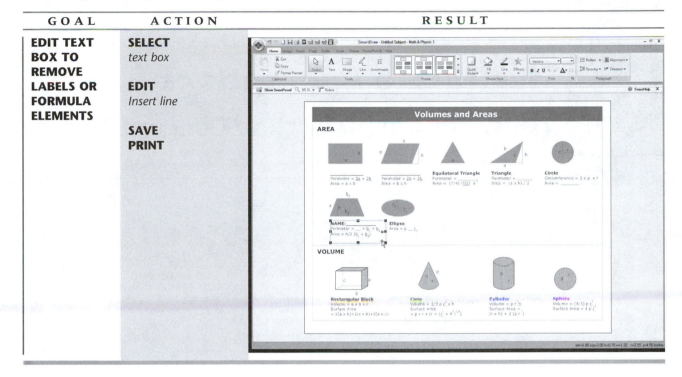

Healthcare Applications
(How Do I Explain that Concept?)

- How Can I Educate My Patients?
  - ▲ *Tutorial—Creating a Newsletter*
- How Can I Create a Medication Schedule?
  - ▲ *Tutorial—Creating a Patient Medication Timeline*
  - ▲ *Tutorial—Changing Arrow Directions and Shapes*

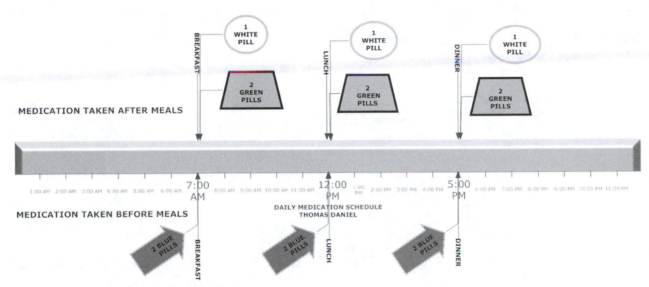

MEDICATION TAKEN AFTER MEALS

1 WHITE PILL

2 GREEN PILLS

BREAKFAST

1 WHITE PILL

2 GREEN PILLS

LUNCH

1 WHITE PILL

2 GREEN PILLS

DINNER

1:00 AM 2:00 AM 3:00 AM 4:00 AM 5:00 AM 6:00 AM 7:00 AM 8:00 AM 9:00 AM 10:00 AM 11:00 AM 12:00 PM 1:00 PM 2:00 PM 3:00 PM 4:00 PM 5:00 PM 6:00 PM 7:00 PM 8:00 PM 9:00 PM 10:00 PM 11:00 PM

7:00 AM   12:00 PM   5:00 PM

MEDICATION TAKEN BEFORE MEALS

DAILY MEDICATION SCHEDULE
THOMAS DANIEL

2 BLUE PILLS   BREAKFAST

2 BLUE PILLS   LUNCH

2 BLUE PILLS   DINNER

Source: Created using SmartDraw Timeline SmartTemplate

HOW CAN I EDUCATE MY PATIENTS?

There are different reasons for, and methods of providing patient education. Some information is general in nature, like newsletters; some is issue oriented, like treatments for ear infections in children; and other information is geared toward patients' specific needs. The following tutorials illustrate how issues-oriented information may be prepared as handouts to patients and used in flyers or mailing pieces. The following content is from the Healthcare version of SmartDraw.

Creating a Newsletter

GOAL	ACTION	RESULT
MODIFY EXISTING DOCUMENT	**CLICK** *Healthcare tab* **CLICK** *Pediatrics* **CLICK** *Pediatrics Newsletter*	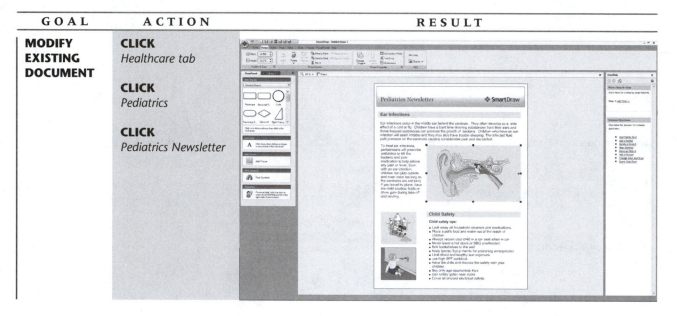

Creating a Newsletter (*continued*)

GOAL	ACTION	RESULT
CHANGE HEADLINE BANNER AND PERSONALIZE	**SELECT** *shape (Pediatrics Newsletter)*	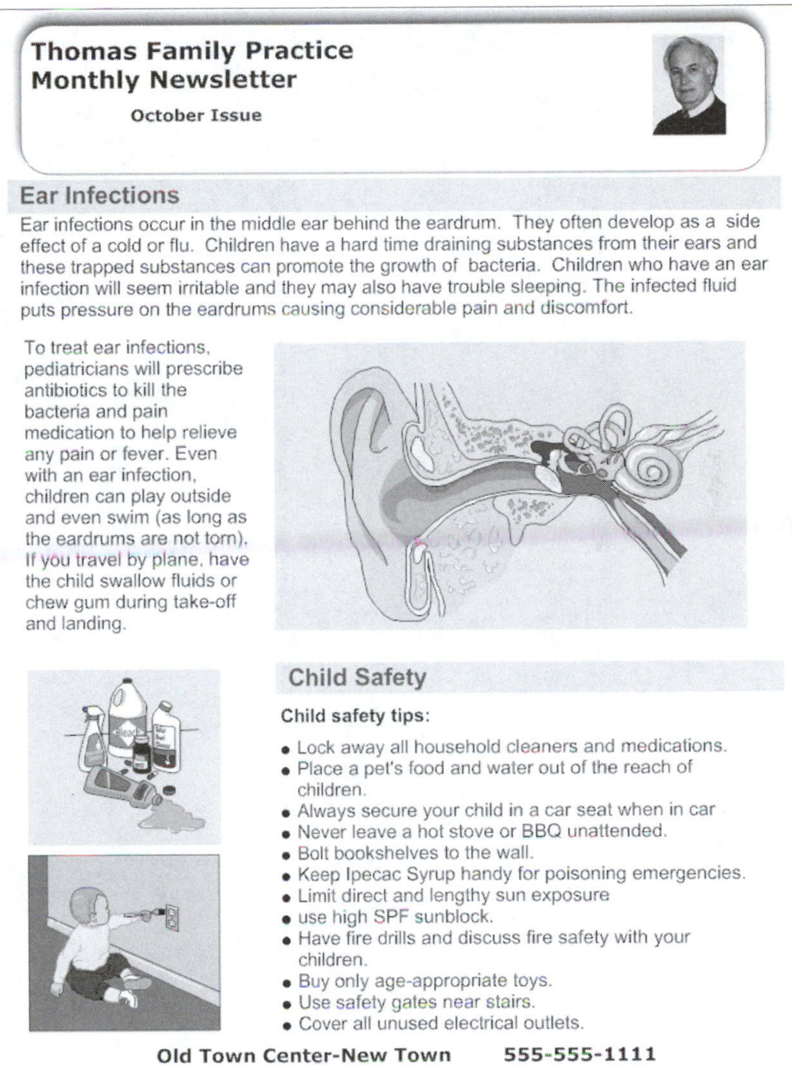
	PRESS *Delete key*	
	CLICK *Shape in SmartPanel*	
	STAMP *shape at top of page*	
	RESIZE *to cover top of page*	
	CLICK *Add Text in SmartPanel*	
	TYPE *new text in banner*	
	CLICK *Add Text*	
	CLICK *Insert tab*	
	CLICK *Picture*	
	CLICK *desired picture*	
	CLICK *OK*	

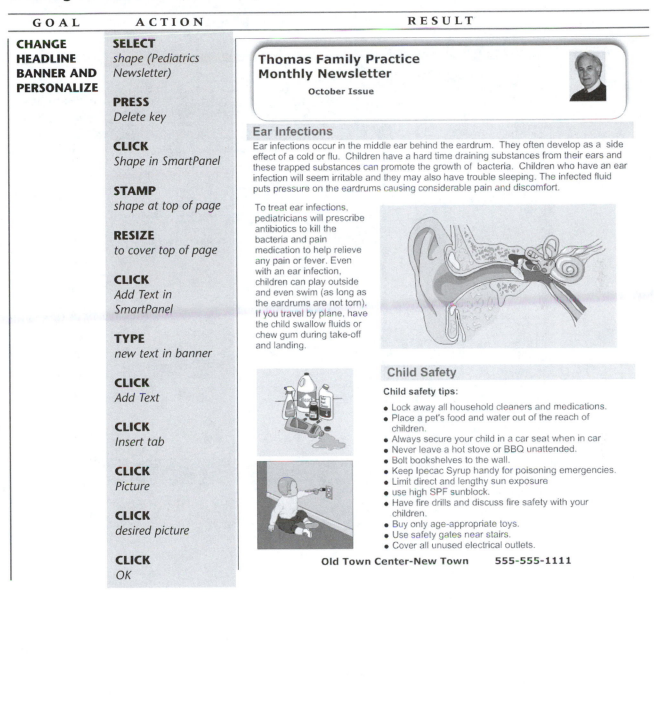

Thomas Family Practice
Monthly Newsletter
October Issue

Ear Infections

Ear infections occur in the middle ear behind the eardrum. They often develop as a side effect of a cold or flu. Children have a hard time draining substances from their ears and these trapped substances can promote the growth of bacteria. Children who have an ear infection will seem irritable and they may also have trouble sleeping. The infected fluid puts pressure on the eardrums causing considerable pain and discomfort.

To treat ear infections, pediatricians will prescribe antibiotics to kill the bacteria and pain medication to help relieve any pain or fever. Even with an ear infection, children can play outside and even swim (as long as the eardrums are not torn). If you travel by plane, have the child swallow fluids or chew gum during take-off and landing.

Child Safety

Child safety tips:

- Lock away all household cleaners and medications.
- Place a pet's food and water out of the reach of children.
- Always secure your child in a car seat when in car
- Never leave a hot stove or BBQ unattended.
- Bolt bookshelves to the wall.
- Keep Ipecac Syrup handy for poisoning emergencies.
- Limit direct and lengthy sun exposure
- use high SPF sunblock.
- Have fire drills and discuss fire safety with your children.
- Buy only age-appropriate toys.
- Use safety gates near stairs.
- Cover all unused electrical outlets.

Old Town Center-New Town 555-555-1111

Creating a Newsletter (*continued*)

GOAL	ACTION	RESULT
SAVE DOCUMENT	**CLICK** *SmartDraw button*	
PRINT	**CLICK** *Save As*	
MAIL	**CLICK** *SmartDraw 2009*	
	TYPE *name*	

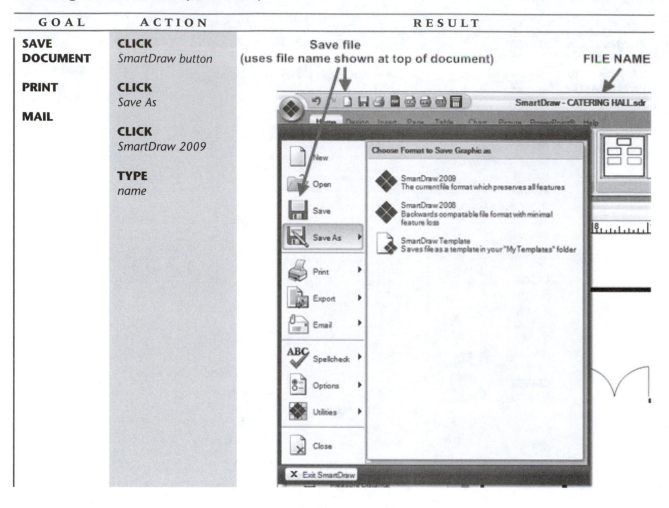

Save file
(uses file name shown at top of document)

FILE NAME

Creating a Newsletter (*continued*)

G O A L	A C T I O N	R E S U L T
CREATE HANDOUT FLYERS	**SELECT** *text boxes and clip art to delete* **PRESS** *Delete key* **SELECT** *text box* **RESIZE**	

**Thomas Family Practice
Monthly Newsletter**

October Issue

Ear Infections

Ear infections occur in the middle ear behind the eardrum. They often develop as a side effect of a cold or flu. Children have a hard time draining substances from their ears and these trapped substances can promote the growth of bacteria. Children who have an ear infection will seem irritable and they may also have trouble sleeping. The infected fluid puts pressure on the eardrums causing considerable pain and discomfort.

To treat ear infections, pediatricians will prescribe antibiotics to kill the bacteria and pain medication to help relieve any pain or fever. Even with an ear infection, children can play outside and even swim (as long as the eardrums are not torn). If you travel by plane, have the child swallow fluids or chew gum during take-off and landing.

Old Town Center-New Town   555-555-1111

Creating a Newsletter (*continued*)

GOAL	ACTION	RESULT
CREATE HANDOUT FLYERS	**OPEN** *saved newsletter* **EDIT** *Create new content* **SAVE**	

Thomas Family Practice
CHILD SAFETY

Child safety start in the home.
Following the following simple tips may avoid a trip
to our office or to the emergency room. Please call us if
you have any questions.

Child Safety

Child safety tips:

- Lock away all household cleaners and medications.
- Place a pet's food and water out of the reach of children.
- Always secure your child in a car seat when in car
- Never leave a hot stove or BBQ unattended.
- Bolt bookshelves to the wall.
- Keep Ipecac Syrup handy for poisoning emergencies.
- Limit direct and lengthy sun exposure
- use high SPF sunblock.
- Have fire drills and discuss fire safety with your children.
- Buy only age-appropriate toys.
- Use safety gates near stairs.
- Cover all unused electrical outlets.

Old Town Center-New Town   555-555-1111

Creating a Newsletter (*continued*)

GOAL	ACTION	RESULT
CREATE TEMPLATE FOR MONTHLY NEWSLETTERS	**CLICK** *All tab* **CLICK** *Flyers category in Document Browser* **CLICK** *Tri-fold Brochure* **ADD** *standard recurring information* **CLICK** *SmartDraw Button* **CLICK** *Save As* **CLICK** *SmartDraw Template* **TYPE** *name (i.e., Monthly Newsletter)*	

Outer Panel 1

The front inside panel is the most important. It is a location to summarize why the customer should choose you. It is also a great location for a glowing testimonial.
It is also a good place to include the telephone number of the company and its web site.

[Back/Cover]

Back cover of the brochure must contain all the information about how to get in touch with the company.
No important message should be included here since people do not pay too much attention to this panel.

Thomas Family Practice
Monthly Newsletter

BACK TO SCHOOL ISSUE

Dr. Thomas
Dr. Owen
Nurse Practioner Mason
Nurse Practioner Emily
Nurse Caitlin

OLD TOWN CENTER·NEWTOWN
555-555-1111

OLD TOWN CENTER·NEW TOWN
555-555-1111

Inside Panel 1

The three inside panels are perfect for a detailed description of the different activities, products and services of the company.

As this is where most of the text will be concentrated, it is important to organize information hierarchically to make the main points of the message perfectly understandable. The harmony of text and image is essential, too.

Bulleted Lists
[Inside Panel 2]

bullet lists allow a viewer to scan and understand easy

- Provide a list of your products and services
- Keep each item short
- Use power words such as new, easy, results, proven
- AVOID ALL CAPS, it's difficult to read
- Use bold and italics sparingly
- Use high quality images that match to your content.
- call to action, step by step tell the viewer what they need to do after reading

Check List:
[Inside Panel 3]

- Is it **Intriguing**?
- Is there enough **white space**?
- Can viewers understand the **intent of the brochure** in under ten seconds?
- Are images **effective**?
- Does the viewer have a **reason** to pick it up?
- Does it provide **value** to the viewer?
- Does it **tell** the viewer what to do next?

[Front/Cover] [OuterPanel1] [InsidePanel2] [InsidePanel3]
[Back/Cover] [InsidePanel1] [InsidePanel1]

HOW CAN I CREATE A MEDICATION SCHEDULE (TIMELINE)?

A timeline can be used to show medication schedules in a graphic format that may be easier for a patient or caregiver to follow. In the following tutorial the basic features for creating a timeline for medication are shown. An alternate view is shown with variations in presentation (different shapes and different colors) for each medication. A color printer could provide the patient with a calendar that uses a color code related to the colors of the medications.

NOTES

The date is not needed for a daily medication timeline.

The label lines in a timeline may be edited by using the end or middle handles to move, rotate, or bend the line.

TIP

If a color printer is available, each medication's color may be used as the color fill of its related shape.

Creating a Patient Medication Timeline

GOAL	ACTION	RESULT
USE DAILY TIMELINE STYLE	**CLICK** *All tab* **CLICK** *Timelines category in Document Browser* **CLICK** *Day with Hours Blank Timelines*	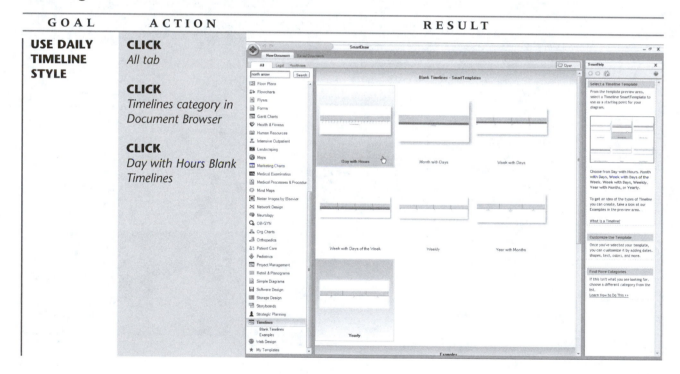

Creating a Patient Medication Timeline (*continued*)

GOAL	ACTION	RESULT
EDIT TEXT TO PERSONALIZE	**SELECT** *timeline* **RIGHT CLICK** **UNCHECK** *Do Not Allow Text Editing* **CLICK** *Text Line* **TYPE** *text*	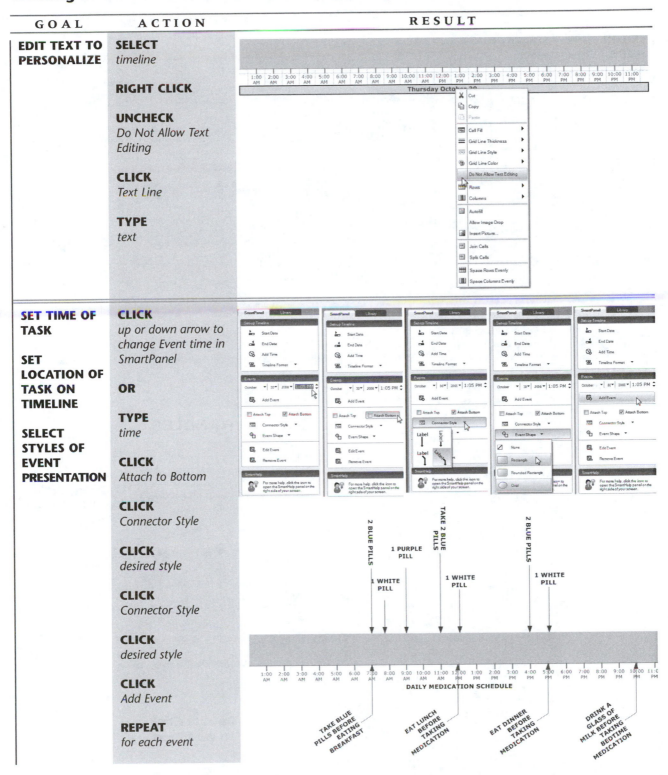
SET TIME OF TASK **SET LOCATION OF TASK ON TIMELINE** **SELECT STYLES OF EVENT PRESENTATION**	**CLICK** *up or down arrow to change Event time in SmartPanel* **OR** **TYPE** *time* **CLICK** *Attach to Bottom* **CLICK** *Connector Style* **CLICK** *desired style* **CLICK** *Connector Style* **CLICK** *desired style* **CLICK** *Add Event* **REPEAT** *for each event*	

Changing Arrow Directions and Shapes

GOAL	ACTION	RESULT
COLOR CODE MEDICATION LIST	**SELECT** *shape* **RIGHT CLICK** *Use menu options to change shape, border color, and fill color.*	
EDIT LINES IN TIMELINE	**SELECT** *Arrow* **CLICK** *handles* **DRAG** *to new location*	

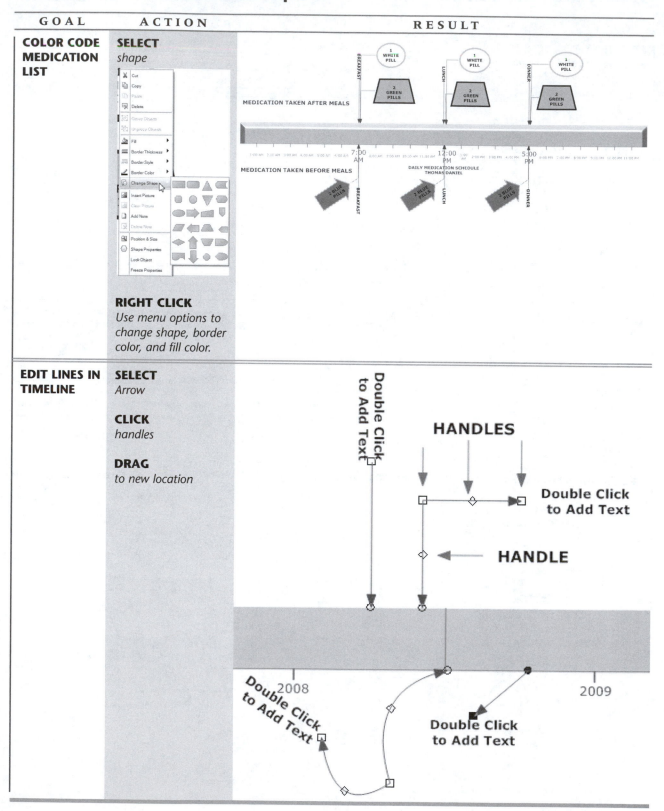

Real Estate Applications

- How Can I Create a Floor Plan of Each Property?
  - ▲ *Tutorial—Creating a Floor Plan*
- How Can I Show the Dimensions of the Property?
  - ▲ *Tutorial—Showing Dimensions of Area*
- How Can I Use the Floor Plan Template to Show How Furniture Will Fit?
  - ▲ *Tutorial—Show a Furniture Layout*

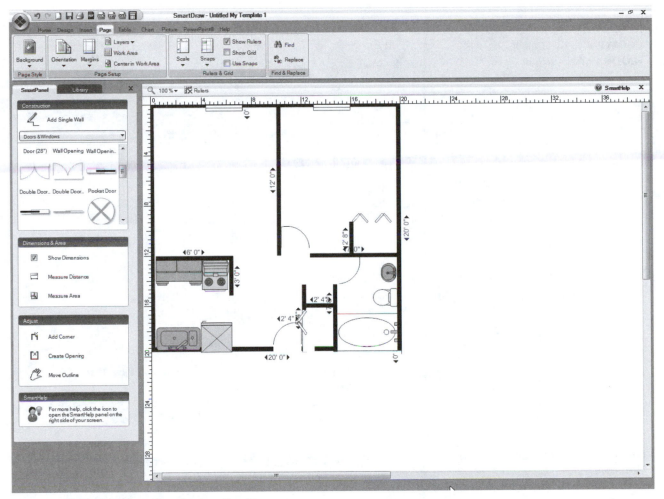

Source: Created using SmartDraw Floor Plan SmartTemplate

HOW CAN I CREATE A FLOOR PLAN OF EACH PROPERTY?

You can very quickly create custom templates for each property with SmartDraw, save them, print them out for brochures, or enlarge them for posters.

TIP

Walls have a width of 2 inches in SmartDraw. Adjust accordingly for interior or exterior dimension.

Creating a Floor Plan

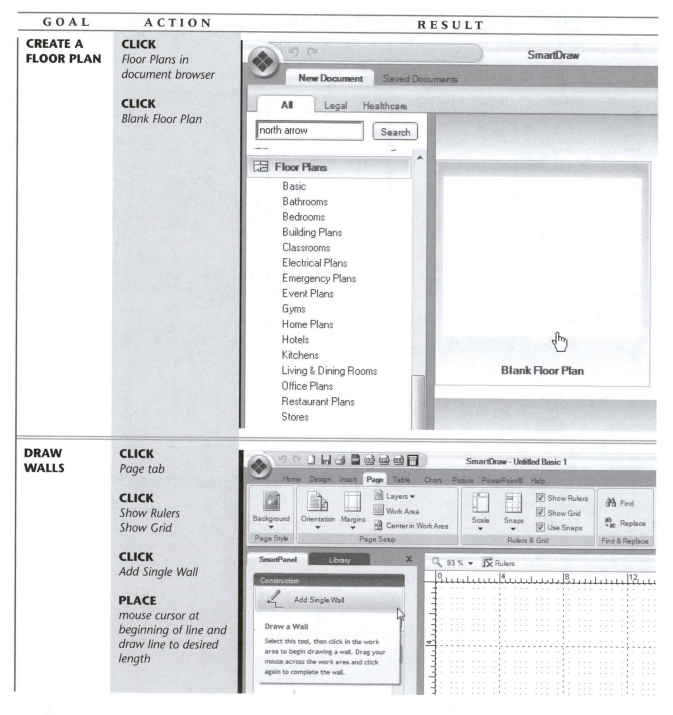

GOAL	ACTION	RESULT
CREATE A FLOOR PLAN	**CLICK** *Floor Plans in document browser* **CLICK** *Blank Floor Plan*	
DRAW WALLS	**CLICK** *Page tab* **CLICK** *Show Rulers* *Show Grid* **CLICK** *Add Single Wall* **PLACE** *mouse cursor at beginning of line and draw line to desired length*	

Creating a Floor Plan *(continued)*

GOAL	ACTION	RESULT
ADD ADDITIONAL WALLS	**CLICK** *Add Single Wall in SmartPanel* **DRAW** *wall* **REPEAT** *for each wall*	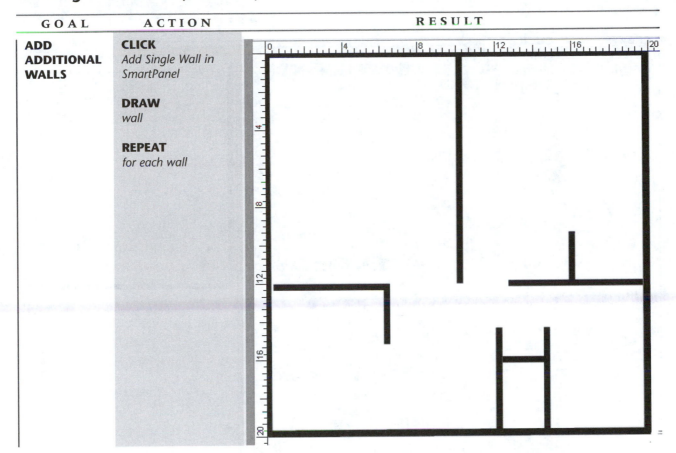

Creating a Floor Plan *(continued)*

GOAL	ACTION	RESULT
CREATE WALL OPENING	**CLICK** *Create Opening in Adjust group in SmartPanel*	
INSERT WALL OPENING IN WALL	**PLACE CURSOR** *at wall opening location* **CLICK** *to insert opening*	

Creating a Floor Plan *(continued)*

GOAL	ACTION	RESULT
ADJUST SIZE OF WALL OPENING		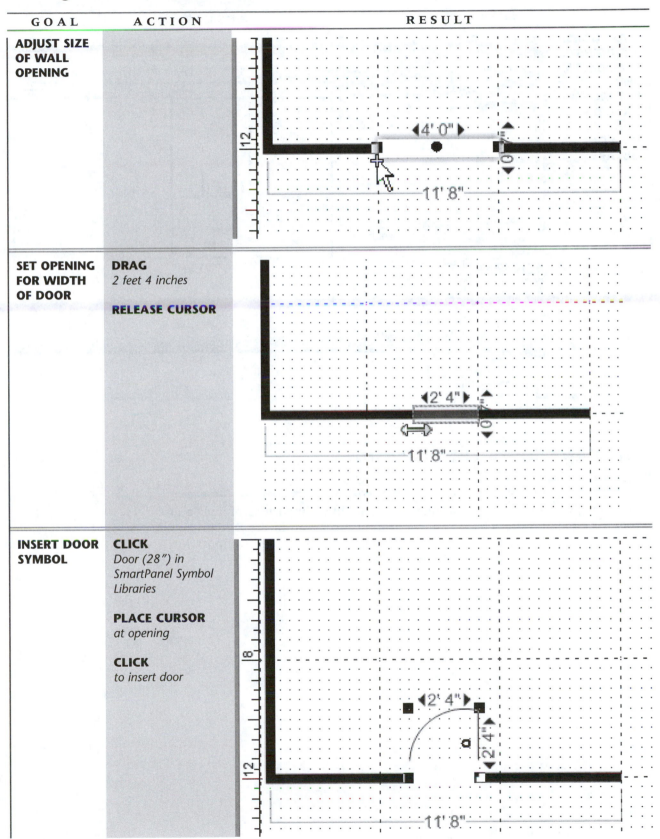
SET OPENING FOR WIDTH OF DOOR	**DRAG** *2 feet 4 inches* **RELEASE CURSOR**	
INSERT DOOR SYMBOL	**CLICK** *Door (28") in SmartPanel Symbol Libraries* **PLACE CURSOR** *at opening* **CLICK** *to insert door*	

Creating a Floor Plan (continued)

GOAL	ACTION	RESULT
ADD DOORS, WINDOWS, APPLIANCES, AND BATHROOM FIXTURES FROM SYMBOLS LIBRARY	**CLICK** *More in the drop-down menu* **CLICK** *in Symbol Libraries Windows* **Insert** *as shown* **REPEAT** *for Appliances and Bathroom Fixtures*	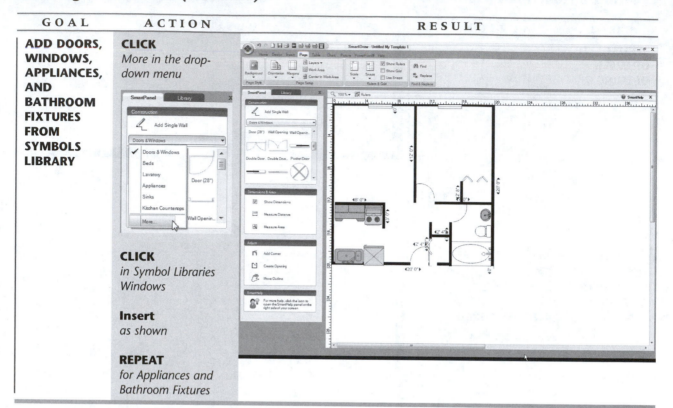

Do not close the file. This drawing will be used in the next exercise.

HOW CAN I SHOW THE DIMENSIONS OF THE PROPERTY?

As previously shown, you can display the individual dimensions of lines and symbols by making the selection in the Dimension menu in the Design tab's Shape Properties group. This menu also allows the automatic computation and display of the total area of an object.

Showing Dimension of Area

GOAL	ACTION	RESULT
SHOW DIMENSION OF AREA	**SELECT** *Outside walls* **CLICK** *Design tab* **CLICK** *Dimensions in the Shape Properties group* **CLICK** *The area of the shape*	
AREA OF SHAPE DIMENSION	**CLICK** *OK*	

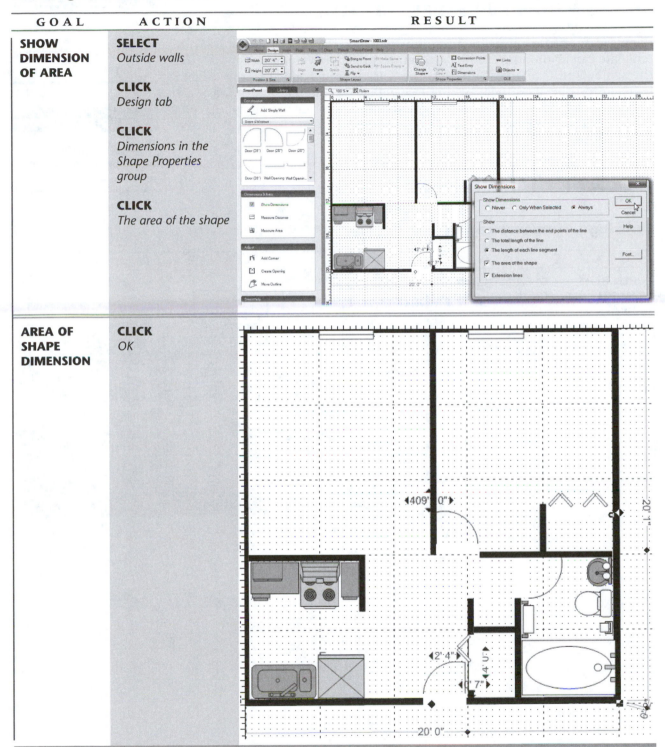

Do not close the file. It will be used in the next exercise.

HOW CAN I USE THE FLOOR PLAN TEMPLATE TO SHOW HOW FURNITURE WILL FIT?

Clients want to know how their furniture will fit in the new property. A layout template can be modified to show furniture, appliances, and accessories using the symbols in the SmartDraw symbols library. Items added to the original template can be rearranged without changing the original floor plan. Each variation can be saved or printed. Enhanced floor plans showing color combinations can be used in sales literature or printed and left for prospective renters or buyers.

N O T E

All the furniture can be filled with color as previously shown and the results printed in color.

T I P

Resize the symbols as needed to reflect actual furniture dimensions.

Showing a Furniture Layout

GOAL	ACTION	RESULT
OPEN BEDS SYMBOL LIBRARY	**OPEN FLOOR PLAN** **CLICK** *More in SmartPanel Symbols Library* **CLICK** *Beds* **CLICK** *OK*	

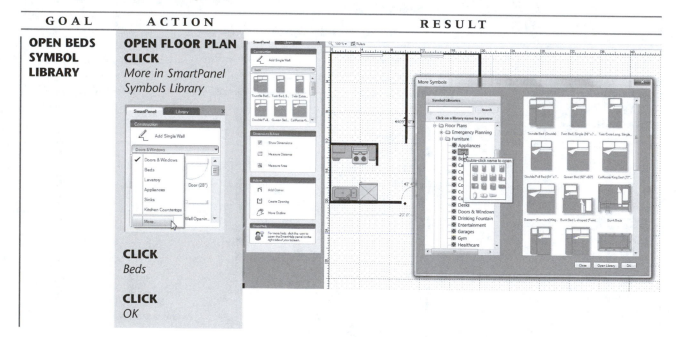

Showing a Furniture Layout *(continued)*

GOAL	ACTION	RESULT
ADD BED	**DRAG AND DROP** *Queen Bed to bedroom* **ROTATE** *By using rotation handle*	
ADD SOFA AND CHAIR FROM SYMBOL LIBRARY	**OPEN** *Sofas symbol library* **DRAG AND DROP** *Sofa* **DRAG AND DROP** *Chair*	

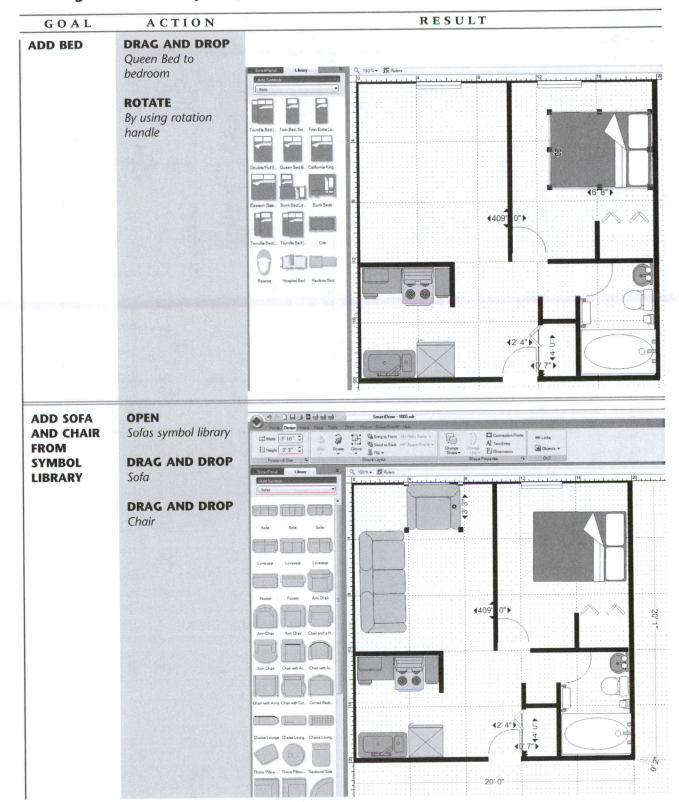

Showing a Furniture Layout *(continued)*

GOAL	ACTION	RESULT
ADD TABLES AND RUG	**OPEN** *Tables symbol library* **DRAG AND DROP** *Tables* **OPEN** *Rugs symbol library* **DRAG AND DROP** *Rug* **CLICK** *Design tab* **CLICK** *Send to Back*	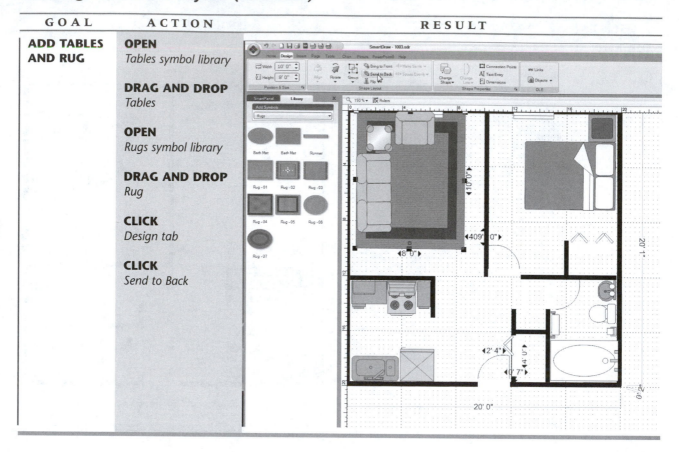

Appendix

A. SMARTDRAW VERSION COMPARISON GUIDE

STANDARD	LEGAL	HEALTHCARE
Accounting & Finance	Accident Reconstruction	Accounting & Finance
BPM & Six Sigma	Accounting & Finance	Ambulatory Care
Calendars	Admissibility and Use of Evidence	Anatomy Illustrations
Cause & Effect	Cause & Effect	Anatomy Worksheets
Certificates	Charts	Anger Management
Charts	Coalitions	Assisted Living
Decision Trees	Contract Action	Asthma & Pulmonology
Education	Corporate Entities	Cancer
Engineering	Crime Scene Investigation	Cardiology
Event Planning	Crime Scene Reconstruction	Cause & Effect
Family Trees	Criminal Law	Charts
Financial & Estate Planning	Decision Trees	CPR
Floor Plans	Electronic Trip Preparation	Decision Trees
Flowcharts	Federal Bankruptcy	Dentistry
Flyers	Federal Court	Dermatology
Forms	Financial & Estate Planning	Diabetes
Gantt Charts	Floor Plans	Diseases
Human Resources	Flowcharts	Disorders
Landscaping	Flyers	Family Trees
Maps	Forms	Fitness
Marketing Charts	Gangs	Floor Plans
Mind Maps	Judgments	Flowcharts
Network Design	Juvenile Justice	Flyers
Org Charts	Law Enforcement Tools	Forms
Project Management	Legal Assistants	Health & Fitness
Retail & Planograms	Maps	Home Care
Simple Diagrams	Marketing Charts	Human Resources
Software Design	Medical Examination	Infections
Storyboards	Mind Maps	Intensive Outpatient
Strategic Planning	Org Charts	Long-Term Care
Timelines	Paralegal Practice	Maps
Web Design		

B. VIDEO TRAINING

The SmartHelp panel has a number of video tutorials. These automatically become available when a template for which a video is available is selected to be worked on. You don't have to do anything else except click the play button. You will need a speaker or headphones if you want to listen to the instructions.

The following is list of the templates that have videos available.

- Calendars.wmv
- cause-and-effect.wmv
- charts.wmv
- decision-trees.wmv
- ecomaps.wmv
- family-trees.wmv
- floor-plans.wmv
- flowcharts.wmv
- gantt-charts.wmv
- genograms.wmv
- hierarchy.wmv
- landscape.wmv
- LDAP.wmv
- marketing-charts.wmv
- mind-maps.wmv
- network-design.wmv
- org-charts.wmv
- software-design.wmv
- timelines.wmv
- website-maps.wmv

C. SELECTED EXCERPTS FROM SMARTDRAW MANUAL

SmartDraw Tech Support Knowledge Base

For instant, 24-hour information about the most common user questions, visit the SmartDraw Knowledge Base at

http://www.smartdraw.com/support/knowledgebase/index.aspx

How to Get Technical Support

Technical support is available to all SmartDraw users, including trial users.

To access technical support from the SmartDraw program click the Tech Support button on the Help tab. To contact support on the web go to http://www.smartdraw.com/support/contact.htm. You can also get technical support by e-mail at support@smartdraw.com or by calling (858) 225-3300 between 8 AM and 5 PM USA Pacific time.

When reporting a problem, please include the following information:

1) Your system configuration (version of Windows, printer, display type, etc.)

2) A description of how to reproduce the problem.

3) A sample file that exhibits the problem (if possible).

Downloading the Latest Version

We frequently offer free updates that include bug fixes and new features. To check for updates click the Updates button on the Help tab or visit the SmartDraw support web page and click the link that says Free Updates.

http://www.smartdraw.com/support/updates.htmSmartDraw Knowledge Base Article #1051

Downloading SmartDraw Installation Files

Category—Downloading, Install/Uninstall, Web Site Features
Updated—11/27/2007 8:32:48 AM

Many times when our customers report that they can't download their software successfully, it is the result of one of the following:

• Download Managers

• Corporate or Personal Firewalls

• The QuickTime Plug-in

• Download extension of .htm or .cfm

DOWNLOAD MANAGERS

Programs such as:

• GetRight

• RealDownload

• Gozilla

• Internet Download Manager

as well as many other others allow users to resume broken or interrupted downloads. These download managers will not work with the SmartDraw.com downloads.

SmartDraw's downloads (except for the Trial Edition) are located on a secure server. These programs are prohibited by law to download from Secure Web Servers (HTTPS) so they are not compatible with our download files. If you are using a download manager, please disable it (usually under the Options menu or Disable Browser Integration) or uninstall it. After doing so, you shouldn't experience any further problems.

Corporate or Personal Firewalls

If your office or personal computer is behind a firewall check with your System Administrator for download rights regarding ".exe" files. Some firewalls have settings to block this file type from downloading because some malicious Internet users send viruses that run when an unsuspecting person runs the file. If your system has a personal firewall, check your settings for this situation.

The QuickTime Plug-in

After clicking the Download button, some users are redirected to a new browser page with a QuickTime movie icon on the screen. The URL ends in the ".exe" filename, but you are never prompted to Run / Open from Location or Save the file. This occurs because at some point you downloaded and installed Apple's QuickTime Player (and subsequently their built-in QuickTime Download program) to play movie files (".mov" or ".qt").

What is happening is that this program has confused the system into thinking that it should handle ".exe" files instead of the system default of prompting to Save and Download. You must disable or uninstall the QuickTime Download or Browser Integration and restart your machine for changes to take effect.

Once you have disabled or removed this Plug-in, you should not have any further problems downloading your software.

Download extension of .htm:

Some Internet browsers have trouble downloading files through our secure server. When trying to download your purchased copy of SmartDraw, instead of getting the installation executable (.exe), you will download a file called **download.htm**.

If this occurs, visit your download page and choose "Download". When you click on the "Download" button, select "Run" or "Open" to open the .htm file, then on the next screen (which will look exactly the same) select "Save" to save the actual .exe installation file.

IS SMARTDRAW COMPATIBLE WITH WINDOWS VISTA® 2007?

Yes, SmartDraw 2009, 2008, and 2007 are fully compatible with Windows Vista®.

WHAT IF I OWN AN OLDER VERSION OF SMARTDRAW?

Only SmartDraw 2009, SmartDraw 2008, and SmartDraw 2007 are fully compatible with Windows Vista®. SmartDraw 7 and older versions of SmartDraw are not.

Known issues with SmartDraw 7 and older versions:

- Floating libraries don't draw correctly

- Graphical menus don't draw correctly

- Installation issues without administrative rights

- Transfer to PowerPoint® 2007 doesn't work correctly

If you're upgrading to Vista® 2007, we recommend you also upgrade to SmartDraw 2009.

D. SHORTCUTS

The SmartDraw Button

Print (Ctrl+P)—Print your document. Displays the Print Dialog to select the printer, number of copies, and other properties before printing.

Print Preview—See how your printed document will look.

Export as Graphic—Export drawings in a number of common graphics formats, such as JPG, EMF, and many others.

Email—Open a new email message in your default email program and automatically attach the current SmartDraw document.

Publish to Web—Share files and publish your SmartDraw documents as web pages.

Spelling—Change the way SmartDraw checks the spelling in your documents.

Libraries—Open, create, or automatically build symbol libraries.

SmartDraw Options—Set the properties (such as line linking and shape linking) of your document, and general SmartDraw options.

Select New Template—Go back to the Document Browser to select a different template.

File Conversion Wizard—Automatically convert files from other programs into SmartDraw files.

Close Document (Ctrl+W)—Close this document. Does not close other open SmartDraw documents.

Close SmartDraw (Alt + F4)—Quit the entire program.

E. HOW TO PURCHASE SMARTDRAW

When your trial period expires, you can continue working by purchasing the full version of SmartDraw, which will replace your Trial Edition. Any drawings you created with the Trial Edition will be preserved, and you can open them with the full version.

SmartDraw offers deep discounts for multiple copy purchases and multi-seat licenses. For more information, please visit:

http://www.smartdraw.com/buyinfo/volume/index.htm

Activation

You can activate your trial version of SmartDraw by clicking the Buy button on the Buy tab and purchasing the full program.

Clicking this button enables you to conduct a secure, online purchase that activates your trial copy. Activation means there's no need to download anything further or wait for any media to arrive to continue working. You simply make your purchase, and pick up where you left off.

Activation removes all restrictions on printing and editing, and removes any watermarks from every document you made with your trial version. At the time of activation you can also order an optional CD and Quick Start Guide to be shipped to you.

If you have any questions or prefer to place your order over the phone, you can always call SmartDraw.com directly at 1-800-817-4238 (in the United States and Canada) or 858-225-3300 (outside the United States).

If you wish to purchase SmartDraw with a Company Purchase Order, print out an order form and mail or fax the order form with a copy of the Purchase Order.

SmartDraw.com only accepts Purchase Orders from entities in the United States and Canada.

Order Online

Visit www.smartdraw.com and order online with a credit card. You can download your software immediately and order an optional CD and Quick Start Guide to be shipped to you.

If you have any questions or prefer to place your order over the phone, you can always call SmartDraw.com directly at 1-800-817-4238 (in the United States and Canada) or 858-225-3300 (outside the United States).

If you wish to purchase SmartDraw with a Company Purchase Order, print out an order form and mail or fax the order form with a copy of the Purchase Order.

SmartDraw.com only accepts Purchase Orders from entities in the United States and Canada.

Order by Phone

You can order by phone and still receive the benefits of downloading the product immediately after purchase. Call 1-800-817-4238 within the United States and Canada, or call 858-225-3300 outside the United States.

You can also order the optional CD if you like.

SmartDraw.com does not accept Purchase Orders by phone. If you wish to purchase SmartDraw with a Company Purchase Order, print out an order form and mail or fax the order form with a copy of the Purchase Order. SmartDraw.com only accepts Purchase Orders from recognized entities in the United States and Canada.

Order by Fax or Mail

Visit http://www.smartdraw.com/buyinfo/forms/index.htm for the latest up-to-date order forms. Fill out the order form and fax it to:

858-549-2830

If sending a check, please mail the check and order form to:

SmartDraw.com
9909 Mira Mesa Blvd
San Diego, CA 92131
USA

If you have any questions or prefer to place your order over the phone, you can always call SmartDraw.com directly at 1-800-817-4238 (in the United States and Canada) or 858-225-3300 (outside the United States).

If you wish to purchase SmartDraw with a Company Purchase Order, print an order form and mail or fax the order form with a copy of the Purchase Order.

SmartDraw.com only accepts Purchase Orders from entities in the United States and Canada.